A step-by-step guide for parents

RAISING
A BILINGUAL
CHILD

Barbara Zurer Pearson, Ph.D.

LIVING LANGUAGE®
A Random House Company, New York

Published in the United States by Living Language, an imprint of Random House, Inc.

www.livinglanguage.com

Editor: Zvjezdana Vrzić, Ph.D.

Production Editor: Lisbeth Dyer

Production Manager: Thomas Marshall

Interior Design: Sophie Ye Chin

First Edition

ISBN: 978-1-4000-2334-9

Library of Congress Cataloging-in-Publication Data available upon request.

PRINTED IN THE UNITED STATES OF AMERICA

10 9 8 7 6 5 4 3 2 1

I dedicate this book to my parents, Raymond and Selmajean Zurer; my husband, Wilbur; our children, Sam and Steve and Zach and Miri; and our grandchildren, Daphne, Eli, Ella, Ezra, Hazel, and Seth.

Acknowledgments

Amherst, MA, July, 2007

I want to express my appreciation to my colleagues in the University of Miami Bilingualism Study Group: the original kernel—Kim Oller, Vivian Umbel, and Maria Fernandez—and then those who joined and improved our efforts—Alan Cobo-Lewis, Virginia Gathercole, Rebecca Burns-Hoffman, Rebecca Eilers, Batya Elbaum, Erika Hoff, and students Sylvia Fernandez, Ana Navarro, Rosana Resende, Vanessa Lewedag, Arlene McGee, Mike Lynch, and so many others. My current research colleagues at the University of Massachusetts, especially the DELV team members Harry Seymour, Tom Roeper, and Jill and Peter deVilliers, are also a source of inspiration for me. I should acknowledge the National Institutes of Health, which supported much of our work. I am also grateful to the members of the congenial international research community here in Amherst and bilingualism colleagues around the world, among whom I have been honored to work. You will see many of their names in the text and notes.

For their help in whipping the chapters into shape, I thank my earliest readers, who waded through the roughest of drafts: my sister Carol Kline (my strictest taskmaster), daughter Sam Pearson, neighbor Pat Schneider, and coworker Loren Walker. Later, friends Zahava Koren and Beth Berry, sister-in-law Diana Zurer, and brother-in-law Dennis Pearson also contributed their eyes and insight to help shape the text. Thanks also go to neighbor Marielle Lerner, who was home just long enough this year to step in as fact-checker, and my editor, Zvjezdana Vrzić, who kept the question "Why do parents need to know that?" foremost in my mind at every chapter. Finally, I thank my husband,

Wilbur, who gave me the encouragement and the space to devote so much time to this project—all of my days and nights, as the deadlines drew near.

The project itself took less than a year, but I feel I have been preparing for this book my whole career. It's much more demanding to write for parents than for other scholars. I thank Random House for making it possible for me to attempt it.

CONTENTS

Tables

Figures

Introduction

If you are bilingual and you are thinking about or are currently raising your children to be bilingual, this book is for you.

If you are not bilingual, but wonder if you might be able to raise your children to be bilingual, this book is also for you.

Or if you are just interested in the amazing story of how children learn two or more languages at the same time, this book is for you, too.

Raising a Bilingual Child is a guidebook for what to do and what to expect when you're parenting a bilingual-to-be.[1] It also contains general background information that will take you beyond the *how*, to the *why*. Sometimes you will use the book as a quick reference to help with a specific strategy. At other times, you may find that you are fascinated, as I am, with the miraculous achievements of small children on their path to language and literacy, and you will want to hear a fuller account of what is happening at different stages. The book gives you this bigger picture as well.

In *Raising a Bilingual Child*, I want to share with you my passion for languages and my hopes for universal bilingualism. "Universal" might

---

[1] I use the word "bilingual" as a synonym for speaking more than one language, whether it's two or more, just as I follow the convention of calling any language after the first a "second" language, whether it is the third or the tenth. Occasionally, I use the word "multilingual" when I refer specifically to individuals who speak more than two languages. Similarly, I alternate the use of "he" and "she" in reference to "baby" or "child" by chapter.

be too strong, but why not? We all grow up speaking a language.[2] Why don't we all grow up speaking two (or more)? When I speak to people from Guatemala, Denmark, Israel, or India, for example, they say that children are expected to grow up bilingual. It is not at all unusual. In the U.S., the families of diplomats, international businesspeople, and movie stars do it. Their lifestyles may not be typical, but their children are typical children. They are born with the same language-learning equipment as your children and mine.

Personal Fascination and Professional Interest

My own interest in bilingual development is both personal and professional. I was not raised bilingually myself. I first became bilingual as a university exchange student. Maybe it was just the magic of being twenty years old in Paris, but I felt transformed when I discovered a larger world through living in another language. Because I could speak to the French in their language, I heard stories from people whose unique lives I would never have been able to imagine at home in New York. Somehow I found myself more outgoing when I was speaking French and even surprised myself by writing poetry in that language—which is not something I typically did in English. Although I was technically beyond the age for learning a second language like a native speaker, I was often mistaken for one. It felt like winning a medal in the language Olympics—bronze if I was taken for someone from a province in France, and silver if the listener thought I was Swiss. (Gold would have been passing for a Parisian. I never won that one.)

Nor were my children raised bilingually from birth. (After all, I didn't have this book!) Fortunately, we lived in the language-rich city of Miami, Florida, and they showed great interest in language as young children and teens. Now, as adults, they, too, are bilingual—but not "near-native," as they might have been had they learned their second languages earlier.

---

2 When I talk about languages, I say "speak" and "listen" but do not mean to exclude sign languages, which are "spoken" with the hands and "heard" with the eyes. People who know both a sign and spoken language (or two signed languages) are an important subgroup of bilinguals, and the ideas expressed in this book apply equally to them.

Although speaking two languages has been an important part of my adult life, I missed out on the early childhood experience of living in two languages. Happily, my career as a university researcher gave me the gift of sharing closely in the experiences of twenty-five families committed to raising their children bilingually. These families generously permitted my colleagues at the University of Miami and me to record as many aspects of their babies' language growth as we could without becoming downright intrusive. We met the babies when they were around three months of age, before they were babbling, and we watched them grow up learning to speak two languages right before our eyes. Through their frequent visits to our lab, we became friends with many of the families, and several parents continued bringing their children back to see us long after the funding for the study had ended and many of the results had been published. Our project was one of the first studies of a large group of young bilinguals, rather than a case study of a single child. In many ways, it was like twenty-five case studies. How different the twenty-five experiences were from each other was as fascinating as the general developmental patterns that we have reported in the scholarly literature.

This infant study was another kind of first as well. It was my first bilingualism research endeavor. Eventually, the University of Miami Bilingualism Study Group (BSG), which I coordinated with D. K. Oller, was funded to work with bilingual groups at many ages, from those first bilingual babies to bilingual toddlers, bilingual schoolchildren, bilingual university students, and a few bilingual adults. The BSG was a wonderfully collegial group, and from those studies, we jointly wrote an academic book and a significant number of presentations and articles for peer-reviewed publications. This experience has enabled me to sift through the growing and sometimes contradictory information on bilingualism now available and to present to you what I think is most helpful to parents.

Who Is This Book For?

Raising a Bilingual Child is for parents or future parents and their friends and relatives. If you are a parent, this book will give you the information you need about choosing two languages for your children—how and why—and will reassure you that science is on your side if you do. If you are a relative or friend, you will learn to understand the needs of bilingual families. I will also be happy if this book finds its way into the hands of people who have not given bilingualism any thought. This book will teach you how you, as a caregiver, can recognize or create an environment where children will flourish in two languages. It offers both a broad overview of the phenomenon of bilingualism and detailed steps you can take to provide your children the motivation and the opportunity for meaningful interactions in two languages within the normal routines of your life.

Information, Encouragement, and Practical Advice

In many would-be bilingual families, even in those where two languages are spoken by the adults, parents may lack practical guidance for the journey. This step-by-step guide gives you information, encouragement, and practical advice for creating and maintaining a bilingual environment for your children.

Many readers already have the vision to see the advantages for children of being bilingual. Some of you are reproducing for your children the conditions that led you to become bilingual as a child. Others of you want to improve on the language experience you had in a monolingual home and smooth the way for your children to grow up speaking two languages.

This book will confirm your feeling that raising your child to speak two languages has distinct advantages. It provides studies to demonstrate this, as well as advice from people who have successfully raised bilingual children or who were themselves raised bilingually from childhood. Whenever possible, I include resources that can help parents build a household that fosters bilingual growth.

I also play the "devil's advocate" to examine arguments against childhood bilingualism that you may have heard—that two languages confuse children, or that learning a second language too early will weaken a child's first language. The information and examples[3] you will find in

---

3 Specific references for each chapter are found in the back of the book, beginning on page 319.

this book will enable you to refute those contentions and will boost your confidence in your decision to raise your child to speak two languages.

Because I am in the U.S., I use the U.S. throughout as my frame of reference, but the information and advice you will find here are by no means limited to this country. In fact, all of the suggestions may be even easier to implement elsewhere.

I want to excite you about the possibility of raising a bilingual child and help you do it. Personally, I am still holding out for a few bilingual grandchildren and godchildren. Perhaps this book can be some help to their parents as well as to other readers!

How to Use This Book

The eight chapters of this book follow a logical sequence, but I also expect that busy parents will consult its sections in different orders, depending on their current need. The "What's Inside the Book?" table below follows the order of the pages and lists the basic themes of the chapters. You may also decide to skip around, in which case we refer you to the Frequently Asked Questions and Alternate Table of Contents following chapter 8.

Let's begin.

What's Inside the Book?	CHAPTER
The arguments and the research to support your decision to raise bilingual children	1
Language-learning basics for your child's first language	2
The basics of being bilingual	3
The major strategies for bilingual homes and communities	4
Testimonials from bilingual families (who follow the strategies in Chapter 4)	5
What to watch out for: Raising a bilingual child that you suspect has special needs	6

CHAPTER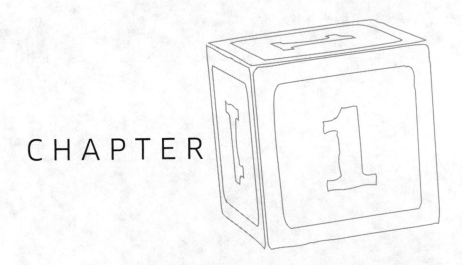

The Benefits of Childhood Bilingualism

IN THIS CHAPTER, YOU WILL LEARN the advantages for children of being bilingual and will find the research to support the decision to raise your child bilingually. We'll look into

- the major reasons given by other parents like you for wanting their children to speak more than one language,

- what the child gains intellectually and creatively from being bilingual, and

- what the family and the community stand to gain from it.

The reports of the research are organized according to how bilingualism has been shown to benefit

- bilingual children's precocious knowledge of language,

- their enhanced cognitive development in general, and

- the social and cultural growth they experience.

You will also see that you do not have to be bilingual yourself to have a bilingual child.

How Common Is Bilingual Upbringing?

Children learn their first language naturally and without instruction through loving interaction with their caregivers. With a little planning and forethought, that is how they can learn a second (or third) language—informally and without lessons.

Many people, especially in countries like the U.S. with a monolingual mainstream culture, think that being monolingual is the most natural way to grow up. In fact, far from being the norm, monolingualism is the exception. There are very few, if any, places in the world where a society can exist in complete isolation from contact and interaction with people of other cultures. The arguments about language and language education that rage in the American press make it seem as if the U.S. is monolingual, but before and since colonial times, there have been many languages other than English spoken here.

You may be surprised to discover that in the U.S., the "language diversity index"—a rough guide to the number of different mother tongues spoken by a country's citizens—is not particularly low. Compared to other countries, it is, in fact, around average. At 35%, it is lower than that of Canada, at 55%, but higher than those of two-thirds of the European countries, like France, Germany, Greece, and the U.K. So, there are many more potential bilinguals in the U.S. than are generally taken into account; more than 300 languages are spoken here. According to the 2000 census, almost 20% of Americans are speakers of languages other than English (and about 11% are foreign-born). Multilingualism is a fact of life—a fact you can take advantage of to benefit your family.

Many people who grew up outside the U.S. report that the ability to speak more than one language is highly valued in their home countries. Parents in several countries expose their children to additional languages early so they will speak them natively. Linguist Anthea Gupta reports that, in India and Singapore, for example, most families speak two or three languages almost interchangeably in their homes and expect children to learn them all. According to Gupta, a child who arrives in preschool with only one language is considered the exception.

In many countries, the formal study of languages in school begins earlier than in the U.S., and even before their children enter elementary school, many families hire caregivers who will teach their children a language other than the parents'. These families may also take their children abroad so they can learn about other cultures, hear other languages being used, and be motivated to learn them. The parents feel strongly that early second language experiences will make the child a richer person, and they are likely to be more than a little puzzled to see what seems so natural and unremarkable elsewhere being called into question, as it often is in the U.S. press.

Advantages of Bilingual Upbringing:
Why Did They Do It? Why Do They Like It?

Jane Merrill, author of *Bringing Up Baby Bilingual,* poses the question, "Do we do everything we do to make our children bilingual for their sakes or for our own?" The beauty of it, she decides, is that it does not matter. Both parent and child benefit.

Later in this chapter, we will consult the published research to learn about the intellectual benefits, enhanced creativity, and mental flexibility gained from a bilingual upbringing. Social scientists have confirmed for us that parents' positive ideas about openness toward other cultures and respect for others can often be traced to experiences in learning other people's languages and having the close interactions with people of other cultures that a common language permits.

First, let's hear what people who have experienced bilingual households have to say. Why did they do it? What did they hope to gain? In the research for this book, in addition to published reports, I consulted more than one hundred families to find their answers to these questions. Their responses appear throughout the book, but see in particular the testimonials in chapters 5 and 6.

Advantages of Bilingual Upbringing from the Parents' Point of View

I have found that people who are from bilingual backgrounds themselves rarely refer to the many cognitive and intellectual benefits that research tells us about when they discuss the advantages of bilingualism for their children. For many of them, language is about the heart—about family, intimacy, and cultural identity.

Christina Bosemark of *www.multilingualchildren.org* says,

*"I had not started out raising my child to speak my native
language. But when we visited her grandparents for the first
time and I saw her play with her cousins, I realized that
an important link to her past would be completely lost
if she couldn't speak Swedish. So I started right
then speaking Swedish with her."*

Others are simply being practical, especially those who are staying in a new country temporarily. By using two languages with their children, they are keeping the door open for the children to step back into the school system in their home country. For others, the chance for their children to learn another language early and painlessly was a factor in their decision to take a job abroad. One couple sees it from two points of view:

*"We think it is a great opportunity, from my own positive experience
being bilingual and because of my husband's struggle with
mastering two languages as an adult."*

When parents adopt as their household language a language they speak fluently but not natively, they are making an even more deliberate choice than those who choose to speak their native language to their children even when it is not a language spoken by the wider community. Their optimism about bilingualism is equally great:

"The knowledge can only benefit children; it can't hurt."

*"In a multicultural society, bilingual children will be more socially
aware—more open to other cultures and practices."*

*"It will ease their travel and give them more opportunities
in education and business."*

*"They won't have to struggle like I did to learn another
language so I could study abroad."*

For parents who do not have a family connection to a second language, the decision is perhaps less emotional. To them, the intellectual benefits are more apparent. Loren, now a writer, says,

*"I feel I owe my enhanced facility for language to the study of Spanish.
To me, this was a big unexpected benefit."*

Even if these parents were not childhood bilinguals themselves, they have in common a passion for travel and a comfort with foreign languages. The nonnative parents who create bilingual households are often those who as teenagers chose to study abroad or who gravitated toward the foreign-born child who arrived midyear in their classroom. When we hear their stories, we can understand how many of them became language teachers or linguists and where they find the motivation for conducting their family life in a second language. Author and teacher George Saunders, who learned German as his second language in school, is a model of a warm and loving father with a passion for German. He imparts this love of German to his children and gets new people with whom he can speak the language in the bargain. In chapter 5, you will meet a couple from Cambridge, Massachusetts, with a similar motivation. They are not language teachers, but they discovered the wonders of different languages as teenagers. Now, as parents, they see no reason for their daughter to grow up without learning three languages, and they have acted intentionally to make it happen for her. At age eleven, the child is so comfortable speaking Spanish and American Sign Language, in addition to English, that she herself chose to start Chinese as her fourth language.

Finally, parents with no second language background may be attracted to excellent schools and programs that will train their child in another language. One family states,

> "We might not have been so keen to send our son to the bilingual elementary school if the school didn't also have an excellent reputation for academics. But it does, so we can get the best of both—an excellent language experience and a solid academic foundation."

Advantages of Bilingual Upbringing from the Children's Point of View

I have heard from many people who regret they did not learn more languages as children, but I have only rarely, if ever, heard of anyone who resents having learned an extra language. Most people who became bilingual as children consider their bilingualism a gift. They remember the experience of growing up speaking two languages as easy and natural. "English (my second language) must have been easy," says Ana, who also speaks Spanish, "because I don't remember learning it. I feel like I've just always known it." People like Ana are hard-pressed to come up with anything negative to say about having learned two languages when they were young. Many of them have told me they see only advantages:

"I am incredibly lucky to be raised in a bilingual household."

"I was greatly envied by my friends."

"It has enriched my life . . . given me an appreciation of foreign cultures."

"I want to bestow the same fortune on my children if I can."

Different Types of Benefits of Bilingual Upbringing: For Money or for Love

Gardner and Lambert, Canadian pioneers of language-learning research, classify people's reasons for learning a second language into two basic types: utilitarian and emotional. The former involves using language as an instrument to achieve something else, like a job, while the latter involves learning the language for the love of it and to become part of the group that speaks it. Both help us understand people's drives to make a bilingual home.

Practical Benefits

Some major utilitarian motivations include getting jobs that are open to bilinguals but are not available to monolinguals and easing travel to or education in other countries by knowing the language there. Another important utilitarian reason is to be able to communicate with more people. For example, a businessperson might be able to add whole nations of potential customers. Similarly, a researcher might want to be able to understand research findings written in other languages.

Other utilitarian, or instrumental, benefits of a bilingual upbringing are found in expanded professional opportunities. Chilean-American author Ariel Dorfman muses about the prehistoric traders who first discovered that "anyone who knows both tongues could sell and buy, swap and acquire on far better terms." He may have been imagining the unusual career niche of my Japanese friend, Ichiro, a fluent Japanese-English bilingual. Ichiro spent two years as a youth in the U.S. and later worked as a translator before he got his degree in international law and became an executive in a large multinational corporation. When he retired, he became a "cultural broker," working as an intermediary between Japanese and American executives. He not only knew the business goals of both sides, but he could also advise both sides on appropriate behaviors to win the favor of the other, how to show appreciation, and how to stand firm in ways that would not be misunderstood. These are things that he learned as an adult, but for which he acquired the sensitivity growing up as a bilingual child.

A team of political geographers at the University of Miami compared the earning potential of bilinguals with that of monolinguals and concluded that bilinguals had an edge in lifetime earnings. There are whole branches of professional and service careers that are open only to those who can navigate freely in more than one language community. Bilinguals gain part of their advantage not just from knowing a second language but also by understanding their clients' needs better than those who do not share a language with them. Careers in diplomacy and international publishing in particular help bridge the gaps in cultural understanding between members of different language groups.

In the European Union (EU), which currently has eleven official languages, childhood bilingualism has become a necessity. Efficient administration of the EU will become impossible unless large numbers of its members become bilingual or even multilingual. Their best hope to accomplish this lies with their children. Likewise, government and trade concerns of the U.S. make bilingual speakers of strategic languages valuable to the national interest. It is no accident, for example, that one of the FBI agents closest to tracking Al Qaeda before 9/11, Ali Soufan, was a childhood bilingual from Lebanon.

Emotional Benefits

Emotional motivation, on the other hand, refers to the desire to learn a language as a form of intellectual and cultural enrichment or to integrate with and have a sense of belonging to the social group that speaks that language. Children who grow up speaking languages without an accent are more readily accepted as insiders in the areas where those languages are spoken. This kind of motivation is especially important if speaking only one language in the nuclear family would cut the children off from a sense of belonging to a larger, extended family.

The Benefits of an Extended Family

Indeed, the most often-cited motivation of the bilingual parents I spoke with was to secure the benefits of contact with their extended family for their children. They are making the effort to help their children learn the language of their own parents and siblings. They want their children to have a sense of closeness and connection to both of their families and to participate in conversations with their friends. They feel it is important for their children to

". . . understand who their parents are and where we come from,
so they can feel proud."

"It will give them a sense of their roots and let them be at home in both
cultures. They won't be outsiders either here or at home."

Because extended family, when it is available, plays such a large role in the emotional well-being of the nuclear family, this reason alone is often enough to motivate two family languages. Children can feel the love and caring from their grandparents, uncles, and aunts, and they can enjoy the companionship of their cousins. The grandparents get the deep satisfaction of knowing their children's children. (Those of us who have experienced being grandparents would not give it up lightly.)

Moreover, parents who speak a language with their children that is different from the community language often report an especially close bond that comes from their "private" communication. Parents who are not in their home country will not want to close the door on moving home, so they, too, find it worthwhile to maintain a second language in their home.

Many monolingual parents of children adopted from abroad are also concerned that their children be able to identify with their ethnic group and eventually relate to their birth families. In chapter 5, Rosemary and her Guatemalan daughter tell us about their language goals and how they have accomplished them.

Access to Cultural Heritage

The language also gives children special access to the artifacts, customs, and rituals that define their heritage. One childhood bilingual (now grown) said,

"I don't know if I would have understood my parents' culture as well if I had learned about it in English. I certainly would have been a spectator at the celebrations that were the high points of my visits to India. Since I spoke the language, I was a participant. I played a role in making them happen."

We can also appreciate this reason if we think of enjoying iconic literature in the language in which it was written. One may want to read Pushkin in the original Russian, Shakespeare in English, or Cervantes in Spanish. These are not, of course, motivating forces for a small child—who may be more interested in Tintin in France or Monica in Brazil—but the parents can be looking ahead on the child's behalf. Similarly, the child's eventual ability to read religious texts is potentially very motivating for people in a number of cultures. Whether or not they live in an Arabic-speaking country, many Muslim Arabs will be eager for their children to participate in prayers. They will want them to be able to read the Koran easily and natively so that they can appreciate the richness of its imagery and interpret its teachings for themselves, much as many Christian parents find spiritual meaning from reading and rereading their Bible and many Jews from studying the Torah.

The strongest tie to traditional practices and folklore—medical beliefs, songs, jokes, benedictions, curses, and the like—is through the language in which they developed. They may be translated for outsiders, but they are most deeply felt when experienced in the original language. Without native speakers to practice them, these traditions lose their authenticity and are eventually dropped. Folklore may be lost. Jewish children who know Yiddish, which was for centuries the language of everyday life for Eastern European Jews, have access to the rich stories in that language that translate weakly, if they are translated at all, into other languages. Poetry, of all the arts, demands to be read in the original language. No translation can capture the entire sense of words in another language, especially the precisely chosen words of a poem. The bilingual Irish-English poet Nuala Ni Dhomhnaill suggests that different translations each "underline different facets of the original, like differing cuts of a diamond can bring out different lights in a stone."

Retaining the Parental Role

If children learn their parents' language, then parents whose language is not the language of the community can remain involved in thei children's lives and interests outside the home. The children will be less likely to be alienated from parents who do not make the transition to the new language and culture. I always feel intense sadness when I reread Richard Rodriguez's moving memoir, *Hunger of Memory*. His parents, immigrants from Mexico, followed outside advice to speak only English in their home, and in so doing, lost their role as leaders of the family. Dinner table conversation was in the hands of the children. The parents' limited English kept them from joining in, and the lives of their children grew more foreign to them. Rodriguez describes lively gatherings with his siblings in the years after the schools convinced his parents not to speak Spanish with them anymore. The mother follows the conversation a little wistfully, like a spectator at a tennis match; the father retreats into himself completely. If these family meals had taken place in Spanish—which the children all spoke very well—this isolation of the parents within the family would not have happened.

WHAT PARENTS ENJOY MOST

For many parents, behind the desire to raise their children in a language that is not the community language is the desire to raise their children the way they were raised—in what is, for them, the language of intimacy and affection.

"We want to relate to them in our best language, what is, for us, the language of home and comfort."

"It feels so good to speak my mother tongue."

"I can tell them what is most important to me in the way I want to say it."

"It feels more natural to me to speak with babies and young children in the language I was spoken to in, to sing the songs that were sung to me, and play the little games that I played."

"The [Tamil] language is such an important part of my identity. I have a deep level of comfort in speaking it—and my toddler doesn't seem to care which language I speak."

ılinguist Virginia Gathercole and her colleagues at the University were funded by the Welsh Language Board to explore what it ıts enjoy most about speaking their minority language with their children. Many say it "just feels better" to speak in the language in which they were spoken to as children. It is also often the language in which they can "feel the most themselves." One father remarked that if he didn't speak to his children in Welsh, his children wouldn't really know him.

The native language is also the language that parents can speak with the most authority. They are naturally more comfortable speaking a language in which they won't make grammatical mistakes that their children would not hesitate to point out to them (or roll their eyes at). In one of our University of Miami Infant Studies, which followed twenty-five babies for about three years, one parent reported that if he found himself in a dangerous situation, he switched unconsciously into Spanish, in which his reflexes are faster. The same thing happens when parents need to scold. Their language of origin often turns out to be the language of anger as well as of affection. My neighbor Marielle says she could always tell when her mother was really angry, because she switched into French.

On the other hand, there is no single pattern for everyone. Sometimes, but more rarely, it is not the parent's native language that has the greatest emotional impact. People—like author George Saunders—who have had intense pleasures and intellectual fulfillment associated with their second language want to provide that experience for their children. Such individuals will have a special feeling from using their adopted language.

Benefits Even for the "Accidental Bilingual"
Many bilingual families—parents and children—are not aware of any particular benefits of bilingual upbringing. They have no special affinity for language or specific language goals, but they become bilinguals by an accident of fate.

Whether parents choose bilingualism for their children or have it thrust upon them, their children reap the benefits of the experience. Many of them stay involved in language when they grow up and choose language-related careers. Many linguists, teachers, translators, and international businesspeople had early bilingual or trilingual exposure as children Being a childhood multilingual does not turn all children into linguis or language teachers—but whether they sought the experience or not, it opens their mind to the possibility and promise of other cultures and gives them a head start on learning their next language. There are many studies that show that childhood bilinguals, even those whose families did not really choose it, can learn an additional language better than monolinguals, are better problem solvers, and have a host of other talents we will explore next.

How Two Languages Are Better Than One: Support from Research

Research shows that children who know at least two languages have expanded capabilities with respect to all three of the main functions of language: communicating, thinking, and learning about one's culture. My goal in this section is to lay out systematically the benefits of bilingualism that science has established and, in doing so, confirm your own intuitions about what you and your children will gain from the experience. I present the research evidence about additional linguistic, cognitive, intellectual, and cultural benefits that you are bringing to your children in the process of helping them become bilingual. (Chapters 7 and 8 will expand on concerns parents may have about linguistic and cognitive development and identity issues.)

People don't make the decision to raise bilingual children by calculating advantages and disadvantages in so many months of development. Nevertheless, these cognitive and intellectual benefits of bilingual households are important for parents to know about. Then they can feel reaffirmed in doing what matters most to them—providing entrée for their children into their extended family or into a culture broader than that of the one community where they happen to find themselves.

The research we are about to discuss in the remainder of this chapter shows that knowing a second language brings tangible benefits to children on three levels:

- ~y acquire precocious *knowledge about language,* a capacity called ~linguistic awareness," which is one of the foundational skills for ~ how to read and write. Metalinguistic awareness will also help ~hen they want or need to learn a third (or fourth or fifth)

..ıld

Bilinguals also get enhanced skills *outside of language* that stem from learning and processing two languages—especially in the realm of thinking skills. New findings even indicate that bilingualism is a hedge against mental aging.

The bilingual child also develops a broader worldview and social understanding, which we fervently hope will lead to a more tolerant society.

Precocious Knowledge *About* Language

Bilingual children have an advantage in the way they think *about* their languages. They become aware of the formal properties and structures of language, such as the fact that words consist of syllables and sounds, earlier than monolinguals. Neurologists tell us that both of the languages of a bilingual are always active in the mind. Therefore, bilinguals must make a decision about language at some, usually subconscious, level every time they open their mouths to speak and their brains must choose which language to tell their mouths to use. Every time they hear something, they have to determine which language it is in before they interpret it. Not surprisingly, then, because bilinguals must think about language so often, they excel in a skill that involves knowing about language, "metalinguistic awareness." They both use language and "see" it.

WHAT IS METALINGUISTIC AWARENESS?

What is it to "see" language? To understand this idea, we can think of words as windows that let us see through them to the objects or concepts they provide labels for. So, if I say "dog," the picture this word raises in your mind is of a furry, barking animal often kept as a pet. The sound of the word "dog" itself does not claim your attention: it directs your attention *through* the word to the idea of your pet. But if I ask how many sounds the word "dog" has, the word is no longer a transparent window into the pet shop. The word is now the object you have to think about in order to count its sounds. Being able to focus on the sounds of the word itself is the basis for learning to read and developing other academic skills. Until we learn to read (or start getting the skills that will let us learn to read), words are like the pane of glass in the window that we look through, without thinking of it, to see the pet we want.

Figure 1. **Using language vs. "seeing" language**

We use words; we don't typically talk about them. However, in order to write and to read what is written children must know *about* the symbols we call "letters" and understand how they are related to the sounds that words are made of. They need to understand that these squiggles on the paper stand for specific sounds that they need to re-create in their minds, while those other similar squiggles are just a pretty design.

Young bilingual children, who choose between languages many times a day, develop greater awareness of the languages involved and are better at establishing this abstract connection between letters and sounds. They often become better writers and more effective users of language because they have a better understanding of how language works. (In chapter 8, we will hear more about this benefit directly from some bilingual writers themselves.)

We will now look at the research, much of it the work of psychologist Ellen Bialystok of York University in Toronto, showing us that bilingual children see the glass pane in the window, as well as the dog beyond it, sooner than monolingual children of comparable intelligence.

Words in Sentences and Words in Minds

One illustration of this precocious metalinguistic awareness that bilingual children commonly possess comes from an experiment looking at the difference between typical adult and child responses to word association tests. What is the first word you think of when I say "dog"? Children most often make the match as if they were *using* the word in a sentence—for example, "dog-bark." Adults tend to give more "dictionary" responses, offering words of the same type—for example, "dog-cat"—that are associated according to their abstract relationships in the adults' mental vocabularies. The adult isn't responding with how he or she would use the word in context but with how he or she might talk about it.

The shift in preference from "sentence matches" to "dictionary matches" has been well established as taking place between the ages of five and eight, but bilingual children give more dictionary responses sooner than their monolingual peers. This shows that they are able to think *about* a word independent of the sentences it usually appears in. When children can do that, they show that they are organizing their mental vocabularies so that they can make better use of the words they know. Children with "metaknowledge"—knowledge *about* what they know— have a better sense of what words mean because they can relate them to similar or opposite words, much like a printed dictionary does.

Words Are Arbitrary Symbols

Another important aspect of metaknowledge about language is an awareness of what is called "referential arbitrariness." This is a fancy phrase to say that there is no predictable link between the sound of a word and what it means; their pairing is arbitrary. Except for a small set of onomatopoeic words that are the names for sounds—e.g., *meow* is the sound a cat makes, and *whoosh* is a fast movement through air or water—there is no relation between a word and its meaning. *Dog* can stand for "dog," but something else could too, like *chien,* the French word for "dog." In contrast, when we say that "smoke *means* fire," there is a necessary connection between them. The fire produces the smoke, and so, universally, smoke tells us that there is a fire. In contrast, the specific word that "means fire" in a language is not universal, and it can be changed—either by convention in different languages or by a temporary agreement between people who need a private code. We could, for example, agree that if I say "ubleck," it means "fire." Bilingualism helps children to see that a word is this arbitrary kind of symbol.

The Swiss psychologist Jean Piaget tested children's understanding of this arbitrary relationship between words and concepts in a famous experiment. He asked children if it would be possible to exchange the names of the sun and the moon, and if so, what would be up in the sky at night. He found that most children could switch the names and say correctly that the "sun" would be in the sky at night. However, the hard part for the children was to then say what the sky would look like at night. They insisted that the sky would be light at night. Because only the names, not the objects themselves, were switched, Piaget's subjects should have recognized that it would still be dark at night (even with the "moon-now-called-sun" up in the sky).

Many years later, one of the pioneers of bilingualism research, Jim Cummins of the University of Toronto, showed that bilingual children were better at Piaget's sun-moon problem than monolinguals were. After all, they are used to changing the names for things: this is "a book" for Mommy and "un libro" for Daddy. In one variation of the task, psychologists Feldman and Shen taught five-year-old Head Start children new names for objects and then asked them to use the new name in a sentence. So, the child would be shown a car and told that in this name game, its name is "airplane." Later, they were told to put the "airplane" on the "plate" (where the "airplane" was a car and the "plate" was a cup). The monolinguals and bilinguals were able to learn the new names for things equally well—either switched real names, like Piaget's "sun-moon," or invented nonsense words—but only the bilinguals were successful in using them in sentences. This is because bilinguals exercise that capacity every day. They learn early that the word and the thing are separate. The word *book* is not made of paper; the word *snake* is not long and thin. The word *red*, even when written in green ink, still refers to the color of blood and roses.

Why Metalinguistic Skills Are Important for Children: Reading and Writing

Parents may wonder why psychologists and educators think meta-linguistic awareness is such an important skill. Here's why: Understanding language structure and functioning gives children an important tool for developing their thinking skills. As we mature and develop more abstract thinking, we are learning to separate the ideas and concepts in our minds from the symbols that convey them.

Reading and writing are the most common, and perhaps the most important, skills based on this awareness of the elements of language, but they are by no means the only ones. They are two of many "meta" skills that we learn as we mature. In general, "metathinking" is an important increase in children's power of thinking. For example, when children verbalize their own thought processes, they are then able to plan how to solve problems, keep track of their successful strategies, and avoid those that did not work in similar situations in the past. As you can imagine, these "meta" skills will make them better thinkers.

Time and again, this ability to think abstractly about language is related to academic success. The better the child does on metalinguistic awareness tasks, the better the child does in school. Children with less of this awareness do worse. Properly controlled experiments make it clear that being bilingual makes a difference. Their bilingualism gives bilingual children a greater ability to "see" language and helps them better understand nonliteral language, the use of one word to call up another, as in literature or poetry. Bilinguals get a lot of practice doing this—using one word for another—on a daily basis. As we see below, it helps propel them into reading and writing earlier than monolingual children with the same amount of experience in the language they are all learning to read.

From Sounds to Letters

Before children can actually read, they exhibit a "meta" skill called "phonemic awareness." That is, children are becoming aware of the units within words—the sounds, or "phonemes." To use my image from above, they must look at the glass pane in the window, not the meaning beyond, and they must see what the different designs on the window itself are.

One commonly tested phonemic awareness skill is counting syllables within a word: clap for each syllable you hear—once for "ball," twice for "to-day," three times for "to-mor-row." Another common pre-reading task requiring phonemic awareness is taking off the first or last sound of a word: say "pant" without the *p*, (that is, "ant"). Note that reading poetry and making rhymes, like being bilingual, can also facilitate this sound-based (rather than content-bound) understanding. That is why nursery rhymes are in such demand everywhere. They are great preparation for reading.

Another key concept for learning to read is called the "concept of print," which refers to the idea of how marks on a page represent words. It is not about any particular words, it's *about* writing in general, so it's a "meta" skill, too. When children learn to write and read, they must learn what the units are in the writing system (graphic symbols for single sounds, syllables, or whole words) and appreciate that there is a predictable and consistent relationship between the letters (or other symbols) used to represent the meaning of a word.

Several systems for how graphic symbols represent meaning have evolved in different parts of the world. To make use of the letters of an alphabetic script, where characters stand for single sounds, children must learn to segment a word into smaller units (its sounds) and to associate them with symbols or letters that stand for them—for example, when you see *s*, say "ss"; when you see *i*, say "ih"; when you see *x*, say "ks"; so when you see *s-i-x*, say "s-ih-ks." The letters are cues to saying the sounds. You put the sounds together and you get to the word, and then from the word, you go to the meaning. By contrast, with whole-word symbols, or "logograms," a symbol stands for a word; for instance, the number 6 stands for the word *six*. So, the "rule" here is, "if you see 6, say 'six.'" It might seem easier to go directly from the symbol to the meaning without going through the step of translating the letters into sounds and then connecting the sounds into a word on the way to the meaning. In fact, some writing systems, such as the one used in Chinese, do exactly that. While that saves the trouble of segmenting words into sounds to be translated into letters, Chinese-speakers need to memorize all of the symbol-word pairs individually. By contrast, when you learn to read an alphabetic script, you have an extra operation, but you only have to remember some thirty or forty symbol-sound pairings.

Ellen Bialystok compared monolingual English speakers with three sets of bilinguals—Spanish-English, Chinese-English, and Hebrew-English—on a phonemic awareness task. Six-and-a-half-year-old children were asked to count the sounds within a spoken word—e.g., "p-a-t" has three sounds, and "a-g-ai-n" has four sounds. All of the bilinguals spoke both languages well and were learning to read in both of their languages. Bialystok statistically corrected for any differences among the children in memory and vocabulary skills so that differences in performance between the groups could not be attributed to those factors.

The groups that did the best were the Spanish-English and Hebrew-English bilinguals. They were both learning two alphabetic scripts, so they had double practice in breaking words down to the units of sound that correspond to the letters of the alphabet. The English monolinguals scored the lowest of all four groups, and the Chinese-English bilingual group scored lower than the Spanish-English and Hebrew-English bilingual children but higher than the English monolinguals. The Chinese-English bilinguals were learning only one "alphabet," the English one, but they still had practice with two writing systems—one based on alphabetic letters that represent the individual sounds in a word (English) and one in which each symbol stands for a whole word (Chinese). It appears that even though they had only one alphabet under their belt, they still had the advantage of the extra experience in mastering how to pair written symbols with words in order to read them.

The Concept of Print

In order to learn to read and write, children also need to recognize that a certain sequence of letters always stands for the same word, even when the written word is upside down or does not match a picture it is found with. Bialystok (who is the undisputed expert in this type of study) used the "moving word task" to find out whether monolingual and bilingual children understood how writing works. She pretested children ages four and five on their knowledge of letters, and then she chose to work only with the ones whose reading skills had started to blossom but had not completely flowered. They knew their letters and could say their sounds, but could not yet read independently. Even though they couldn't yet read, she wondered how much they knew about how reading works.

For this task, the experimenter showed children pictures of two objects—for example, a king and a bird. Then a card with the name of one of the objects was brought out. The experimenter said, "This card has the word *king* on it. I'm going to put it here," and she placed it under the picture of the king. Then she asked the child what was written on it. Most emergent readers were able to say that it was "king." At this point, the experiment called for some confusion—two stuffed animals in a scuffle, or an elephant sneezing very hard—so that the items would shift about and the card with the word on it would end up under the wrong picture. The experimenter again asked the child to identify what was written on the card.

The key question was the second one, when the printed word was temporarily under the wrong picture. Bialystok estimated that the bilinguals were more than a year in advance of the monolinguals in recognizing that the print did not change what it said when it moved to a different picture. This is a very crucial piece of the reading puzzle for a child. Among monolingual subjects, only 38% gave the correct answer, compared to 82% of the bilinguals at the same stage of emergent reading. The four-year-old bilinguals were ahead of the five-year-old monolinguals.

My own studies with colleagues at the University of Miami, Florida, of elementary school children who learned to read in two languages also demonstrated a bilingual advantage. In this *Language and Literacy in Bilingual Children* study of 960 English-Spanish bilingual and English monolingual schoolchildren's language and literacy capacities, we looked at three groups: one monolingual group and two different groups of bilinguals. The first group of bilinguals consisted of children in "one-way," English-only schools, learning Spanish at home, while the second group of bilinguals were in "two-way," dual-language programs, with half the day taught in Spanish and half in English. The children in the two-way program learned to read in two languages from the very beginning.

Not surprisingly, in kindergarten, the two bilingual groups were different neither from each other nor from the monolingual group with respect to how well they did on the standardized reading tests we used. At that age, no one is expected to know how to read yet, so the reading test for the kindergarteners just checked how well they identified pictures and recognized the letters of the alphabet. But by second grade, differences in reading skill between the groups had emerged. Differences now favored the group with instruction in two languages, and the advantage was still found at fifth grade (the oldest group tested in the study). It is not surprising that the two-way group did better in Spanish reading, because the one-way group had had no instruction in it. The more striking observation was that learning to read in Spanish as well as in English had clear benefits for the children's reading scores in English, where on some tests they surpassed the monolinguals as well. It seems that the experience of working out rules for two different writing systems—once they have done it—makes the rules more explicit and accessible to bilingual children than to those learning to read in only one language.

Enhanced Mental Flexibility

DIVERGENT THINKING

Another area of thinking where bilinguals have been shown to excel is divergent thinking, the ability to come up with many different solutions rather than just one. Divergent thinking is considered to be one of the basic elements of creativity. In early tests for this type of mental flexibility, the bilingual subjects thought of more uses for typical objects (like a paper clip, a brick, or a cardboard box) and generated more possible solutions to problems than did the monolingual subjects. Later experiments explored bilinguals' ability to apply that mental flexibility in a science inquiry program. The bilinguals were able to generate three times more high-quality hypotheses for solving science problems than the monolingual students. The bilinguals did better even when they were less advantaged socially and economically than the monolingual participants (a condition that is often associated with lower academic results) and had lower reading scores.

Psychologist Sandra Ben-Zeev found that the increased mental flexibility of bilinguals, which has been shown in the verbal domain, extends to tasks requiring analysis of nonverbal patterns as well. She matched groups of children between ages five and eight in Israel and the U.S. on IQ scores and then gave them tasks that required them to see two patterns of organization at once in pegs on a pegboard. The children had to complete patterns with pegs that varied in three levels of height and three levels of width and then explain what they did. The hardest task was to rearrange the pegs in a different orientation while still preserving the pattern. Monolinguals and bilinguals performed the reorganization equally well, but the bilinguals' descriptions were more analytical and systematic than the monolinguals'. They more consistently referred to both dimensions of the pegs and kept track of how they were related. Ben-Zeev interpreted her findings as showing that the bilinguals were seeking out rules behind the patterns and using the rules to organize their understanding when the patterns changed.

SELECTIVE ATTENTION

Recently, researchers have discovered a new area of thinking where bilinguals are consistently faster and more accurate than monolinguals. With different language pairs, at different ages, bilinguals consistently excel in selective attention. Bilinguals do better than monolinguals on tests that require them to focus on just one or two aspects of a task while *suppressing* attention to its other aspects. To be successful, the participant must ignore conflicting or extraneous information. The more misleading the material to be ignored, the greater the bilingual advantage.

A classic measure of selective attention is called the Stroop test. This test displays lists of color names printed in colors that do not match the names. If the word "blue" is written in red ink, you are supposed to name the actual color you see (red), but most people mistakenly say the written word (here, "blue"). They find it hard to inhibit that automatic response. Bialystok explains that from the beginning of their use of two languages, bilinguals must constantly control which of their languages they will use at any given moment and at the same time turn off the other. Thanks to this extra mental exercise for their brains, bilinguals are better able to control what they focus on than monolinguals are.

The bilingual advantage in selective attention is not restricted to verbal tasks. It is also seen in tests of perception that involve misleading cues. To test people's ability to pay attention to one aspect of a scene while ignoring another, Frye, Zelazo, and colleagues developed the "dimensional change card sorting task." Children are shown two cards, one representing, for example, a circle in blue, and the other, a square in red. Subsequent cards switch the pairing—red circles and blue squares. When first sorting the items according to one dimension—say, color—everyone finds it easy. Bilingual and monolingual children complete the task equally well. However, when the children are asked to sort the cards again, this time according to shape, bilingual children respond more accurately and more quickly. Their minds are more agile. Their selective attention is better. That is, it is easier for them to put the old response aside and pick up the new one.

Another test for enhanced selective attention is based on the "Simon effect." John Simon was an engineer in the 1960s trying to design better cockpits for pilots. Fast responses for pilots are a matter of life and death, so every fraction of a second counts. Simon found that if pilots need to respond to information coming to them from their right side, they will do it faster if they can make the response on their right. Information from the left side is responded to better on the left. One version of Simon's test for this has a red and a blue light that can come from either side of a screen, the left or the right. There are two buttons to push, one on the right for one color and one on the left for the other color. When the blue light and the button for blue are both on the same, "congruent" side, the task is easier than when the blue light is on the right and the button to press for blue is on the left, "incongruent" side. The difference in response speed between congruent and incongruent sides is measured in milliseconds, but over many trials the differences add up. The bigger the difference, the stronger the effect. When you are an air passenger, you want your pilot to show as small a Simon effect as possible.

Bialystok found that bilingual children as young as four showed a smaller Simon effect than the monolinguals they were matched with. Bialystok and her colleagues tested monolinguals and bilinguals of all ages. The bilinguals performed better than the monolinguals across the life span. An unexpected finding was that the elderly bilinguals (with an average age of seventy) maintained an advantage over their monolingual peers.

Bialystok followed these experiments up with a study of mental functioning in the real world. She and her coauthors studied the medical records of 184 monolingual and bilingual patients with dementia. They found that the onset of dementia was delayed by an average of four years in people who had spoken two languages throughout their lives:

onset age was seventy-five for the bilinguals, compared to seventy-one for the monolinguals. The difference remained statistically significant even when the researchers took into consideration the possible effects of gender, cultural differences, and educational level. One expert on Alzheimer's disease commented that there is no known drug that produces as dramatic an improvement as this.

Selective attention is controlled by a mental process called "executive function." "Executive function" refers to the general ability to coordinate the many distinct activities that must be integrated in order to carry out any goal-oriented task. It is thought to develop between two and five years of age and to continue improving through adolescence and young adulthood, but then it declines with age. (It is also diminished by excessive alcohol consumption.) Simply put, bilinguals build their powers of executive function whenever they choose and switch between languages in conversation. Their executive function has a greater opportunity—and much more need—to improve.

Understanding the role of executive function helps clarify what may sometimes seem like contradictory results in the research. One study would find bilinguals doing better, the next would show no advantage, and so on. So, you might ask, does being bilingual help or doesn't it? Yes, it does, but only on tasks that require "metaknowledge" and a high degree of executive control. Work is now underway to investigate the limits of the bilingual benefit. Questions under investigation include the following: How bilingual does one have to be to experience the smaller Simon effect? Is this benefit greater for proficient bilinguals? Does the strength of the benefit differ between childhood bilinguals and those who become bilingual later in life? We do not have the answers to these questions yet, but we have enough evidence to see that the benefit is real and available to us when we pursue it.

A Broader Perspective and Understanding "the Other"

Linguistic and cognitive benefits are very real and important, but they do not represent the whole of the bilingual benefit. We turn in this section to benefits that stem from having a broadened worldview. Francois Grosjean, a Swiss psycholinguist who has written extensively on bilingualism, stated, "[Bilingualism] broadens your scope. It means you have two worlds instead of one." He was referring to friends, cultural traditions, and job possibilities, but he might have added that the bilingual also gets two worldviews. In the words of a Czech proverb, "Learn a new language: get a new soul."

Linguistic Relativity: The Influence of Language on Thought and Perception

The relationship between one's worldview and one's language was first discussed in the early part of the twentieth century as the concept of "linguistic relativity." This theory says that your language determines the way you think and how you perceive the world. Benjamin Whorf, one of the early scholars associated with this idea, was impressed by the way the Hopi language seemed to express a worldview of its speakers that was very different from that of his own language community. For example, Hopi verb forms do not mark a linear sequence of time— past, present, and future—the way English verb tenses do ("was/were," "is/are," and "will be"). In the Hopi culture, time is conceived of as a cycle, where past, present, and future are recurring points in time. The Hopi language obliges Hopi speakers to pay attention not to the time of an event but to whether an event is actual or potential—whether it is "objective" or "subjective"—in order to use the appropriate markings on the verb. This distinction is less commonly encoded in English, except perhaps in the subjunctive mood to talk about events that haven't happened. (English speakers usually learn about this form only if they study a different language, like Latin or Spanish, in which the subjunctive is more prominent.)

According to one way of understanding linguistic relativity, people are *confined* by the worldview encoded in the structure of their language. That claim is not only hard to test, but is most likely false. For example, it was thought for a time that the names for colors determined how people saw color. If a language didn't have two distinct words for "blue" and "green," but only had, say, "grue," a strong interpretation of linguistic relativity would say that blue and green would look the same to speakers of that language. In fact, experiments with languages that have different color-naming words have shown that this does not happen. In a language with a term for "grue" instead of "green" and "blue," speakers can perceive the difference between these colors, but they tend not to consider it a prominent contrast.

A weaker version of the role of language in shaping how we think has been receiving considerable attention and support in recent research. According to the weaker sense of linguistic relativity, a language can modify how its speakers view and remember objects and events, but it does not imprison them in that view. It is a common experience that having a word for something helps you remember it. If you cannot name something, it is harder to hold on to the concept. Consider, for example, looking at clouds and admiring the patterns they make in the sky. If you were to be asked to describe the patterns three days later, you probably wouldn't be able to do so. But if you had "seen" a lamb, a face, or a boat there, it would be easy. So at the very least, having a word for something makes it more present in our minds and easier for us to retrieve.

The categories of the grammar of a language also influence speakers' attention so that habits of perception develop over time. Looking at pictures seems like a universal activity that would be the same for all people, no matter what language they speak. You might suppose that if people were to look at the same picture or video of an action—like a girl running out of a house—everyone would see the same thing and describe it the same way. But linguists have found that people who speak different languages describe different parts of the same scene in ways that match the vocabulary and grammar patterns of their language. For example, in languages like German and English, verbs that describe motion (like "walking," "running," or "skipping") tend to include the *way one moves* in the meaning of the verb. The *direction of the motion* is less central, and it is expressed in a prepositional phrase that follows the verb—"She ran *out of the house*." The verb describes how she moved ("at a run"), and the "out of" phrase indicates where ("out of the house"). Romance languages, like French and Spanish, do it the other way. They include the directional information in the basic meaning of the verb and then use a phrase to describe the manner of motion if it is relevant. So the same sentence as above in Spanish would be *(Ella) salió de la casa corriendo*—literally, "She exited the house, running." That is, the verb specifies the direction (in, out, up, or down), similar to the English verbs "ascend" and "descend." Spanish speakers can optionally indicate that she ran—*corriendo*—as well. German and English have directional verbs like "enter" and "exit" too, but they are less common, more specialized words than "running," "walking," etc., and they are learned later and used less frequently.

If these different language patterns had no effect on people's perceptions, German and Spanish speakers would be equally likely to describe the *way* a character moves, and equally likely to denote the *direction* in which the character moves, if, as in the example above, they are both represented in the picture. Letty Naigles, a psycholinguist at the University of Connecticut, tested whether Spanish- and English-speaking adults actually do that. She showed them short videos of an action, gave the action a nonsense name (like "kradding" for English and "mercando" for Spanish), and asked the subjects to say what the verb meant. The English-speaking subjects were more likely to notice the manner of motion and use that in their definitions of the nonsense verbs, while the Spanish-speaking subjects noticed and spoke about the direction. The answers followed a pattern reflecting the aspects of meaning most commonly expressed by verbs in the subjects' language. A few English speakers mentioned the direction first, and a few Spanish speakers talked about the manner of motion, but there was a strong tendency among subjects to find most salient those aspects of meaning that were expressed by the verbs in their language.

Several experimental techniques, which I illustrate below, show the strength of these effects and the extent to which they can be changed with further language experience.

Psycholinguist Lera Boroditsky elegantly demonstrated the difference between English and Indonesian interpretations of the same events. She showed people three pictures of an action—like "a person kicking a ball." In picture 1, a man is shown with his leg back, about to kick the ball. In picture 2, the same man is shown having just kicked the ball. In picture 3, a different man is shown in the same position as the first man, with his leg pulled back, about to kick the ball. Participants were asked which two of the three pictures were the most alike. The English-speaking subjects would describe pictures 1 and 3 by saying, "the man is about to kick the ball," but would say, "he has kicked the ball" for picture 2. So, they most often said that pictures 1 and 3 were most similar. Not the Indonesian speakers. In their language, marking the verb for tense (the difference between "is about to kick" and "kicked") is optional; both phases of the kicking action are labeled just "kicking," and all three pictures would be described by saying, "a man kicking a ball." (Indonesians can, of course, use another phrase to draw attention to the position of the kicker's leg, but it is less frequent.) Reflecting that pattern, Indonesian speakers overwhelmingly said that the pictures with the same man were most similar, rather than the pictures of different men in the same phase of the kicking event.

Interestingly, Indonesians who spoke English answered more like the English speakers. As the Indonesians became more proficient in English, their answers reflected more strongly the English view of the event. Even more interesting was the finding that bilinguals answered more like the English when the experiment was conducted in England, but more like Indonesians when the experiment was conducted in Indonesia—even though they always responded by pointing and they were not asked to use either language.

How the Influence of Language on Thought Develops

We discussed above just two of many similar demonstrations of different ways of "seeing" the world that mirror lexical and grammatical distinctions in one's language. Some studies show these effects in children's earliest words, even before age two, while other habits of thought formed by language may develop more slowly, as University of Chicago researcher John Lucy's work shows.

Lucy demonstrated that the ways in which Mayan speakers and English speakers sort common objects—combs, pencils, etc.—differ according to the way the objects are grouped in the agreement system of their language. The Mayan language does not just say "two items" but must use a different numeral "classifier" depending on the texture or material the item is made of—"two smooth-stone-type tools" or "two long-wax candles." Mayans typically sort by the material something is made of, whereas English speakers sort by shape.

Lucy's experiments used sets of three objects: One object had a characteristic shape and material, like a sheet of paper. The second object matched the shape but not the material, like a sheet of plastic. The third object matched the material but not the shape, like a book. Preschool children—one group learning Yucatec Mayan and one group learning English—all preferred to use shape as the basis for saying which two objects were most alike. They were more likely to say that the sheet of paper and the sheet of plastic were the same. That remains the preferred pairing for English speakers, even adults. The Mayan children, however, at around age eight, started to show a preference for grouping by material, putting the sheet of paper and the book together as the most alike. By age eleven, like Mayan adults, they matched objects by material almost all the time. Thus, the robust differences in how Mayan- and English-speaking adults sort objects do not emerge until around age eight, when children are experienced users of their respective languages.

HOW BILINGUALS BENEFIT FROM LINGUISTIC RELATIVITY

The two languages of bilinguals focus their attention on more aspects of events, so they are able to make a wider set of distinctions in perceiving the world. Bilinguals also profit from having perspectives within more than one language, which can make them sensitive to the fact that each view is only one of many possible views.

Many elements of thought—spatial relations, conceptualization of events, object categorization—that one might think are universal, and thus the same for speakers of all languages, turn out to be closely interwoven with specific languages in complex ways. We might think, then, that the bilingual is doubly confined—bound by two such sets of constraints rather than just one. But the effect is more profound. Having two sets of distinctions for the same phenomenon dethrones each set as the only right way of seeing things. A bilingual is more likely to understand that his or her perspectives are just two out of many. This is the basis of greater tolerance of the opinions of others.

There is an old saying that "the fish is the last to discover the water." This is because water is all the fish knows. Animals that can experience both water and dry land will have a better sense of what is water and what is not water. Being bilingual gives children (and their parents) the opportunity to see each of their languages as one of many others, not better or worse, necessarily. Even given the natural tendency of humans to view our own way as superior, bilingual children have two "superior" ways and a broader perspective overall.

We explore the leap from such an abstract appreciation of the language structure to greater understanding of other cultures and hopefully respect for all people in the next section.

How Language Can Change Social Perceptions

Studies by social psychologists of children who are in school with speakers of other languages show clearly the specific role of language in breaking down prejudice and fostering positive attitudes toward members of other groups. In one experiment by University of Massachusetts professor Linda Tropp and her colleagues, researchers studied English-speaking children in three types of classrooms: Type 1 had all monolingual English speakers. Type 2 had bilingual Spanish- and English-speaking children in the class with the monolingual English speakers, but the language of the classroom was only English. Type 3 had only bilinguals, and everyone—both English speakers and Spanish speakers—was learning in Spanish as well as in English. Note that the classes were all in different schools, so parents didn't get to choose the classroom type. The luck of the draw determined who was in which type of classroom.

To find out how the children thought about the ethnic groups, researchers had them select photos from a stack of pictures of children their age whom they did not know. Some of the children in the pictures looked Latino, and some looked like American children of European background. They were to pick out pictures of children who looked like they might be smart, children who looked like they had a lot of friends, children who looked like someone whose friend they would like to be, and so forth.

The results were strikingly clear. It was not enough for English monolingual children to be in a class with Latino children to develop positive attitudes toward them. The children in classes with no Spanish-speaking Latino students (Type 1) selected a photo of a Latino child as having positive traits very rarely, about 10% of the time. Those in Type 2 English-only classes with Spanish-speaking Latino students in the class chose photos of Latino children for positive traits just a tiny bit more often, about 12 or 13% of the time. However, the English-speaking children learning Spanish (in Type 3 classrooms) chose pictures of Latino children for positive traits 40% of the time. All subjects chose photos of children from their own ethnic group for positive traits more often than pictures of children from another group, but the proportion of those who chose pictures of children from another group was substantially higher for the children of European background who shared not just a class but also a familiarity with the Spanish language with the Latino children. Thus we see that shared language is a very clear mechanism helping children identify with individuals in other ethnic groups.

Just as the experience of going back and forth between languages many times a day is a powerful mental exercise with beneficial consequences for the child's thinking processes, the same experience is a strong cultural exercise, developing the child's powers of cross-cultural understanding and empathy. Many languages have very self-centered vocabulary with which speakers describe themselves and others. They encode their fear of foreigners into the words they use to refer to them. For example, we are "people," but foreigners may be "ghosts," "demons," or "barbarians." People with two languages see that the world does not revolve around each of them, but that, as in the solar system, they all revolve around something more universal.

How the Community Can Benefit from Bilingual Upbringing

Families do what they think is best for their children. If goals for the child and the goals for a community are in conflict, parents are not usually faulted for pursuing the path that benefits the child. But it is a fortunate circumstance when family and community goals converge—as in the bilingual upbringing of children. For local languages losing ground to global languages, passing the endangered language to the next generation within the home is a critical factor in its survival. The world's leading expert on such matters, Joshua Fishman, warns that without bilingual upbringing of children, many minority and endangered languages cannot be saved. So, here is a case where parents can help build their community by speaking the heritage language in their home, with their extended family, and with their friends.

Preserving Linguistic Diversity

This mutual benefit of local (as opposed to global) language use is most clearly articulated in Wales, the region of 2.5 million people in the west of the British Isles. The language of Wales, like local languages in most parts of the world, has less instrumental value in the global economy than does the language it shares its home territory with, English. Thus, almost no one in Wales is a monolingual speaker of Welsh. Nevertheless, Welsh enjoys a relatively strong presence in the form of a growing bilingual English-Welsh community. Estimates of the number of Welsh speakers in Wales fell from 50% in 1901 to 37% in 1931 and 19% in 1981, a drop that alarmed Welsh speakers and policy makers. Since the 1960s, activists have been trying to build Welsh back up, but until the last census, there had been no rise in its level of use. A recent rise in the number of speakers stems, no doubt, from a change in official language policy. In 1988, the Education Reform Act made elementary education in Welsh mandatory in all schools in Wales, and in 1993, the government set up the Welsh Language Board (WLB). According to the website of the WLB, at the latest census, in 2001, the number of Welsh speakers had risen, and the percentage had gone up to 21%, a small but significant amount.

Fortunately, the Welsh put these measures into effect while there were still five hundred thousand speakers. If language maintenance is to be effective at all, it must start well before the time when the language gets down to the last two elders, which happened to many Native American languages.

A key focus of the Welsh Language Board's efforts is getting children to learn the language in the home and at school. The Welsh Language Board provides incentives for the use of Welsh, and, crucially, it provides economic support for parents and schools to teach Welsh. Of these two institutions, the family is considered the more essential. Schools support the parents' efforts, but schools cannot achieve language survival on their own. The family could do it without the schools, but it is even better when schooling supports the parents' efforts. The schools can provide a peer group of speakers, make a broader selection of literacy materials available, and give the minority language higher status within the community. (However, as many readers are aware, or will learn when their bilingual children reach school age, unlike in Wales, schools in most countries are rarely active partners in promoting childhood bilingualism. At best, confident and informed parents will be able to work around monolingual school policies to keep them from being actively destructive of their child's heritage language.)

Why Not Have One Single Global Language?

You may question whether preserving local languages is important, even critical, to the survival of the human race. Wouldn't it be nice, after all, if we could return to a mythical time before Babel when all the people of the earth were supposed to have spoken one language? In modern times, there have been several movements to create a universal language as an instrument of world peace. You may have heard of the invented language Esperanto, which is still active, with as many as two hundred thousand speakers, but it is unlikely to overtake more popular languages, like English or Chinese. At present, English is spoken by one quarter of the people in the world as a first or second language, and its growing use is apparently attributable to natural and commercial forces, without any official policies promoting it. Why would we want to slow its spread?

One reason is that local languages are best equipped to discuss local concerns. It is somewhat of an urban legend that Eskimos have one hundred words for "snow," but they certainly have more than the languages spoken in the balmy South Pacific do. Terms for social relations also develop to communicate the kinds of relationships that are valued in a particular culture. Chinese speakers of English may find it confusing that there is no term to distinguish an uncle on your mother's side from one on your father's side. Quechua speakers of English may miss the advantage their language has of having two words for "we"—one that includes the people you are speaking to and one that does not. Author Eva Hoffman describes how the Polish terms for "friendship" she brought to Canada with her did not prepare her for how she was expected to relate to her Canadian friends. It is impossible to think of a language that would fit all societies.

Another possible reason is that we *need* linguistic and cultural diversity as a survival mechanism for the human race. Michael Pollan's book *The Botany of Desire* makes this lesson clear to us by the analogy to loss of diversity in the plant kingdom. One of his examples involves the humble potato. In the 1800s, both Ireland and the Andes (where the potato originated) depended heavily on the potato as a staple of their diet. In the Andes, there were hundreds of different species of potato as well as a relatively varied diet in general. When blight attacked the Andean potato, the effect on the population in the Andes was almost unnoticed. In Ireland, by contrast, the Andean potato had pushed out other varieties, so by the time of the famine, only one major variety of potato was grown there. Ireland was a very poor country, and few other foods were affordable to much of the population. When blight wiped out this one type of potato, the country suffered a famine in which approximately one million people perished, and many others emigrated, over only a few years. The biodiversity that protected the people in the Andes was absent in Ireland, which was devastated as a result.

A similar principle is at work with languages. Languages express the wisdom of cultures, and different cultures represent different ways of living on earth. As we have seen above, our language shapes the way we tend to view objects and events. The perceptions imposed by our languages do not have to be confining; experience with another language can change those perceptions. Bilinguals have already broken out of the confines of the single worldview of each of their languages and have shown themselves to be more flexible, divergent thinkers and superior problem solvers. If we had just one language and one worldview on earth, the lack of cultural diversity would reduce our margin of adaptability to changing conditions, which is the hallmark of survival of the fittest. Cultural historian George Steiner calls the current power of the "Anglo-American" perspective around the globe *un*natural selection, which threatens to cut us off, he says, from innumerable alternate Odysseys and creation myths or other works that offer an interpretation of our humanity. For Steiner, the stranglehold of the Anglo-American perspective represents a great loss and can only diminish the number of ways people will be able to say "hope."

Besides, it is clearly not language differences that are preventing world peace. George Bernard Shaw described England and the United States as "two nations separated by a common language." Unfortunately, we see all too many countries torn by civil war, with speakers of the same language on opposite sides of the battlefield. The other side of that coin is that countries with many languages are by no means more violent.

The linguistic conflicts we have seen—in Quebec, for example—arise not from a failure of language communities to coexist, but from the efforts of one group to threaten the rights of another.

Bilingualism builds a better world, as well as a better mind. As a linguist, I am well aware that linguistic diversity, like biodiversity, is diminishing at an alarming rate. Childhood bilinguals—people who become bilingual early and know a second language well enough to bring it into the next generation—are our strongest asset in the struggle to preserve endangered languages and the cultures that are associated with them.

Language diversity in the abstract and language planning, like what we have witnessed in Wales, will not by themselves motivate anyone to embark on the challenges of creating a bilingual family, but recognizing language diversity or planning as a common good might reinforce the desires of the individuals in those bilingual families and help them persevere and even garner some outside, governmental support for themselves, as the Welsh have done. Otherwise, without a strong belief in the rightness of what they are doing, many parents succumb to the overwhelming pressure to use the majority language of their region.

These are all very lofty reasons for doing what most parents want to do anyway—speak the language of their parents and their grandparents with their children or recreate for them the rewarding multicultural experiences of their own youth.

CHAPTER

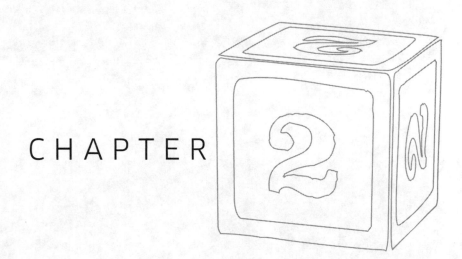

Learning a First Language

IN THIS CHAPTER, I DISCUSS what is involved in learning a first language. We look at what tools children have for the job—which ones they are born with and which ones they have to pick up as they grow. First, we consider how hard it is for anyone—let alone a baby—to learn something as complicated as a language. Then, I tell you how children do it anyway and how you can help them do it. I provide a timetable for children's major language milestones, and at the end of the chapter, I list twelve well-researched ways for you to enhance your child's language development, whether it is in one language or five.

The lessons from this chapter are doubly useful for parents of children learning two or more languages, as the same principles are at work for learning any language or any combination of languages. Children are born with a biological endowment to help lay the framework for learning the rules of language. Parents do not teach their children the basics of language; children use their inborn abilities to "crack the code" of the sound system and then to begin learning words and grammar. Once the process is underway, though, it is language experience that brings children to the level of fluency appropriate for their culture. Parents play an active role in making sure that their children get the right kinds of language experience. They interact with their children to make sure the children are profiting from the experiences to the maximum. Language learning is not a question of nature versus nurture: neither alone is sufficient. This chapter sheds light on many parts of the process—some nature and some nurture—that are often taken for granted.

The Child's Language-Learning Equipment: The LAD and the LASS

Few people appreciate how difficult it is to learn a language—how much more difficult it is than anything else we do. Children learn language before they can tie their shoes. They use and understand complicated grammar rules before they can master the simple rules of "pin-the-tail-on-the-donkey." Without instruction, they learn what the most powerful computers in the world—like those that play world-class chess—have not yet been able to master. Acquiring a first language is incredibly difficult. The physical dexterity and coordination alone that are necessary for it are well beyond the powers of someone who still has trouble pouring juice. The skilled movements of the lungs, lips, and tongue required for speaking have been compared to juggling and acrobatics, but speaking is harder. Understanding language is just as hard. The subtle distinctions encoded in grammar are more like philosophy than like Mother Goose, and listening and speaking call on powers of memory far beyond what young children demonstrate for other tasks.

Fortunately, children have an extraordinary talent for language. The human infant has been called the most powerful learning machine in the universe, and it comes specially equipped to learn the demanding skills involved in language. Before they are two years old, children will use sophisticated statistical analysis and principles of algebra to discover the sounds, words, and syntax in what you are saying to them.

As soon as they can hear, infants begin their language learning and apply their special talents without having to think about it. How long they keep their extra ability in language is a question we'll discuss in chapter 3, but it's clear, just from listening to them, that young children, who are still relatively helpless in most respects, are masters at language learning. They do better at it than the smartest and most capable animals we know of. (They are probably better at it than we are—another topic we discuss in chapter 3.)

To explain children's amazing talent for language, psycholinguists—scientists who study the "language mind"—invented the concept of a Language Acquisition Device (LAD) that children are born with. The LAD is not an actual machine. It's like a black box that we can't see inside of. We can't describe its gears and pulleys (or even its circuits), but

Figure 2. **The Language Acquisition Device (LAD)**

we can see that it is definitely doing something: what goes into the LAD is *not* what comes out. What children hear and what they then say are related in systematic ways that assure us there is a system at work, even though the logic of the system is not always obvious to us. Children's early attempts at syntax follow universal principles of grammar in general as they gradually shape their utterances in the image of the specific adult (or target) grammar that underlies what they are hearing. While we can't see what's in the LAD, by comparing what children hear, the "input," and what they say, the "output," psycholinguists try to figure out the operations that must have gone on between the two.

The LAD, however, cannot account for the whole process. Children are also born into exactly the right social context that fosters language development. Psychologist Jerome Bruner uses the acronym LASS, Language Acquisition Support System, to describe the culture of mutual responsiveness found in families all over the world. The LAD represents what nature provides for the task; the LASS represents what caregivers and the environment provide. With these two "helpers," babies everywhere learn to speak one, or more than one, of the 6,000 or more different languages spoken around the world. They all learn them on a similar schedule in about the same way.

The first part of this chapter deals primarily with the LAD, and the second part with the LASS. Bilingual children are thought to have the same LAD as monolinguals; it is their LASS that must be expanded to support two or more languages. When you understand the broad outline of how the LAD works and what it needs to operate at peak efficiency, then you can tweak the LASS in your home to better provide those elements for your child.

The Steps along the Way: From Syllables to Stories

By the time your baby is born, she's been listening in on your conversations for a couple of months, ever since her ears started to function in the womb at around twenty-five or thirty weeks. She doesn't know what you've been saying, but we know that she already recognizes the sound of your voice, knows what music you like, and can tell when you speak an unfamiliar language. Now that she's born, her language learning will really take off.

Your child travels two paths to language at once. On one path, she builds up her grammar block by block, like the tower in Figure 3. She analyzes the sounds around her to identify the speech sounds in them. Then she combines

- the speech sounds to make syllables,

- her syllables to make words,

- her words to make sentences, and finally,

- her sentences to make paragraphs or texts.

In the meantime, though, on the other path, she is establishing communication holistically. She figures out your general message from your tone of voice, from the way you speak, and from nonverbal cues. It will take a few years to "build" a functioning grammar, but your baby begins communicating with you long before she has the words and sentences to do it with.

Figure 3. **The tower of language**

Going Right to the Top of the Tower of Language

Your child bypasses words and sentences and goes right for the sense or meaning of what you're saying. She hears your soothing voice and your lullabies, connects them with the pleasant stroking sensation she feels, and thinks to herself, "I think these people are telling me they like me and that they will take care of me." That's the only verbal message she needs to understand until she starts moving around on her own a little. Then, at least sometimes, she'll need to be able to interpret that "no" in your voice as well.

She pays attention to your talking, so she can start taking turns with you, responding to your noises with noises of her own. No one, though, is expecting much "output" from her. Her main priorities are eating and sleeping. If she doesn't master those, talking won't matter. Before six months, she can cry (which doesn't count as speech) and do a little "goo"-ing. Then she works on smiling, because it's important for her to give you some feedback until she can tell you in words how much she loves you and needs you. In these first months, if she can manage to breathe so that the vocal cords vibrate and make some vowel sounds (different versions of "aaa" and "uhhh"), she'll be doing well. She'll worry later about how to shape her mouth, tongue, and lips to make some consonants, so eventually she can tell you what's on her mind.

In the first few months, your infant also makes important progress in understanding and responding to the "stage directions" for speaking: She orients to someone speaking, and she begins taking turns. She watches your eyes and gradually learns to look where you look, in preparation for being able to follow where you point. If your baby isn't crying and is "talking" with you in this language of "goos" and "gahs," her contribution to this game counts as her first intentional act of communication. That doesn't mean she knows what intentions are, but she is not acting reflexively. There's not a reflex to say "goo" when you say "goo." She didn't have to respond, but she did—and right on cue.

Building Up from the Bottom of the Tower of Language

She also starts right in on the ground floor of our tower above. She concentrates on breaking the code of the sound system. That's a real priority, because until she does that, she won't have access to the specific words you're saying. She's got a complicated task ahead of her. Imagine that you are at a noisy cocktail party where you can barely hear the person in front of you. Suddenly, you hear your name spoken across the room. In the flood of noise, your ear gets a "match." Your ear has a very strong mental representation of your name from hearing it over and over and will pick up the name in preference to other material. This "cocktail party phenomenon" illustrates the child's need, not to hear more noise, but to be able to pick out relevant signals from an overload of possible messages. The whole enterprise of talking entails sending and receiving speech signals through noise. By having a system already set up in your head, when you receive the signals, you can pick them out of the noise and interpret them.

The baby's first mission is to find the words in the stream of speech swirling all around her. How does she do that? Words don't just start and stop; we could speak one word at a time—"Baby." "Sleep." "Now."— but we don't often do it. We squish them together: "Djeetjet?" ("Did you eat yet?") We adults are readers, so we have a sense of what a word is because we write words with spaces in between them. Your baby has to find the words in the connected stream of sounds she hears way before she can learn to read, so she needs to come up with a different method to find them. She looks first for the sounds so that she can make syllables and then finally words with them.

STARTING WITH SOUNDS

At first, your baby can hear lots of different sounds, probably more than you can, but she has no idea which ones are important to the language or languages she is learning. Luckily, she came equipped with a statistical analyzer, because she's got a lot of statistics to do. To learn the sounds of a language is to learn what *not* to listen for. By the end of your baby's first year, she'll have heard a lot of sounds in her environment and will have figured out which forty or fifty sounds she hears the most. She focuses mainly on those, creating representations of them in her mind to guide her understanding.

The human ear can detect variations between more different sounds than it could possibly process in running speech. Very fine gradations and too many subtle distinctions are not useful for a linguistic sound system that requires rapid, automatic recognition of ten to fifteen speech units per second. So each language cuts up the sound waves into manageable pieces, called "sound categories," and reduces the infinite possibilities to a small number of contrasting sounds. These abstract sound categories, or "phonemes," then combine to carry the meanings relevant to the language. You need to know the phonemes of your language so that you can tell *b* from *p*, *big* from *pig*, or *bin* from *pin*. The name for this principle on which speech sounds are based is "categorical perception." English uses a system of about forty sound categories, corresponding roughly to the letters of our alphabet plus some variations. (For example, the *a* in *bat* represents a different sound from the *a* in *ball*.) Spanish uses about thirty phonemes, and the African language Khoisan has more than one hundred.

Janet Werker, a psycholinguist in British Columbia, devised ingenious experiments in which babies were trained from about five months of age to turn their heads in response to changes in sounds being played for them. Once they were used to a specific sound, they turned toward it significantly less often when, as the second sound presented, it was the same as the sound preceding it. In this way, she discovered the first indication that babies learn sounds by learning *not* to respond to them. She used the following example from Hindi: Hindi has two different *d* sounds, whereas English has only one. At six months, infants learning either language can tell the two Hindi *d*'s apart. By twelve months, infants learning Hindi can still distinguish between them, as it will be a useful contrast for them (like the contrast between *din* and *tin* for English speakers), but babies learning English no longer respond to the different *d*'s because they don't need them for their language. They lump the two Hindi *d*'s together into one sound category. That is, they have learned to ignore the differences between the two different *d* sounds. In exchange, they are now more prepared to pick out your English *d* when they hear you say it. We will see in chapter 7 that bilingual babies at these same ages are going through the same process—in two languages.

Moving from Sounds toward Syllables

Your child will also be developing a sense of the "shape" of your words, even if she doesn't really know any yet. For example, more English words have the stress on the first syllable, like "NAna," than on the second syllable, like "baNAna," or the final syllable, like "girAFFE." French words tend to be like "girAFFE," with the stress on the final syllable. By nine months, in laboratory tests, babies already pay more attention to sequences that follow the stress patterns of the language they have been hearing than to those that follow the pattern of a different language. If a child knows the general shape of words, then in a phrase like "pretty baby," for example, she will be more likely to pick out "pret" and "bay" than the unstressed "y" as the beginning of the words.

Around the time that her perception is getting more selective and more attuned to the fine details of your language (or languages), your baby's babbling is also getting a little stronger. She has developed more control over her breathing and can send air through the vocal cords in the rhythm she will eventually use for words and phrases. She is beginning to control when and how she closes off different parts of the vocal tract with her tongue and lips.

You begin to hear regularly alternating consonants and vowels ("ba" or "baba" or "dadada"). Your child is still producing sounds and syllables that she could use for any language. Soon, though, she begins to home in on the ones found in the particular language (or languages) you are using. She pays less attention to the sounds she won't need and will soon stop practicing them.

Then she figures out—in a general sense—which sounds can go together. For example, consonants in English are more often followed by a vowel than by another consonant, so two consonants together might be the end of one word and the beginning of the next. Your baby figures most of this out on her own, but as a parent, you can help her by using "parentese" (or "caregiver speech").

"Kitty.

Look at the kitty.

Nice kitty.

Do you see the kitty?"

We often do this without knowing it, intuitively adjusting our speech for the baby. The exaggerated stress, the higher pitch of the voice, short sentences, and repetition of words or phrases in parentese guide her to find a word or two. You shouldn't feel funny about it. People in almost every culture speak parentese to babies. Even little children pick it up and do it for their younger siblings. It's a big help for the baby. Once she gets the idea that "kitty" is a unit, something to pay attention to, she can look for it in the middle of a sentence, too, in the fast, connected speech of adults. You can think of her as Ginger the dog from the *Far Side* cartoon, who hears only "yada yada yada yada, Ginger, yada yada yada yada yada, Ginger," and so on.

Once she gets her foot in the door with a few units she can recognize— like her own name, or "kitty," or "baby"—she's got something to work with. Soon she can move on to acquiring vocabulary through associative learning: she will associate the sound of "kitty" with that furry creature with the tail she likes to reach for. For now, though, these units are still just sounds. Combinations of syllables are not words for her until she can attach meanings to them.

From Syllables to Words

It will still take some time to link the syllables to a meaning. When your baby is ready to learn the names for things, she will really begin to use the joint attention skills you practiced with her in your "turn-taking" lessons early on. Her first word might even come from these turns. It may sound like a word, but, to her, it may still be "the noise I make when it's my turn" in a routine. For example, if you are playing with a toy train and you say "choo-choo," then, in the same situation, in the same game, the child may say "choo-choo." You may consider that her word for "train," but if she knows it only in the context of your game, she will not associate her utterance "choo-choo" with a train in her picture book or at the train station, so it is not a true word yet. Similarly, a child who says "uppa uppa" while raising her arms to be picked up is saying something more like "pick me up" and may not realize that "up" can be used in other contexts, like going "up" the stairs or finding a toy "up" high on a shelf.

Even at the next step, when your child progresses beyond using her "words" in just one context, learning words is still conceptually far more abstract than just the association she makes between a sound and one person or thing, like the name for your pet. It's really not obvious to her what goes with what. If she can't follow where you're looking and read your intentions, she'll make a lot of wrong guesses about what words mean. For example, just because you say something in the vicinity of something else, it doesn't mean what you are saying is a name for that thing. Psycholinguist Roberta Golinkoff and her colleagues point out that you might say "shoo" (as in "go away") every time you see a certain dog, but that doesn't mean that it's called a "shoo" or that its name is Shoo. Your child has to be able to tell when you mean "shoo" to be a name and when you don't.

Besides, your child is not just learning the names for specific things, like learning that your dog's name is Pluto. It is more like learning that your car's name is "a Ford." Lots of individual cars are called "Fords." Like dogs, Ford cars come in many different shapes and sizes. What makes them all Fords or all dogs is not something your child can tell just from how they look.

Using Words to Learn More Words

Once your baby has a few words, she can use those words to learn new words. Linguist John MacNamara showed that seventeen- to twenty-four-month-olds, who generally do not produce the articles "a," "an," and "the," can still use those little words receptively to guide their learning. The toddlers in his experiment, for example, could tell the difference between the meanings of "*a* pluto" and "Pluto." The researchers introduced a stuffed dog to the toddlers with the words, "Here's Pluto. Do you see Pluto?" Then, when they brought out another stuffed dog, the child would assume correctly it was not "Pluto," but that it would have its own name. However, if the first stuffed animal was introduced as "a pluto," the child would extend that name to another stuffed dog. When they were shown another stuffed dog and asked, "Is this a pluto?" then the toddler would say "yes."

So, except for proper names, like George and Martha, names for things do not name the specific thing that the name is being associated with; they name the class of objects that are *like* what you are pointing to. This gives rise to an endearing child-language mistake. Children don't automatically know how alike something has to be in order to be a "pluto" or a "doggie," so it's not unusual for them to *overextend* the terms and call a horse or a cow a "doggie" because they are animals with four legs. Or they may point to the full moon and say "cookie" or call their cookie with a big bite out of it a "moon," like the crescent moon.

If they do not understand that "Daddy" is a "proper name" only for their own father, it can be embarrassing when they call the pizza delivery man "Daddy," too. While they are learning what counts as the same or different in their language, children are also as likely to *underextend* terms. So they may learn the word "shoes" when you show them their sneakers but might use it only to refer to sneakers and not to other kinds of shoes.

Learning Verbs: Another Kettle of Fish

Names for things are hard enough, but we can get along with pointing and pictures to learn many of them. Pointing, though, is not much help for learning verbs. Your child will need another system, and that system is grammar. Psycholinguists Lila and Henry Gleitman say, "A picture is worth a thousand words, but that's the problem." They show that even adults can't learn what an unknown verb means from a picture or a video if they don't hear it in a helpful sentence. Picture this scene: you see Ernie with a long belt around his waist on a stool spinning, and Bert is pulling the belt as if to make Ernie spin. If you say "Look, gorping," there are several alternatives for what "gorping" is and no way to choose among them. But if you say, "Oh look, Ernie is gorping," you'll think "gorping" is spinning; if you say, "Look, Bert is gorping Ernie," then "to gorp" is more likely something like pulling the belt or making someone else spin. When you hear the verb in a sentence, with the word endings and word order to tell the relationships, you can make a better guess at what its meaning is. If you hear it in several different sentences, you will gradually zero in on the meaning. My colleague at the University of Massachusetts, psychologist Kristen Asplin, showed that children ages three to five can use different sentence frames to learn the meanings even of words for mental activities, like "thinking"—where there's really nothing to "see" when someone is doing it.

Using the tools the grammar provides for it, your child will learn all the different kinds of words she will need to make her own sentences. The child's skill at word learning is very different from your dog's. Dogs can learn their own names and the names of some other salient objects, like "Frisbee," but although that's where your toddler's word learning starts, your toddler goes way beyond that. Unlike your dog, what she learns does not have to be obvious in the environment—it can be invisible, like "honesty," or imaginary, like "unicorns" or "ghosts." From there, she can learn essentially anything.

FROM WORDS TO SENTENCES

Around eighteen months, once your child has a tidy stock of about fifty words, she starts putting them together, both in complex words, like "sleep + -ing," and in sequences, like "mommy shoe." She is now working toward sentences and their meanings from the bottom up. Once she has simple sentences, she will soon figure out how to put sentences inside of sentences to make more complex sentences; for example, "I love John" grows to "Why do I love John?" or "You know that I love John." She will also eventually begin to create understandable links across sentences to make paragraphs, or texts.

Some children take a different route to sentences. They start out skipping the word stage and jump right to phrases, which they break down into words only later. They say "gonna-get-you" or "lemmeseeit" before "going" or "you," progressing perhaps to "lemmeseeit car" before pulling the "see" out to use with other objects ("see dog," "see dolly," and so on). Eventually, though, these children tune in to words like everyone else and proceed from there. Because they take a roundabout route, they may reach words later than usual, but that doesn't keep them from being ahead in other areas (and going on to become star students).

Going Beyond Single Words

So just getting to the words of the language is pretty amazing, and it's not surprising that this process could take a year or two. But frankly, animals can get this far. Pets learn their names and the names of salient things of great interest to them, like "Frisbee" or "outside." There are monkeys that have been trained to recognize hundreds of words and use either hand-signs or plastic tokens to express them. Words are helpful, but we don't usually speak one word at a time. To start seriously making sense, your baby needs to get into sentences. That's the really hard stuff. Before she's two, she'll need to be able to do a little "algebra" on top of the statistical analysis of the sounds she's been doing since day one.

It's a common idea that adults teach children language. Parents report that they tell children the names of all the things they see in their houses and that this is how they teach the child. The process that they describe is called "associative learning," and it's a good technique as far as it goes. We use it all our lives for learning words, but your child also needs other strategies. Associative learning doesn't work for learning the sounds of the language. There's too much that has to be ignored in the sounds that are coming to you, so figuring out the relevant sound categories or phonemes involves a much more complicated analysis. (Fortunately, our ears are designed for just that kind of analysis.) Most especially, associative learning doesn't work for learning sentences. Plain old, ordinary sentences, like the ones you are reading now, turn out to be a much more complicated system than anything else we learn.

So, how *do* you learn the sentences of your language? You don't learn them one by one or memorize them like you might learn all the kings and queens of England. It entails much, much more than just repeating what you have heard. True, there is considerable memorization and repetition. You learn all exceptions to the rule, like saying "spoke" instead of "speaked," one by one from having heard or seen them. Instead, it's a little like the times tables in math. When you learn the times tables, at the beginning, you might just memorize all the combinations: 6 x 7 is 42, 6 x 8 is 48, etc. Memorization works fine for the table of numbers up to about 12, and is probably easier than learning how the system works. But you can't go too much further just memorizing. At some point, you are going to have to learn the process of how to multiply. The same is true of grammar—rather than learn all the sentences, you learn how to make them. You start out with some ready-made phrases like "what's that?" or "lemme see." But before too long, you need your own sentences, not someone else's.

Before she can make her own sentences, your baby has to discover the process used by the people around her for making all sentences—without being told that there is a process or what it is. First, she has to uncover the invisible abstract structure of sentences just from hearing them. These invisible abstract structures and the rules for forming them and then interpreting them make up the "syntax." The rules of syntax tell you how the words of your language fit together and what they can mean. Parents can't and don't explain syntax to children, because although we can all use it, no one can describe more than small parts of it in the detail children need to make sense of your sentences.

More on Grammar
When most people hear the word "grammar," they think of their junior high school English teacher and of rules like "Don't say 'Him and me went out.'" Grammar rules within linguistics are called by the more specific term, "syntax." First you learn the words. Then the syntax provides the rules for combining the words. Syntax tells you what is a sentence of a language and what isn't, and it tells you the relationships between the words. "The dog is barking" is an English sentence; "Is dog the barking" is not (although it might be the literal translation of an acceptable sentence in a language I do not know).

Imagine that a toddler is looking at you in the presence of a dog and says, "Dog bark." She hasn't given you any directions to interpret how the words (or the meanings they refer to) are related to each other. If the dog is barking, you may take "Dog bark" as a description of the event. If the child is looking at you and the dog is quiet, you might take it as a general comment about what one can expect of dogs. If the child is looking at the dog, it could be a command asking the dog to bark. As an utterance outside the grammar, the phrase is just a string of words, and you, the language-using listener, try to match it to one of the structures you know that is closest to it and that fits the situation. But when the child knows a little syntax, she can say, "Dogs bark" or "This dog is barking," or "Dog, please bark." Using the order of the words and the little "grammatical bits" in complex words (like the "s" on "dogs" or the "-ing" on "bark*ing*"), now it is the child guiding the interpretation.

Crucially, your child can also say a completely novel sentence, such as "In my dream, the dog put pizza in the treetop," an unlikely sentence that neither she nor you nor I have probably ever heard before. The ability to make and understand novel sentences is what you need to really be talking. Until your child makes novel sentences, she is really not a speaker of a language. So, while syntax is just one piece of the language puzzle, it is the key piece. Without it, we do not like to give an individual credit for knowing a language, even though he or she may know lots of other pieces of it. Syntax is the crux of the argument currently being waged by those who claim that monkeys (or a trained grey parrot) can talk. These nonhuman creatures can learn, and have learned, hundreds of words and even phrases, and they appear to use them in appropriate structures. But can they combine them into sentences in systematic ways without relying on having heard the exact sentence before? Probably not. The jury is still out on whether animals are capable of syntax.

Abstract Structure

To be able to make novel sentences of their own, children have to learn what they cannot see or hear in what you say. When I say the syntactic structure in sentences is "abstract," I mean you cannot see it but you know it is there. You need to know the structure of a sentence to figure out what someone just said to you, but most of the structure does not show in the string of words you are hearing or reading. The structure is like the skeleton in your body. It does its work supporting the parts of the body that we can see. Our trunk and especially our limbs could not work without something like a bone inside, but we don't get to actually see the bone unless we apply special x-ray tools of analysis or unless a bone breaks and pokes through the skin.

Some sentences put a little of the structure out in plain sight: "Give that *to* me." That little "to" gives a clue to what goes with what—who gives what to whom. But what about: "Give me that"? Where are the clues now? Am *I* being given away together with *that*? An early language experiment used example sentences that differed by only one syllable but had totally different structures: "John is eager to please" and "John is easy to please." In the first, John is the one doing the pleasing; in the second, he is the one we need to please. Who taught you that difference? You understand it immediately, but I doubt you had a lesson on it. Likewise, two sentences can sound exactly the same and mean completely different things. "Visiting relatives can be boring." We can be doing the visiting, or the relatives could be visiting us.

These invisible structures of a language are described by rules that are like equations in algebra. They set up the relationships into which you can fit any values or meanings. In "x + 2 = y" in algebra, you can substitute any number for the variables, "x" or "y." Once you fill in one of them, though, it reduces the set of possibilities for the other variable depending on what "operators" (+, =, etc.) are in the equation. The set of numbers that can fill in the variables is vast—actually infinite—but the set of operators is very small. Both variables and operators are crucial for interpreting the equation. In addition to the actual values, we have to know a little *about* equations. We have to know that we can only use a number as a variable, not another equals sign and nothing from outside of the number system, like "Mickey Mouse." In language, there are similar restrictions that the child must pick up. If I ask, "What color is your favorite animal?" *green* and *purple* are acceptable answers, but *melody* is not. So the child needs to deduce what the "equations" are and also what roles the different elements or words are allowed to play in them.

When you are a speaker of a language, you can identify what goes with what even when there are no explicit clues to guide you. Consider this statement: "He told me, 'Go upstairs,' but I didn't want to." Didn't want to what? Because we know English, it is obvious to us that the "to" in "didn't want to" points to "go upstairs," as if the original sentence had been, "He told me *to* go upstairs." Then the "to" of "want to" could be a signal to tell us which part of the previous sentence the "to" must hook up with. You cannot understand this exchange unless you recover what has been left out, and you not only have to recover the gaps, but you have to find the clues for them, too—all on your own.

You might think that these rules are too abstract and too difficult for infants, but linguist Gary Marcus showed that babies at seven months are capable of picking up on these kinds of algebraic rules and relationships.

INFINITY

So, your baby is learning sophisticated structures all on her own. She is also grappling with infinity before she can reliably count to ten. Thanks to the influential modern linguist Noam Chomsky, we are aware that the set of sentences in any language is logically infinite. You can never learn every last sentence of your language. Actually, he argued that sentences themselves are potentially infinite because of a special property of their rules (called "recursion"). A sentence can contain a sentence, which can contain a sentence, which can contain a sentence, and so on, until we run out of breath or get bored. We do not happen to speak in infinite sentences because our memories are not good enough to keep track of where a really long sentence is going or has been, but our understanding of our language is such that, in theory, we would be able to process a nearly infinite sentence were we to encounter it. So, the language-learning problem is acute. We need to explain how your child can learn unseen and unknown things of unlimited length.

Clearly, when you listen to your child, you will see that she tries to use repetition and memory as much as she can. But even toddlers show us that they are indeed analyzing what they hear and not just parroting what we say. They give away their rule-making skills when they say things like "it goed," "I haved it," or even "I had-ed it." To make those forms, which she has not been taught and probably has not heard, your child has to apply a rule ("the base form + '-ed' = past tense"). If she immediately knew the exceptions to the rule, you would not get to see the operations she is applying to the elements she is learning. While she is learning the exceptions, you get to observe her rule-making capability in action.

COMBINING SENTENCES INTO "TEXTS"

It used to be said that your child would essentially master the adult grammar by age five. This is largely true for the basic grammar of sentences. After age five, the greatest challenge is learning how to combine sentences to make even longer sentences and connected passages longer than a single sentence. As we have seen, learning a grammar of sentences, or syntax, is no small feat. Still, your child will have much further to go to master how to make paragraphs, or "texts." The key difficulty in making texts is making them coherent, relevant, and interesting. Your child's texts can grow with your help—as in conversation—or in "extended solo turns," as in stories.

Actually, it's misleading to say that your child does not start working on stories until age five. She starts working on stories as soon as you start telling them. But you should not expect her to make very much progress in creating links across sentences until after age five. You can expect her to sound somewhat adult in her words and sentences by about age three when she talks about the here and now, but her ability to maintain a reciprocal conversation throughout several turns or tell a story with an identifiable point will still be underdeveloped. Your child's language does not become literate and "decontextualized" (talking about past and future or hypothetical abstract concepts) until she has had a lot of experience talking with others about the past, future, or hypothetical situations. Reading storybooks, for example, trains her language about faraway places "once upon a time." Engaging her in discussions about what you did together yesterday or will do tomorrow at Grandma's house is her path toward telling her own stories about things you did not experience with her.

For making texts—unlike syntax—there is not a mysterious innate LAD (Language Acquisition Device) available for help: your child is your apprentice and, with your guidance, will learn by doing. When you see ads for materials to "increase children's language abilities," they typically aim to increase their abilities with texts—to make their texts longer, more complex, and yet still easy to follow. This is what you are doing every day when you converse with your child and help her improve her turns in the dialogue.

THE USES OF LANGUAGE

Your child also learns other things about language that are above the level of the sentence. To be a competent communicator, your apprentice speaker has to learn about the different ways you and the other people she knows *use* language in different situations. "Communicative competence" means she knows to speak one way to her brother and another to her granddad or the salesperson at the store, just as adults modify their language based on who they are talking to and where the conversation is taking place. You might want to show her how to be more formal when talking to your clergyperson or your boss. She has to learn *not* to ask why the person in front of you in the grocery line is so fat—and other details of politeness that will keep her (and you) out of trouble with others. She needs to understand that she should repeat herself, or maybe switch languages, if someone hasn't heard well or hasn't understood her.

Once your child knows how to make questions and becomes adept at using them to get new information, she will also need to know when a question is not a question—for example, "Do you know the time?" Answering "no" is all right, but answering just "yes, I do" would be distinctly odd; the question is actually a request to tell the person the time. Finally, one of the hardest uses of language for your child to catch on to will be irony or other nonliteral language. In irony, what you say is the opposite of what you mean, and there are no cues to that in what you say, except maybe a look on your face or a tone in your voice. When you say, "Great car you have," how does the child know whether you're admiring it or whether you're making a comment on what a jalopy it is?

Bilingual children are introduced early to "communicative competence." They learn to speak to different people differently—that is, in another language. Their speech patterns show they are sensitive to the language of other speakers even before age two, and they generally learn to identify who speaks which language(s) between ages two and three.

The Timetable for Learning a Language

When Does Your Child Know a Language?

Because language is always capable of incorporating new elements, it is an "open system." It is not a fixed target. You cannot say that on May 1, 2002, at 12:15 p.m., you finished learning Japanese. Unlike climbing a mountain or cleaning your room, it is hard or impossible to say when you're done. Language learning is not an activity with a recognizable product, or even a process with a recognizable finish line. The best we can do is impose a framework that allows us to identify several different smaller finish lines or landmark events by which we judge our progress. For each of the components of language—sounds, syllables, words, sentences, and texts—there are separate timetables for *understanding* when someone else says them (what we call "receptive" language) and for *producing* them (that is, speaking, or "expressive" language").

Language Milestones

Even though we appreciate how difficult and abstract children's task in learning a language truly is, we still expect them to meet their deadlines in doing it. The first three years especially are full of target dates for the many milestones involved. In chapter 7, we will look at laboratory findings about children's milestones when I compare bilinguals to monolinguals for those developments. Here in Table 1, I list a few of the major landmarks that parents should be able to see and hear for themselves.

All of the ages I give are very approximate. Although we say language learning is universal, each child interprets the universal principles slightly differently. It is always hard to prevent yourself from comparing your child to your cousin's child, who may have walked sooner and speaks more clearly than yours. But you must not do it. It is not a race, and in any event, what you can see of the children's learning is only the tip of the iceberg. There are many more "behind the scenes" skills that do not factor into such comparisons. One child may repeat a lot and come to two-word utterances early, while another—equally advanced—may come to two-word speech later because she is building the grammar word by word rather than relying on several fixed phrase patterns. Some children will use a form, like plural "s," as soon as they are aware of it but before they know all the details, so you might hear "childs" or "feets" along with "cats" and "dogs." Another child may do it later but be more correct from the outset.

(At the same time, if you are very concerned about your child's development, it is worthwhile to seek out an expert opinion—or two. In chapter 6, I discuss the special precautions parents of bilinguals must take in choosing which experts to listen to.)

Table 1. **Landmarks on the path to language**

AGE	LANGUAGE YOUR CHILD UNDERSTANDS ("receptive language")	LANGUAGE YOUR CHILD PRODUCES ("expressive language")
Sounds: Birth–5 months	Your baby starts tuning in to the "stage directions" for speaking and has begun taking turns. She follows your gaze to each side, but doesn't yet turn to see where you are looking when you look above her head.	Your baby produces vowels, gooing (with a vaguely "g" sound), and some poorly timed babbles (like "b-waaa"). She smiles, sometimes in response to external events.
Syllables: 6 to 9 months	Your baby turns toward her name, and she can start learning "no." She can look where you point (and not just at your finger).	Your baby starts making real syllables: "bababa," "dadada." You may hear "raspberries"– forceful trilling of the lips (especially exciting with a mouthful of solid food).
Babble and words; routines: 12 months	Your baby starts recognizing words for things of interest to her.	You'll hear the easy sounds of the language like "ba" or "da," and an occasional "sh" or "f," but not the more difficult sounds, like the "r." Your baby takes part in (but does not lead) "routines," like patty-cake, bye-bye, and itsy-bitsy spider. Some children will have started saying a few words.

AGE	LANGUAGE YOUR CHILD UNDERSTANDS ("receptive language")	LANGUAGE YOUR CHILD PRODUCES ("expressive language")
Words: 16 to 18 months	Average number of words[4] your boy understands at 16 months: 140, with a range from 50 to 350. Average number of words your girl understands at 16 months: 190, ranging from 60 to 400.	First words come, on average, between 10 and 18 months. Average expressive vocabulary your boy has at 18 months: 75, with a range from 13 to 420. Average expressive vocabulary for girls at 18 months: 112, ranging from 17 to 475. We do not worry if the child does not have any words (or signs) until after 18 months. It is more of a concern if the child does not *understand* any words at that age.
Two-word sentences: 24 months	Your child understands most of what is spoken to her, especially with a lot of support from the context.	Major milestone is two-word combinations ("more cookie," "mommy shoe"). Average for two-word "onset" is 18 months or around 50 words; almost all children have some combinations by 26 months.
Sentences: 36 months	Your child understands more of the language she hears, even when it is at odds with the context. She is beginning to understand more language of mental states, what people are thinking or feeling. She can follow two-step directions.	Your child speaks in simple sentences, mostly about the here and now. She recounts simple events in the past. She is largely intelligible. She is beginning to take longer turns in reciprocal conversation (but there is still a lot of "parallel talk"– talking side-by-side, but not necessarily to each other).

---

4 These averages are from the latest age normed for comprehension on a standard parent report form. Note that average figures for girls are slightly higher than for boys at these ages. These gender differences become less evident by school age.

AGE	LANGUAGE YOUR CHILD UNDERSTANDS ("receptive language")	LANGUAGE YOUR CHILD PRODUCES ("expressive language")
Complex sentences and conversation: 5 years	Your child is doing well understanding and speaking "on the playground." Her basic interpersonal communication skills are well in place.	Your child is doing a pretty good job with complex sentences—"No, I don't want that because it's yucky," or, "Why can't Lucas come over to play with my dinosaurs?" Only a small percentage of five-year-olds have difficulty with articulation, mostly of harder sounds like "r" or "s." Your child is getting the hang of reciprocal conversations.
Texts and academic language: 8 years	Your child is making progress in academic, or abstract, language. She probably understands some indirect requests and irony.	Your child organizes her speech in paragraphs, to tell coherent stories. By eight, your child is also able to manage a joke that you will actually laugh at.

By age eight, your child is between an apprentice and a master. She still has a lot to learn, especially in making texts, both spoken and written. Texts will also introduce her to longer, more complex syntax than she will generally hear in casual speech. So she will continue to learn how to express more complex ideas in different kinds of texts or discourse valued by your culture. She is probably also being the expert speaker for younger children and siblings.

LAD versus LASS: How Much Is Nature? How Much Is Nurture?

Babies' achievements in learning language are impressive, both in what they bring to the task and what they draw from their environment. How much of what they acquire is "hard-wired" from birth, and how much is contributed by the environment?

The Role of Nature

THE "LANGUAGE GENE"?

Scientists estimate that about half of the individual differences in children's language abilities are explained by heredity. One sign of the role of genes is that certain kinds of language impairments run in families—a child with a diagnosed language delay is more than six times more likely to have another family member with a similar impairment than a child without an impairment (20% versus 3%). Researchers have discovered an unusual family in Britain in which one-half of the family members in three generations exhibit the same kind of grammatical impairment. Their sentences lack the important little grammatical words such as "to" or "the," and their words are missing their endings, like the "-ing," as in "Girl is cry." The pattern of the occurrence of the impairment suggests that it is controlled by one dominant gene. With modern gene tracing methods, scientists have in fact found that the impaired members of this family share a mutation on chromosome 7. That is not to say that chromosome 7 is the "grammar gene," but something on 7 is necessary for the grammar of the language to be learned properly.

Twin studies have also allowed researchers to estimate the hereditary component of language development. This is done by comparing the variation in language scores between groups of identical twins (who share 100% of their genes) and fraternal twins or siblings (who share only 50%). The scores of identical twins who are raised together as opposed to those raised apart are compared to the scores of fraternal twins raised together and apart.

Both kinds of twins are more alike when reared together than apart (.51 versus .38 and .20 versus .07). But identical twins reared apart are still more alike than siblings reared together (.38 versus .20). Scientists' calculations end up showing that about 50% of the similarity in children's language scores can be attributed to having the same genes and 50% to having the same environment.

Parents Don't Teach Language

Before linguistics redefined the study of language acquisition in the 1960s and 1970s, a leading psychologist, the behaviorist B. F. Skinner, maintained that language was a behavior, no different from other complex behaviors. According to Skinner, you could use the same kind of training to teach children language as you used to teach pigeons which lever to press to get food. If you just broke the behavior down into its smallest parts and gave children the right rewards for imitating you, that would work.

In a 1959 article, linguist Noam Chomsky showed quite convincingly that language was not the kind of behavior you could make training and reward schedules for. The behaviorist principles were especially irrelevant for learning the abstract structure of sentences. For one thing, as we saw above, you as the parent speak in accordance with grammatical structures in minute detail, but you aren't aware of them. Therefore, you cannot be systematically teaching sentence structure through the kind of steps Skinner described. Also, your child's language does not match your adult language but differs from it in systematic ways that behaviorism does not address. Children's errors are not just random lapses; they substitute and simplify according to universal grammatical principles. Even their earliest two-word combinations show relationships and structure ("show Mom," "dog here"). They do not just use garbled words: "man, man, dog, no." Their sequences of errors show remarkable consistency, so much so that linguists speak of the intermediate grammars children go through on their path to the adult grammar.

In Chomsky's view, parents cannot be said to teach language to their children any more than you teach a seed to become a flower. In fact, according to Chomsky, syntax cannot be learned; it is "hard-wired" in infants at birth in the "language organ," and it "matures" at about age two to three. This happens just like walking "happens" between ten and twenty months, when all the relevant muscle groups and nerve pathways have matured and there has been sufficient opportunity to practice in a supported situation. Although there are areas of the brain specialized for language (as we see in chapter 3), the "language organ" Chomsky is referring to is not a physical structure but an organized, behavior-controlled network of nerves that act together.

Since Chomsky's article, it has been pretty well accepted by linguists, and even most psychologists, that parents do not teach their children syntax. Once babies sort out the sounds, parents help them learn words and provide them with a body of sentences to analyze and discover the syntax from. Parents are crucial for helping babies find those first words and break into sentences, with a lot of give and take and back and forth in the process. You as the parent can do some helpful things, like modify your speech to your baby to draw her attention to such things as the ends of sentences and the ends of words. You may speak in "parentese" (as in our kitty example above), but "parentese" is only helpful, not critical. Not every parent, and not even every culture, uses "parentese," but in every culture, people talk to babies, and in every culture, babies learn to talk.

A Role for Nurture

Even with an innate, "hard-wired" view of language acquisition, many scholars recognize a role for language "input" from the child's environment beyond what was included in Chomsky's early formulations. Input has always been recognized as critical for "jump-starting" language acquisition and for learning vocabulary, but new work argues for the role of input in children's discovery of some of the complexity in their grammars.

Interestingly, grammatical studies of bilingual children have demonstrated that differences in both quality and quantity of speech addressed to children make a difference in how fast and how well children learn all the fine details of their language. The findings from the studies of bilinguals have identified areas of the grammar where similar effects can be shown in monolingual learning. Effects of differing quantities of input are seen especially in learning word order irregularities and word endings, or the "grammatical" pieces of words. Quantity of talk from adults, which includes the various structures being learned, can affect how quickly children accumulate enough experience with forms in many different contexts to be able to arrive at the correct idea of how to use them in that language.

According to psycholinguists Virginia Gathercole and Erika Hoff, frequency of structures in the input affects how quickly children reach a "critical mass" of instances of a structure in order to get all the details of its use correct, but the structures themselves and the state of the child's internal grammar dictate how large the critical mass for a given structure needs to be. In general, children need less exposure to structures that are regular, but need more if the structures are irregular—that is, when the forms being used have exceptions or when the same forms have different uses in different parts of the grammar. (See examples in chapters 3 and 7, where I discuss these issues under the term "morphosyntax.") Equally important, a child can be more ready or less ready to attend to different structures. When learning Spanish articles, for example, children have to already be using them in regular cases before their attention can be focused on the irregular ones. That is, they will be using the article "el" with masculine nouns like "el perro" (the dog) before they learn to use it in irregular cases, with some feminine nouns, as in "el agua fría" (the cold water), where you might expect "la agua."

Things Parents Can Do to Help Children Learn Language

If, as I report above, 50% of language learning is controlled by genes, there may be some factors that are beyond your control, such as the speed of your child's nerve impulses or the capacity of her phonological short-term memory. Still, the remaining 50% leaves parents a lot to work with. Very large differences in how children learn language are explained by more obvious factors in a child's environment that you do have control over. The environment in this case is *you*, the people speaking to the child.

There is considerable research that shows which behaviors of parents can make a difference in children's growth in their first language. These are principles that parents of bilingual children can apply in two or more languages. So, while you specifically do not want to drill your children on the parts of speech or diagram their sentences, there is much you can do to facilitate their learning. It matters

- how much you say (and how well you listen),
- whom you say it to,
- what you say, especially praise, and
- how you say it.

I summarize advice based on these principles in the "Twelve Steps" in Table 2 at the end of this chapter.

How Much You Say Matters

Talk to your child (a lot). A landmark study by psychologists Betty Hart and Todd Risley has made it very clear that how much you speak with children makes a difference in how much they learn to speak with you. Hart and Risley followed forty-two toddlers monthly from ten months to thirty-six months, recording the children for an hour each time in their home environments. They audio-recorded and transcribed everything said *by* the child, *to* the child, and *to other* siblings or adults in whatever location in the house they found the child. In addition to studying the carefully detailed cumulative lexicons for each child and the child's caregivers that were made from the transcripts of the sessions, the researchers gave the children verbal IQ tests at thirty-six months, and in a follow-up study, verbal IQ and language tests in the third grade. The biggest difference between the families, which turned out to have an enormous influence on the children's language development, was just the sheer number of words addressed to the child in an hour. Averages ranged from 600 words per hour in the lowest group to 2,100 words per hour in the highest group. Overall and within subgroups, the number of words spoken *to* the children was positively correlated with their verbal IQ scores at age three and again at age eight.

The relationship was not one-to-one. Every 100 words per hour of the parent did not translate into so many more words from the child, but the overall effect was astounding. Even if children are using their innate Language Acquisition Device (the LAD) to figure out by themselves the rules of syntax and identify the sounds of the language they are learning, that does not mean parents have no role to play in their children's language learning. Hart and Risley's demonstration shows a very strong role for interaction with parents. The effect of early experience on academic development six years later is all the more remarkable because by the third grade, there are many influences on the children other than their parents.

Listening Is Important, Too

Parents need not only speak to children but listen to them as well. A dissertation by linguist Rebecca Burns-Hoffman at the University of Colorado compared the communication styles of different adults in interaction with small groups of children in a Scottish preschool. The naturalistic data (transcriptions of spontaneous speech) had been collected in a format that mimicked an experimental situation. Four adults—three teachers and a parent aide—interacted in two situations each with three sets of four children: three-year-olds, four-year-olds, and five-year-olds. The two situations were designed to contrast a "lesson" and a free play activity, where the children were seated around a table engaged in building with Legos.

Burns-Hoffman found that, in general, there was more talk from the children in the informal activity but more complex language from them in the lessons. Their most complex talk was in their stories. The four adults were consistent in the two situations. In both the lesson and the free play, the lead teacher spoke the most to the children and the parent aide spoke the least. The teacher who consistently elicited more speech and more complex speech, however, was not the lead teacher. It was the teacher who was the second least talkative of the adults. Burns-Hoffman concluded that if adults talk too much, they do not leave any time for the children to talk, but if they talk too little, they do not stimulate the children to say anything. Teacher 3 seems to have struck just the right balance. In addition, she used more open-ended questions to encourage longer answers from the children. She used more positive feedback and less "management talk," that is, fewer directions to the children on how to do the task and how to behave.

Live Interaction

Interaction is key. For children to learn their language from the talk of others, that talk has to be directed at them in an interactive situation. Overhearing something doesn't work for early development (although it may be crucial later at the dinner table and in the lecture hall). Hart and Risley recorded whether the words they transcribed were addressed to the children as opposed to someone else and were just overheard by the children. Their second book based on these materials emphasizes that the crucial factor in the growth of the children's vocabularies was the speech addressed *to* the child in interaction generally with the parent. I find it striking that there were no words reported in the children's vocabularies (tallied monthly) that were not previously recorded in the parents' transcripts. Hart and Risley also confirmed that other adults spoke less *to* the child until the child was already a speaker—that is, until the child spoke at about the same rate in the hour as the parents did (as opposed to the earliest sessions, when even the child's unintelligible contributions were far below the level of the adults' talk).

These results about the quantity of words spoken to the child do not count TV or audio recordings. Actually, studies show that children learn language poorly, if at all, from TV as compared to live interaction. Daniel Anderson, a psychologist at the University of Massachusetts, has been a leader in studies of learning from TV since the 1970s. He reports that there is substantially less learning from a video display compared to seeing the same demonstration in person. For very young children (under age two), it does not appear that TV helps them learn vocabulary, although some learning of vocabulary from TV has been shown in older children. More damaging, he found that just having TV on in the background decreases parent-child interaction by more than 20%, even though neither parent nor child was actually watching what he calls "background TV." There is also no evidence of phonetic or syntactic learning from TV.

As bilingual children, too, have demonstrated, children need more than just a few hours a week of exposure to a language to become "users of the language." Children need to get a full enough body of sentences in a language to do the "analysis" that is required for learning. (I look more closely at how many hours are required in chapter 4.) We have a real-world illustration of this point from the experiences of hearing children of deaf parents. As recently as the late 1970s, it was thought that deaf parents needed to have their children exposed to just a few hours of contact a week with hearing people. This idea was based on a misinterpretation of the Chomskian idea of needing just a little input to jumpstart the child's innate LAD.

Deaf parents have also been given other poor advice. According to psycholinguist Steven Pinker, they were sometimes told to put their hearing children in front of the TV so they would learn to speak that way—but they didn't. A case study of one such child by Letty Naigles at the University of Connecticut confirms that although the child had actually picked up some words, his grammar was severely dysfunctional. Also, many deaf parents were not informed that it is worthwhile to teach their hearing child sign language. This is also a big mistake. Children need language input (that is, communicatively competent "free speech" directed at them) as soon as possible for their first language development, and sign language is perfectly suitable for this purpose.

Recently, toy manufacturers have started making "talking books" that read themselves to the children. This sounds like a reasonable idea, but this too doesn't work very well. A study of mothers using talking books with their children was presented at a recent conference on language acquisition. The researchers compared the content and quantity of the mothers' speech with children during talking-book reading as compared to regular book reading. The quantity of talk was not that much different, but it was disheartening to see that most of the talk from the parent to the child in the talking book condition was devoted to behavior management—"don't touch it," "let it go," etc.—compared to the much richer conversations around the children's reactions to the events in the stories while they were reading the regular books together.

Books are already language-promoting tools par excellence, and they are not improved by making them read themselves. Parents reading with their children can engage children's attention and contribute to their learning about texts by making comments on the events that relate the reading to the child's own experience. It is also very useful to ask what the child thinks will happen next, or probe why things are happening and what the characters' feelings are about the events that are taking place in the story. Talking books create the same problem, or rather, "missed opportunity," as stories presented on TV or videos. Even when parents watch TV *with* their children (as many parent guides suggest), the pace of the story on TV is not influenced by the child's pace. You cannot start and stop when it is useful, and so TV watching becomes a passive activity as compared to the active event that reading together is.

What You Say Matters
The other striking difference in Hart and Risley's study between the children with higher and lower IQ and language scores was the seven times greater number of *positive* statements—praise or other positive feedback—addressed to the higher scoring children per hour. By contrast, the lower scoring children heard twice as many negative statements and prohibitions—"You're stupid" or "Don't do that"—than the higher scoring group. Once again, the difference in the children's early experience was evident many years later (although it might be that the same kind of negative verbal environment still surrounded them many years later).

Watch How You Say It, Too

You will want to treat your child like a conversational partner, someone whose thoughts you are interested in. Your tone needs to be interested and supportive. Child psychologist Hyam Ginott many years ago suggested you talk to your child as you would to a friend. You would hesitate before criticizing a friend. You wouldn't correct the friend's grammar in the middle of a conversation, for example. The kind of feedback you give when engaged with a friend is also the kind that is most helpful to children.

That is, what is most helpful appears not to be focused on the correction of children's "grammar." In fact, researchers who have specifically looked at how often parents comment on children's utterances report that parents correct the content of what children say but rarely the form. You probably find yourself doing what are called "recasts" or "turnabouts." A helpful recast takes the child's error, for example, "None of them trucks is working," and provides an expansion like, "Oh, none of those trucks will work for you? Let's see. How can we get those trucks to work?" First the parent models a correct structure. At this point, the child might (after she had heard a similar recast many times) say "those trucks." The other thing the parent has done is turned it around and set up the child's next turn in the conversation, sometimes called a "turnabout." The parent takes the child's utterance, incorporates it into his or her own, and then sends the idea back with a clear direction for where the child *might* take it, but doesn't just get the child to "fill in a blank."

No single recast "teaches" a grammar point, but it does not just let the child's error pass. Most important, it encourages the child to continue communicating. You want to avoid focusing on how the child says something, but you do want to reinforce the child's attempts and encourage her to go on through your response to the child's genuine act of communication. In chapter 4, we look at similar motivations for parents' responses to errors in bilingual conversations.

Scaffolding Language

The stories children are learning to tell very directly build on the kind of interactions the parent (or teacher) and child have in the children's early attempts at speaking. I still recall my daughter's first "story" when she was about seventeen months old. We had been to a lake where people were playing with small motorboats. One of the small boats turned over, and the riders made a big happy ruckus that really drew her attention. That evening, we "recounted" it together to her dad:

Mom: And what did we see today? Were there fast boats?

Child: Zoom zoom.

Mom: Yes, they were going very fast. And then what happened?

Child: Zoom zoom.

Mom: And after that? Did it turn over and they went in the water?

Child: (raises and lowers her arms as if splashing in the water)

Mom: Yes, they fell in.

Child: Zoom zoom.

Granted, it's a stretch to call this the child's story. For me, the key is that for days afterward, she would prompt me with her two little pieces of the story, and we would go through the little routine a few times until something else caught her attention.

An unlimited number of collaborative stories can be told by the caregiver, with the child "taking the parts." Our friend Jake's earliest story was one he told (or "co-constructed") with his grandmother shortly before he was two. It began as a comforting recitation of something that had happened.

Jake, remember when

Mommy had to go to work.

She told us good-bye.

She went to her car.

You ran outside.

The sprinkler was on!

You got all wet.

BB picked you up and brought you inside.

And BB was all wet, too.

Jake would do short stylized pantomimes for each line as the grandmother (BB) told the "story." Over the course of several weeks, it continued to fascinate him as they told it and retold it to each other and to others.

You can draw out stories more obviously when the child is a little older and has more language resources to contribute: "What did you do in school today?" "Nothing." "Who was there?" "Joey." "And what did you do with Joey?" "Play airplanes." "Did he share his airplane with you?" and so on. Before you know it, that child will be providing you with information on her own. One key is for you as the parent to *extend* what your child starts and help the child extend what you've given her. It is very hard for children to learn how to make their contributions relevant to what has gone before. So this is one system parents can use to put a protective scaffold around the child's attempts.

You can compare this "scaffolding" of children's communication to how you and your child work with puzzles. You start out with one the child can do. After the one-piece-at-a-time puzzles, you move on to four to seven pieces for you to do together. Until the child can do the puzzle all on her own, you point to where a piece goes or you help turn it to make it fit. Then you work on another four-to-seven-piece puzzle and do it together until the child can do it on her own. Now you're ready for ten to sixteen pieces, and you repeat the process. The puzzle for developing texts works the same way. You stay with the child—giving her just a little more than she can do on her own, and you do it with her until she can do it by herself. Then you raise the bar. Vygotsky, the Russian psychologist, called this technique "moving in the zone of proximal development." I call it "parenting for independence." Sooner than you think, you'll be listening in amazement to what is on your child's mind that she tells you from a fresh perspective you never dreamed about.

All of the strategies discussed above are summarized in the twelve steps of Table 2.

Table 2. **Twelve steps that promote language development**

Step 1: Treat infants and young children as conversational partners.
Respond to children's earliest vocalizations as if they are meaningful turns (you supply the meaning). Pay attention to the child's attempts. Your tone needs to be interested and supportive.

Step 2: Use positive reinforcement.
Use positive statements rather than prohibitions: "I like how you're sitting quietly" instead of "Sit down and don't talk."

Step 3: Continue the topics introduced by the child.
The best place to start a conversation is from the child's interest—which you infer from where a child is looking, what she is showing you, or what she is trying to say.

Step 4: Never laugh at the child's attempts to communicate.
You want to laugh with the child, but never at the child, and never because of how she says something, even if you think it's cute.

Step 5: Do not correct; instead, recast children's utterances.
Direct your attention to *what* your child is saying, not *how*.

Step 6: Expand your child's utterances.
The best way to expand the child's vocabulary and syntax is by expanding or recasting what the child says. For example, when the child says, "Ball," you respond, "Oh, do you see the ball? What a pretty blue ball. Can you throw me the ball?"

Step 7: Give the child a chance to talk.
Balance your own talking with listening: a patient attitude encourages the child to take her turn.

Step 8: Ask open-ended questions.
Ask, "What was the horse doing in the parade?" or, "What did you like best about the parade?" rather than, "Did you like the parade?"

Step 9: Provide scaffolding for your child's stories.
Co-construct stories with your child, and then tell them together (repeatedly).

Step 10: Use books and media interactively.
If you watch TV, watch it together. As with books, use it as an opportunity for complex talk back and forth.

Step 11: "Teach" through play.
Children learn best through play. (Keep it light!) When you do want to be a little more teacherly, do it in very small doses.

Step 12: Use movement with speech.
Singing and finger-play are especially helpful. Dances like the hokey-pokey are fun and instructive. Incorporate repetition and refrains.

CHAPTER

Learning Two (or More) Languages

WHILE LEARNING A FIRST LANGUAGE WOULD BE IMPOSSIBLY HARD if babies didn't have special biological equipment for the job, learning a second (or third) language is not that much harder for them. Linguist David Crystal suggests that the Language Acquisition Device (LAD) we talked about in the previous chapter is really a Multilingual Acquisition Device (MAD). Whatever helps babies learn their first language helps them with the second (or third) language, too,

- provided they are exposed to the second language during the time when their brains are most open to learning new languages and

- provided the routines of their daily life are adapted to accommodate meaningful interactions in more than one language.

This chapter looks at how acquiring a second language is both the same as and different from acquiring the first. I describe different ways of becoming bilingual, especially the difference between acquiring the second language at the same time as the first language (bilingual first language acquisition, or BFLA) and adding a second language early in childhood but after the first language is already firmly in place (early second language acquisition, or early SLA). We will consider when children's brains are most open to new languages, and how strong the arguments are in favor of learning the second language before the start of school or after. We look at the consequences of different amounts of exposure to the second language at the different levels of the language tower introduced in chapter 2 and discuss how it is that children could learn two languages as easily as one. Finally, we set the stage for chapter 4, where we will consider how to arrange children's language environments so they get the exposure they need in order to acquire both (or all) of their languages.

Different Ways of Being Bilingual

Bilingual First Language Acquisition (BFLA) and Early Second Language Acquisition (Early SLA): A Metaphor

Parents raising bilingual children are essentially choosing between having them learn two languages at the same time ("infant" bilingualism) or beginning a second one after the first language is already established ("childhood" bilingualism). If children learn two languages simultaneously, as in Bilingual First Language Acquisition (BFLA), they will have two "first" languages. As we shall see later in this chapter and in chapter 7, given sufficient exposure to each language, the two first languages of a bilingual will be essentially the same as a single first language for a monolingual.

Children who learn their languages sequentially have one first language (L1) and one second language (L2), so this kind of bilingual learning includes First Language Acquisition (FLA) as well as Second Language Acquisition (SLA). However, if children learn the second language before puberty (early SLA), their skill in it is often the same as or better than in the first language; it is usually also comparable to the skill of children who started the second language at birth. The distinction between BFLA and SLA is an important one that I will try to clarify throughout this chapter.

Bilingual First Language Acquisition (BFLA)

You could picture two first languages in the human brain as two trees in a forest. If each tree (or language) has its roots in the ground and grows from the ground up independently, we can say they are both "doing" first language acquisition. Two first languages are generally planted at the same time, at birth, and depending on the nutrients each receives, we may expect parallel growth (see Figure 4a).

The two trees can have all independent branches and roots (as in Figure 4a), or they can have some intermingling of branches and roots, analogous, for example, to a person mixing elements of what are essentially separate languages. For each to develop as a first language, both must be "planted" around the time of the child's birth.

Figure 4a. **Bilingual First Language Acquisition (BFLA)**

SECOND LANGUAGE ACQUISITION (SLA)

To visualize the coexistence of a first language and a second language in an individual, we could also use a botanical analogy. The ficus tree, for example, does not take root in the ground, but on another tree. (See Figure 4b.) The ficus has its own trunk and branches, but it grows on top of the roots and main trunk of its host tree. It may eventually overshadow the first tree, but more often, the two trees (or languages) live entwined until a ripe old age.

Another image of SLA is derived from grafting: one species of tree can be grafted onto another by a gardener so that the roots and the trunk and many branches are from the original tree (or first language), but there will be one grafted branch (or second language) sharing those same roots and trunk. (See Figure 4c.)

The grafting image more neatly parallels the situation of second language learning in a school setting. The roots and trunk are clearly

Figure 4b. Early Second Language Acquisition (SLA) (Ficus tree)

from the first language, and an outside agent—not the tree itself—initiates the learning. Unlike the ficus tree, which may have its own root-like and trunk-like elements that surround the host's trunk and parallels more closely FLA, the grafted portion has no roots or trunk of its own. Still, the grafted branches of the second language can easily attain the strength and stature of the first language branches, and, in fact, may even overshadow the "native" branches.

Following the tree metaphor a little further, we might see that our two trees are potential competitors for nutrients and light, but competition will rarely arise. That is, both trees are planted in the same rich—or rocky—soil. When it rains, it rains on the whole forest, not just on one tree. When the sun shines, it reaches half the earth at a time. It does not strike one tree and pass over that tree's neighbor. On the other hand, in a forest, when trees are mature, they can block the sun and prevent the growth of any new plants below them, so even two trees

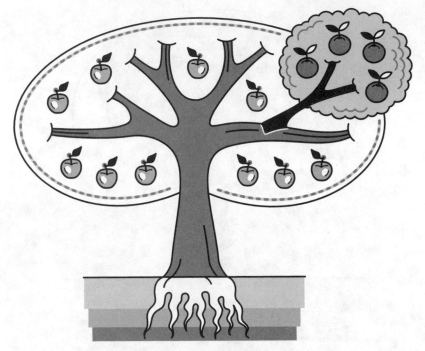

Figure 4c. **Second Language Acquisition (SLA) (Grafting)**

together in the same forest in the same climate may grow at different rates.

BFLA and Early SLA: Which Is Better or Easier?

Second language acquisition is both harder and easier than first language acquisition. It is easier because, for example, the child already "knows" the basics of language learning: he knows he is looking for words to talk about classes of things and that he should pay attention to the ends of words (either prefixes or suffixes), where many languages put important information about how to interpret the words within its sentences. He also knows it matters how people put words together into sentences. Other things work to his benefit, too. When the language learner is a little older, not a newborn or a toddler, his memory is better; his tongue is more dexterous, and he is more able to repeat longer stretches of what he has heard and stored in his mind. He also has more reference points for interpreting new words and sentences.

But learning a second language after the first is in place already is also harder for two reasons: In the sound system, for example, in order to learn the important sound contrasts for the new language, you must set aside the ones you know already for the first language and try to start from scratch. For example, English has a *b* versus *p* sound contrast, used to distinguish between minimal pairs of words, such as "bill" and "pill." French also has a *b/p* contrast, but the French *p* and the English *b* have the same values acoustically. So, when French speakers are learning English, they often sound like they are saying "bill" when they mean to say "pill." They do that until they learn to switch the French contrast off and use the English contrast instead.

Another difficulty arises from the idea that the LAD (Language Acquisition Device) may be less available to us for second language acquisition than for first language acquisition. It might be such a costly device that the brain makes a trade-off. You can have all that brain space and extra glucose early on in life, but the LAD has to move out when a new tenant arrives. Once we have a language, we can then use that first language—imperfectly—to learn another one. One hypothesis is that the LAD is not available for second language learning, so we must use general cognitive processes, which are not as well-adapted for the complications of language stimuli. On the other hand, for very young children, there is some evidence (still being debated) that the LAD is available to them for second language as well. As we have seen in chapter 2, children's processing in their first language is less automatic than for adults, and so they also may be able to "override" their first language categories more easily than adults, whose behavior is more efficient, but less flexible.

Note on Early SLA

Although second language learning appears easier for very young learners than for older children and adults, it does not happen completely without effort for them. The common notion that "children soak up language like sponges" has to be modified. Patton Tabors, an educational psychologist at Harvard, summarizes the four stages young children typically go through when they are thrust into a second language, as when their families move to another country.

In Stage 1, young children may start out trying to use their home-language, although they quickly see that it won't work. Then, in Stage 2, they go through what Tabors calls "the nonverbal period." They do not say much, although we know they are listening intently. In Stage 3, children learn a few ready-made phrases and "formulas," latch on to them, and use them whenever they can. They're usually pretty general and appropriate, in a "one-size fits all" way, and they make a good stepping stone to Stage 4, "productive use" of the second language. The timetable for these stages is very individual. Some children may stay in Stage 1 for only five minutes, so you won't even notice it. Similarly, Patton reports that some children go through Stage 2 so fast you don't see it, and others may stay silent for an entire year. (A year is probably an exception. Case studies 15 and 16 in chapter 5 talk about this silent stage.)

The formulaic speech of Stage 3 can often pass for fluent. "Me, too" or "What's happening?" are useful to give the impression that the children understand, so they will get more input. They may adopt phrases like "I want" + an object. "I want water" works; "I want book" sounds less good, but it works to get started. Another common formula is "I do" + something—for example, "I do these," "I do swing," or "I do ice cream," which slowly grows into "I make these" or "I do swinging," and then to "I am swinging."

Children's first productive speech in their second language is not going to be flawless, but depending on the child's age, the communicative demands on the playground are usually quite low. It is rare for second language issues to keep a child on the sidelines for very long. Children who are slow to join in with new children even when the language of the playmates is their native language will find the same problem in a second language. In either a first or a second language, the solutions are the same. Case studies 11 through 16 in chapter 5 show school-age children's responses to school in a new language.

Studies of their ultimate attainment show that childhood bilinguals, when they become adults, almost never have an accent that can be detected outside of a laboratory. An accent is also rarely found in those who began before age six or seven, and is still the exception for children who started learning the second language before their teen years. I know many adults who learned English in their teens or even after who sound perfectly "native" to me, but careful tests by linguist Kenneth Hyltenstam and others show that when you push these near-native-sounding adults—either overload their processing by requiring them to answer very quickly or give them a competing speech task—they are more prone to errors than native speakers. Those of us who have achieved "near-native" status in a second language as adults can tell you that our performance in it goes way down when we are tired or excited (though it is often enhanced with a little wine).

What Does "Bilingual" Mean? Different Classifications

Because there is no universally accepted definition of what it is to be bilingual, I will take some time here to say how different terms may be used to mark distinctions between different ways of being or becoming bilingual.

The term "bilingual" takes on different meanings according to what you want to describe with it. One set of terms, as in Table 3, talks about the languages themselves. It is important to consider whether the language being learned is the language of the wider community or a minority language and what social status is associated with it.

Table 3. **Names for the two languages of the bilingual**

TERMS FOR THE LANGUAGES	Majority language Community language	Minority language Heritage language
STATUS	High	Low (typically)
USE	Used for public and private purposes	Used mostly for private purposes

Other terms, as in Table 4 below, talk about groups of bilingual speakers and distinguish them from each other according to where the languages were learned and the socioeconomic status (SES) of the learner.

Both immigrant and "elite" bilinguals' ability to learn the second language is closely tied to the status of that second language in the community where they live. (See chapter 4 for a discussion of the effect of language status on learning.)

Table 4. **Types of bilinguals according to where the languages are learned**

TERMS FOR BILINGUAL INDIVIDUALS	COMMUNITY LANGUAGE	MINORITY LANGUAGE
Elite speakers • high SES • two high-status languages	Learned at home and school (first or second language)	Learned at home and/or school (first or second language)
Immigrant or ethnic minority speakers • low SES • one high-status and one low-status language	Learned at school (second language)	Learned at home (first language)

Table 5 illustrates how the relative timing of when two languages are learned, whether at the same time or one after the other, gives rise to yet another classification: "early" versus "late" bilinguals, and within early bilinguals, "infant" versus "childhood" bilinguals. Whether they start learning the first and second language in infancy or childhood, as long as the languages are both planted within the optimal planting season (or "critical period"), early bilinguals typically become "native speakers" of both languages, whereas late bilinguals are generally not considered native speakers of their second language, even if their skills are very good, or "near-native."

Table 5. **Terms for bilingual individuals according to timing and skill type**

BY TIMING OF SECOND LANGUAGE	TIMING OF SECOND LANGUAGE (L2)	SKILL	RELATED TERMS
Early bilinguals	From birth, simultaneous to L1, learned at home	Native speakers in L1 and L2	Infant bilinguals Simultaneous BFLA
	After age 2 or 3, following establishment of L1, learned at home; Around age 5, learned in school	Native speaker in L1 and L2	Childhood bilinguals Sequential Early SLA
Late bilinguals	After puberty, (usually) learned in school	Native in L1; nonnative or near-native in L2	Sequential bilinguals (Late) SLA

How Much Do You Need to Know to Be "Bilingual"?

We saw in chapter 2 that there is no magic moment when you can declare, "That's it; I've learned Japanese." It will be doubly or triply hard to know when you can say you have learned each of two (or more) languages.

The consensus is that the ways individuals use two languages in their lives fall on a spectrum. (See Table 6 below.) At one end is the simultaneous interpreter at the U.N. who speaks both languages as well as a native and is literate in both. Without a doubt, such interpreters command two languages and all will agree that they are "bilingual" (sometimes called "ambilingual"). At the other end of the spectrum are newborns whose parents speak two languages to them, but who cannot speak or read one language, much less two. Technically speaking, infants are not even monolingual, but we call them bilingual on the basis of what they are hearing.

In between these poles are all degrees of language proficiency and use. For example, your elderly aunt who came to the U.S. from Russia thirty years ago but has not said a word in Russian since she arrived is bilingual because she *could* use either English or Russian if she had to. Your preschooler who is just being introduced to a new language at school that is different from the one he speaks at home is nevertheless called bilingual because, like the newborn, he is hearing two languages, and he probably *will* speak two languages at some point in the near future.

Two languages cannot reach the same level of development in all areas unless there is sufficient exposure—and for reading and writing, sufficient training—for them both to develop. More often, bilinguals have unequal exposure to the languages, and thus they have one dominant language and one nondominant language. For each language, they may have different arrays of the four language "skills"—speaking, understanding, writing, and reading—and different skill levels (from limited to very fluent) for each language.

In education, people often refer to skill "type"—that is, whether the person can participate only in informal and oral conversation in a

Table 6. Types of bilinguals according to skill level in each language

Balanced Ambilingual Active	This person speaks, understands, reads, and writes equally well in two languages.	Elite bilingual Additive bilingual
Unbalanced Dominant	One language—either the L1 or the L2—is dominant. Proficiency levels in one language approach monolingual levels, but the other language remains weaker, more like a "foreign" language.	
Unbalanced Dominance Unclear	In the typical immigrant situation, the child starts out dominant in the L1 and switches to dominance in the L2. That is, the L2 takes away from the L1. Generally, the child learns all four skills in the L2, but does not learn to read or write in the L1, which remains an "oral" language only.	Subtractive bilingual (Oral only versus oral and literate skills)
Passive	The child learns all four skills in L1, but only receptive skills (understanding and/or reading but not speaking) in L2.	(Receptive only versus both expressive and receptive)

given language (playground language) and has Basic Interpersonal Communication Skills (BICS), or is capable of formal academic learning in it as well, both oral and literate, and has Cognitive Academic Language Proficiency (CALP).

What Is It Like to Be Bilingual?

A major difference between first and second language acquisition is the degree to which learning in the second language is filtered through the first. Another debate focuses on whether the second language can make use of the biological "assist" recognized for first language acquisition (the innate LAD), or whether one has only general learning mechanisms to aid in the process. We see in this section that there are also strong biological arguments in favor of early second language learning.

Where Are Languages in the Brain?

We can translate our botanical metaphors used earlier into maps of the brain to find just where Chomsky's "language organ" (see chapter 2) is

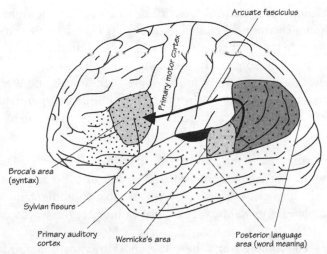

Figure 5. **Language centers of the brain***

located and how the maps are redrawn to accommodate two languages. Metaphors of mind are of two main types: (1) the "real estate" view wants to know where the languages are located, and how much space they occupy, while (2) the "software" view asks how the languages operate there, how the wires connect, and what patterns of activation are visible. Medical studies since the 1800s have given us information about the mind's real estate; modern imaging techniques of healthy brains are shedding new light on the software view.

The Real Estate View of the Mind

Our knowledge of the mind's real estate comes from studies of language disruptions. People who have had strokes or other trauma to the brain often develop aphasia, a condition where they can no longer speak or understand language. Since the mid-1800s, scientists studying aphasics have located the brain's two major control centers for language in its outer layer, or cortex—one principally for syntax and making speech grammatical (Broca's area) and another for understanding and selecting words and making sense of our utterances (Wernicke's area).

* "Language Centers of the Brain" illustration, on p. 355, by Lise Eliot from WHAT'S GOING ON IN THERE? by Lise Eliot, Ph.D. Copyright © 1999 by Lise Eliot. Illustration adapted from A.R. Damasio, "Brain and language," Scientific American, September 1992. Used by permission of Bantam Books, a division of Random House, Inc.

The left hemisphere controls activities carried out on the right side of the body, which are more skilled or dexterous than activities controlled by the left side for most people. ("Dexterous" is actually from the Latin word for "right.") Conversely, the right hemisphere controls activities on the left side of the body. In most people, both Broca's and Wernicke's areas are on the left side (or in the left or "dominant" hemisphere of the brain), although a small percentage of left-handed people have their language control centers in the right hemisphere.

Damage to the area on the forward side of the Sylvan Fissure (a landmark about midway between front and back) will cause Broca's aphasia. A person with this pattern of injury will be able to understand what is said and appears to want to speak, but cannot get the words out—for example, "No . . . uh . . . today . . . uh . . . Mom . . . school . . . yeah." Their speech is labored, and their utterances are mostly content words, with none of the function words and word endings that express syntactic relationships. Their understanding of simple sentences seems normal, but testing of specific constructions, like passive sentences (e.g., "the bear was washed by the boy," rather than the active "the boy washed the bear"), shows that comprehension of syntax can be a problem, too. At first, because the right side of the mouth becomes slack (along with other paralysis on the right side), researchers thought the nerves to the muscles of the mouth had been "cut," but actually the patients can use their mouths for other functions like eating and breathing. The nerves to the muscles are largely intact, but it seems like the syntactic "software" in the patient's brain has been corrupted or erased.

The other main type of aphasia, "Wernicke's aphasia," comes from damage to the "meaning center." Wernicke's area is further back in the brain from Broca's area, behind the Sylvan Fissure (where the lobes of the brain come together). Wernicke's aphasics, with damage in that region, talk freely and volubly in full, mostly grammatical sentences, but they make no sense. "You know the telephone pinkered and I want to get him round and do it like you find before" is a short quote from a Wernicke's aphasic I once worked with. Here the disconnect is to the mechanism within the brain that selects our words. It is as if the stock clerk in the brain is sent to find one set of words and comes back with altogether different ones. Amazingly, the grammar of what receptive aphasics say is relatively good—but they use the wrong words.

Wernicke's aphasics also have trouble understanding what is said to them, and generally have no idea that what they are saying makes no sense.

When bilinguals suffer a stroke, in most cases both languages are affected, but often enough it happens that one language is impaired and the other is spared. This phenomenon suggested to early researchers that the two languages, at least for those individuals, were stored in different places in the brain. When a number of bilinguals with aphasia were found to have damage in the right hemisphere, not the left, it gave rise to the hypothesis that bilinguals might expand their language capacity by appropriating space in the other side of the brain. The most unusual report was of a person who could speak only one of his languages one day and only the other on the next, and back and forth. This led his doctors to speculate that the languages were intact but the mechanism that controlled their retrieval was separate from them and capable of being damaged independently.

SOFTWARE VIEW OF THE BRAIN

Until the end of the last century, we could tell what parts of the brain were involved only after they got damaged, so we had no images of languages in a functioning brain. New, non-invasive imaging techniques like fMRI (functional magnetic resonance imaging), PET (positron emission tomography) scans, and ERPs (event-related potentials) give us revolutionary new data from healthy individuals. This new evidence brings together the real estate and the software metaphors. From experiments that map the activity of the brain while people are speaking or listening to one or both languages, it appears that some parts of both first and second languages occupy different territory in the brain for different activities, like speaking versus listening. We also see two languages "lighting up" within the same space, like two software programs that can be active within the same hard drive.

These new experimental techniques are also pushing down the age at which we can see evidence of bilingual learning in children from bilingual environments. Before they can show us through their own speech and actions what they can understand, sophisticated instruments show babies' different response rates to familiar and unfamiliar sounds in their brain waves and fractions of a second differences in their eye movements. These techniques are showing differences in babies' reactions to different languages within the first year—at a time when babies' production, monolingual or bilingual babbling, sounds the same in any language.

According to patterns of activation in the slides and videos produced by the different instruments, the two languages of adult bilinguals are spread over a larger part of the "neural landscape" than one language in a monolingual brain. A 1997 article in the journal *Nature* showed that when highly fluent childhood bilinguals were processing speech, the two languages activated (or lit up) the same areas of the brain, but when the subjects were late bilinguals, some areas that were activated did not overlap. French researchers have also found some right hemisphere activity specific to the use of the second language. More recently, a report from Laura Petitto's lab at Dartmouth College expanded the comparison. First, she compared monolinguals with bilinguals when they were speaking in only one language. When bilinguals were speaking in just one of their languages, the activity seen in the left hemisphere was the same as for monolinguals. However, when the bilinguals did a task that made them switch back and forth between their languages, they showed activation in the analogous areas of the right hemisphere as well.

In general, then, a second language seems to have at least some functions spread out over a wider area of the brain. Researchers explain this pattern with an analogy to reorganization of brain function during first language acquisition. The pattern of development observed in babies (as well as adults) is for less practiced behaviors to involve a larger area of weaker connections. As the behaviors become more practiced, they become more "focal," with stronger responses from fewer neurons. When the second language is more recent and less fluent, it might take up more space, whereas two highly practiced languages would be handled efficiently in one hemisphere. Thus the neurological evidence seems to suggest that two well-practiced languages are physically in one place, but functionally separate.

Are There Two Separate Languages or One Language with Two Parts?

The new pictures of two languages in the brain shed some light on what has long been an unanswerable question in bilingualism research. For many years, the burning question about bilinguals was whether their languages could be considered "one language or two"; that is, using philosopher Anna Wierzbicka's words, do bilinguals have one set of mental furniture with two sets of labels for the world, or two separate and independent sets of mental furniture—a whole suite for each language.

A key issue in the "one-system-or-two" debate is whether the languages share resources or not. If systems are shared, this might result in cooperation (which would make learning two languages easier) or competition (which would make learning two languages harder). If they are not shared and are completely independent of each other, the second language duplicates everything for itself. If the languages compete for space, one might be squeezed out. On the other hand, if the systems share resources, then those resources "transfer" from one language to the other and don't need to be duplicated for the second language—so two can live as cheaply as one. If the languages are largely independent of each other, as in Figure 4a, learning two languages might be twice as "costly" in space or processing capacity, but not necessarily more difficult.

SHARED AND UNSHARED FUNCTIONS

The "one-system-or-two" question is difficult to answer because there is probably more than one correct answer. There are many factors involved in becoming bilingual, and they change over time. Languages are complicated systems: some subsystems may be shared, others not. Some may be shared with some languages, but not with all.

In a study by our research group at the University of Miami, for example, we found that reading and writing skills were shared between languages, while vocabulary was not shared. In vocabulary, we used the image of concepts being "distributed" between the languages. That is, some vocabulary items are found in one language *or* the other, as opposed to those that are shared or found in both languages. The consensus is that learning two languages is harder for some functions than learning just one, but not twice as hard. Furthermore, each language contributes more mental resources, so there is more dedicated language capacity than if you were learning only one language.

"One-System-or-Two" Debate in Development

Early observers like Werner Leopold, who wrote a four-volume study of his bilingual-learning daughters, proposed that children start with a single, fused system containing both languages and gradually differentiate them. So the question for infant bilinguals was when and how the two languages separated. In an influential article, Italian psycholinguists Virginia Volterra and Traute Taeschner proposed that the separation takes place first in the lexicon and then later in the grammar. New tools of analysis provide new data that have helped us reevaluate that view. Psycholinguists have found that babies' sucking rates and heart rates, for example, change in response to changes they perceive in sounds being played for them in the laboratory. So we can see babies' "responses" to sounds in the lab long before they can make intelligible verbal responses to show their understanding. It appears that all babies are universal learners—in one language or two—until close to the middle of the first year. That is, no matter which language they will eventually speak, they respond equally to sounds from any language until about six months of age. Current consensus is that as soon as you can see any indication that one language is becoming more familiar than others for the monolingual infant, you can see evidence that a bilingual infant is recognizing the sounds of two languages. (More evidence is presented in chapter 7, where there is an explicit comparison to monolingual milestones.)

Monolingual and Bilingual "Modes"

The "one-system-or-two" question no longer seems to be an "either-or" issue. In fact, bilingual individuals appear to move back and forth between one system and two. Neuroscientists tell us that when bilinguals go to say something, both languages are activated. But there has to be an executive decision: will one language be suppressed and one allowed to "go through," or will both stay activated and be used in the same conversation? All bilinguals appear to be able to operate either monolingually—in two languages independently—or bilingually—using two languages within one thought or conversation.

MONOLINGUAL MODE

The Swiss psycholinguist Francois Grosjean protests that a bilingual "is not two monolinguals in one person," but, contrary to this claim, some bilinguals prefer to operate in what he calls a "monolingual mode"— in two languages. That is, they switch between being a monolingual speaker of one language with one speaker (or in one situation) to being a monolingual speaker of the other language with another speaker (or in another situation). Radha, one of our respondents who told about her bilingual childhood, says it feels to her like putting on her "Tamil hat" or her "English hat" as she goes from one language to the other. She might wake up from dreaming in Tamil and have to switch to English for a day of classes. Her mother describes Radha as being adept at moving between monolingual modes in two languages even before age three. She recalls picking her up at her English preschool. She would say something to the child in Tamil, the child would nod and turn to the teacher and tell her what the mom said, but in English. The teacher responded in English and Radha would turn to the mom in Tamil and so on.

BILINGUAL MODE

Many bilinguals do not use their languages so separately from each other, as Radha describes; they use both languages together in a "bilingual mode" or a "rich language stew" when other bilinguals are around. A bilingual mode is only possible if both people in a conversation understand both languages, but they do not have to be able to speak them both. When speaking with monolinguals—or a bilingual who signals by his language choices that he prefers to use one language at a time—bilinguals learn to suppress responses in the "wrong" language. With other bilinguals, those who speak the same two languages, they can operate in a "bilingual mode" adapted to take advantage of the communicative resources of both languages.

Non-Converging Dialogue

Both speakers can use both languages within a conversation, or they can have "non-converging dialogue"—where each person is speaking in a monolingual mode to the other, but in a different language. For example, very often we find that a parent uses the minority language and the child uses the majority language in the same conversation. Both parties are in bilingual mode receptively and monolingual mode expressively. They can understand each other in either language, but choose to speak in only one language.

Bilingual Mode and Code-Switching

In bilingual mode, speakers often switch between languages, or "code-switch." This seamless switching between languages (here called "codes") can happen either between sentences or within sentences at permissible points in the grammatical structure. Code-switching used to be thought of as a failure of bilingual behavior, what people with incomplete knowledge of the two languages did when they found themselves unable to continue in the language they started in. A little bit of it can be filling in words you don't know or can't recall in one language, but code-switching turns out to be a skilled behavior that people master only after they have considerable skill in both languages.

Lexical code-switching can arise from a gap in the individual's vocabulary, for example, "Mira, mira, vi una—a frog," meaning "Look, look, I saw a—a frog" (instead of "una rana"), but often it's a recognition that the term in the other language is not quite equivalent to its translation in the one you're currently speaking. The French "joie de vivre" has a more festive feeling than its literal translation, "joy of living." "Chutzpah" is one of the many terms in Yiddish that need a whole story to communicate the force of what they mean. It is usually translated as "nerve," as in, "She has some nerve!" It may be a little bit of "gall," or a little "moxie," but it's none of them exactly.

Grammatical code-switching—for example, "Sometimes I'll start a sentence in English, *y termino en espanol*" ("and I finish in Spanish")— is a response to an internal or external "trigger." A trigger is a word or grammatical element that is represented mentally in both languages, so it facilitates, or "triggers," the move from one language to the other. Proper names are among the most common triggers. Linguist Michael Clyne gives this example: "Di jungste ist in *Portland*. That's Ruby . . ." (German: "The youngest is in Portland"). The speaker starts in German, then says the name "Portland," an American city, and continues in

English. Words that are similar, even when their meanings are not exactly the same, often trigger switching, too: "an' we reckoned Holland was too *smal voor ons. Het was te benauwd . . .*" ("too narrow for us. It was too oppressive . . ."). *Smal* is pronounced the same either for "narrow" in Dutch or "small" in English, so it was a natural point for the speaker to switch from English to Dutch.

All bilingual speakers have the choice to switch or not to switch. It is as if they have a meter that they can set at either one language or the other—or in between. Generally, a child's setting—closer to bilingual or closer to one of the monolingual poles—reflects the way his environment is set. Children under age two appear sensitive to signals from other speakers, although they may not be very skilled at staying in one language, especially if one is more dominant than the other. As they get older, they become more aware of their language choices and, if it is appropriate, may still choose to speak in a bilingual mode.

Are Children Better Language Learners?

Many people see the difference between second language learning by a child and an adult as psychological or social. They see adults struggling to learn but reason that their poor success is due to either the language-learning situation or their psychological approach to the new language. These people point out that adults, unlike children, are rarely in an immersion situation and they spend a smaller percentage of their time and effort in learning the language. Furthermore, they argue, if adult learners could be as uninhibited as young children, not afraid to make mistakes, they would learn better and faster. There is not a definitive answer to this question, as there is some support on both sides, but to me, the preponderance of both the circumstantial and biological evidence suggests that children truly are better language learners.

Children Are Better Language Learners: Circumstantial Evidence

Some who claim that children *are* better at learning a language sometimes argue backwards from their results. Two areas where child and adult language learners differ are 1) the kinds of errors they make and 2) how well they eventually speak the second language, what is called "ultimate attainment."

Errors: First Language Acquisition vs. Second Language Acquisition

We can learn about processes that take place during language learning by looking at the errors learners make. We talked earlier about the errors that children make when learning their first language, like "he gots" or "he gonna don't worry." Some errors made by learners of a second language are the same errors with the same stages as those made by first language learners. These errors are called "developmental." However, second language learners (L2 learners) also make "transfer" errors, where they try to use the same rules in the second language (L2) as in first language (L1). For example, when you speak a first language that has no articles (like Chinese) and then learn one with obligatory articles (like "a," "an," or "the" in English, or "le," "la," or "les" in French), those small words are among the hardest to master in the new language and are often omitted erroneously under the influence of the first language. Languages with gender systems (like Spanish) are also very difficult for people whose first language (like English) does not require that distinction for every noun or adjective.

One class of strong transfer errors is seen in the sound system, when L2 learners, said to have a "foreign accent," use their L1 sound categories to both produce and comprehend words in a new language. They often fail to recognize a sound in the second language that does not occur in their first language. In the educational video "American Tongues," the narrator goes around asking Americans what "schlep" means (Yiddish for "carry," with a connotation of annoyance). "You mean 'sleep'? Like 'George Washington shlept here'?" was one response. English has both the sound "sh" and the sound "l," but no words that have them together in a cluster, "shl." The English listener unfamiliar with this word was quick to interpret the sounds he didn't know as equal to sounds he did know. Likewise, we have all heard people speaking with a foreign accent. The famous linguist Roman Jakobson, who emigrated to the United States during World War II at the age of forty-two, was said to "speak Russian in seven different languages." He spoke his seven languages brilliantly, but pronounced them all with a recognizable Russian accent. Henry Kissinger, who was President Nixon's Secretary of State, also never lost the strong German accent in English, which he learned as a teenager. By contrast, Madeleine Albright, President Clinton's

Secretary of State, was a childhood bilingual, and one cannot hear the sounds of her native Czech in her English.

The difference is not categorical. Child language learners make transfer errors and adults make developmental errors, but the proportions of each are very different, lending weight to the argument that for younger bilinguals, second language learning is less likely to be filtered through their first language.

ULTIMATE ATTAINMENT

The proportion of adult learners who become native or near-native speakers of a second language is much lower than the proportion of child learners who do so. The proportion of successful adult L2 learners is similar to what one sees for other skilled behaviors—like basketball prowess—and makes it look like a "talent."

Most of us carry the mental image of ourselves as second language learners in high school. A couple of people in each class were superstars, but most of us could barely order a cup of coffee in the new language by the end of three years. In contrast, the acquisition of the first language seems much less susceptible to individual differences (and special talent) than the acquisition of the second language. A small number of individuals have difficulty with their first language development (as discussed in chapter 6), but beyond that tiny minority, everyone seems to be able to do it; everyone becomes a "native speaker." But second language learning in high school, college, and beyond seems more like other skilled behaviors. Most of us are average ball players, a few are very poor at it, and a very few—less than 3%—are very, very good.

There is no age of first exposure after which we can say *no one* achieves native proficiency, but it becomes very rare. For most of us, second language learning in high school and college is effortful and not particularly successful (or even enjoyable!). We do better, even as teens and adults, if we are immersed in a second language environment—for example, if we marry a speaker of another language and our life takes place in the medium of the second language—but most late second language learners, even after fifty years of practice, seem to filter their second language through the first. Research by educational psychologist Catherine Snow shows that older learners are actually faster at the outset than younger learners, but she concedes that, in the final analysis, the child learners surpass the older learners.

Adult SLA, then, has the same success rate as other skilled behaviors, while FLA and early SLA have the more general success rate of a species-wide capacity like walking. What we see is that the distinction between FLA and SLA plays a larger role for older children and adults than for younger children. This universal ability to learn a second language "natively" appears to apply to children under age seven (or whatever research eventually determines the critical age to be). The second language can become as good as or better than the first, and for many individuals, the second language becomes the primary language.

Children Are Better Language Learners: Biological Arguments

Kids Have Special Adaptations for Learning, Including Language

Infants are born with very acute hearing—more so than most young animals. They prefer complex sounds (like speech) to simple tones, and they can make fine discriminations between them. They have shown performance equivalent to adults' from six months or before. They can localize voices immediately—at least from side to side.

Compared to their hearing, babies have poor vision, but they are preferentially drawn to human faces, and they focus especially on the eyes and mouth—both of which are important for their language-learning needs. It helps them to see your mouth moving. Babies have to see your eyes because they need to know where you are looking. When they are learning words, associating sounds with meanings, they know which meaning you intend by checking where your eyes are looking. (See chapter 2.)

What may be the biggest boost to language-learning ability in children is the extra blood flow and metabolic activity in their brains. Their brains are working twice as hard as adults'. The level of glucose they use rises until age two and then stays twice as high as adults' until around age nine. Babies' brains are working in overdrive to make new connections between neurons. It is through those connections that they learn the sounds and words, and then compute the grammar of what we are saying.

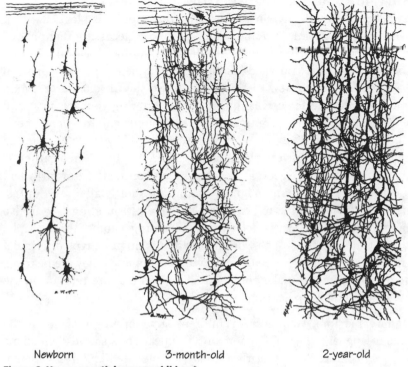

Newborn	3-month-old	2-year-old

Figure 6. Nerve growth in young children*

Children are born with most of the nerve cells in the brain that they will ever have, but infants have vastly fewer connections between nerve cells than adults do. It is as if all of the telephones in a town have been delivered, but none of the wires between the houses have been ordered yet. Children are making so many neural connections in their first five years—on the order of fifteen thousand per neuron—that they end up pruning them drastically by age five to *reduce* them to adult levels. Your child makes lots of connections, but they do not all end up being useful, so only the ones that actually work for your language are kept, and the ones that are not used are allowed to wither away.

* Reprinted by permission of the publisher from THE POSTNATAL DEVELOPMENT OF THE HUMAN CEREBRAL CORTEX, VOLS. I, III, and VI by Jesse LeRoy Conel, Cambridge, Mass.: Harvard University Press, Copyright © 1939, 1947, 1959 by the President and Fellows of Harvard College.

Superior Sound Discrimination

Children's superiority in sound discrimination is legendary, if temporary—on loan, it would seem—until the necessary distinctions for the language or languages they are learning have been made, and then the ear is discouraged (though not completely prevented) from paying attention to new distinctions. As we saw in chapter 2, when you learn the sounds of a language, you are tuning your ear to attend to some differences, or contrasts, between sounds and to *ignore* others. The main point of a famous series of experiments by Janet Werker and colleagues at the University of British Columbia, mentioned earlier, is that infants are very good at hearing sound contrasts from birth and are also good at learning to ignore them from shortly after six months, if they do not continue to hear them in their surroundings. By twelve months, their experience tells English-learning babies, for example, that it is not worthwhile to work on distinguishing one type of Hindi *d* from another. It will not help them with the language they are hearing, so they continue to make only the distinctions that are relevant to the language(s) they are hearing around them.

At the same time, we infer from children's superior pronunciation in the second language that children remain able to learn new sound distinctions for a long time. We saw earlier in this chapter that children's mental representations of the sounds are serviceable, but they tend to be relatively diffuse and unstable. Brain imaging studies conducted while words are being recognized in the brain show that children's responses are more global and involve a larger area of the brain. So before age seven, children seem to be able to override the sound categories that they formed through exposure to their first language. In contrast, adult responses are quicker and originate in a more focused area in the brain. It is also notoriously harder for adults to override their more stable representations of sounds.

Rulemakers

Young children have other excellent linguistic capabilities that they will no longer need and will lose once they have learned a language. They have a heightened grammar-making capacity. Children come prepared to *look* for patterns in what they hear—and have been shown to create more regularity than there is in their input. They expect structure, and if it is not there, they create it. One strong example comes from Elissa

Newport of the University of Rochester, who studied the sign language of a young deaf child, Simon. Simon's parents were also deaf, but they had not had the opportunity to learn sign until they were teenagers, and so their signing remained "ungrammatical," analogous to leaving off the "-s" in verbs like "runs." In spite of this, Simon's signing was more accurate than his parents'. He extracted the rule from their irregular usage and then applied it across the board. This is a fairly dramatic example of the child "going beyond his input."

When Do You Lose the Capacity for Bilingual First Language Acquisition or Early Second Language Acquisition?

There appears to be a trade-off between the child's language-learning facility and mature mastery. Adults can react to sounds more quickly, and their speech movements become more streamlined and efficient—so once the child reaches "automaticity," like "overdrive," the highest gear, there's less (mental) energy involved in the speaking *per se,* and the additional resources get diverted to other purposes. It is as if the mind knows that the learning process takes more resources—and they are sent in on a short-term (five- to six-year) basis. Until efficiency develops, there are energy-intensive measures being taken in the language areas of the brain. Once the brain is operating at near-adult levels of efficiency, its high rate of metabolism goes down.

So, what can we conclude about the comparison between child and adult language-learning strategies? It may be true that children's lower inhibitions and higher levels of engagement contribute to their prowess at language learning, but we cannot ignore the special physical and mental endowments they have for the task.

When Are Children's Minds Most Open to New Languages?

ARGUMENTS FOR A "CRITICAL PERIOD"

Children are so much better than adults at language learning that it has led some scholars to speculate that there is a "critical period" for it that ends at age six or seven (or, others say, at puberty). Technically speaking, a critical period is a window of opportunity with a defined starting time and ending time. Only during that time will a certain experience lead to a desired outcome.

The critical period concept is familiar to us from studies of the animal world. Newborn geese learn to recognize and follow the creature that they see in the first forty-eight hours of life. The image of this animal for the baby geese is fixed in those first two days, and it is not susceptible to change later. No other imprinting will take place after that period. In most circumstances, this is very adaptive. It is usually the mother goose that the baby goose sees, and the baby will not survive on its own if it does not have a strong sense of who it should follow to get food and protection. (The tenacity of the baby geese's imprinting was demonstrated by ethologist Konrad Lorenz, who may be the first male primate ever to have played this role for them. When he was observing newborn goslings' behavior in his laboratory, he was the first creature the little geese saw. After that, whenever he came into their sight, the geese lined up in a row behind him and followed him around.)

Another example, closer to language, comes to us from songbirds, who develop normal song if they hear their species' calls (even from a recorder) during a two-week window shortly after birth. If they are kept from hearing it at that age, it does not matter how much of it they hear later; they will not develop their own song properly and then will not be able to attract a suitable mate. The loss of song may not be fatal for the bird itself, but it will be less likely to reproduce itself, and so its genes will be lost.

First language learning in humans also seems to be subject to such a time limit. We are less aware of the limit because it is so rare for children to be completely deprived of language interaction during the time right after birth and before age ten, when their brains are so primed for it. One horrific case of such deprivation came to light in Los Angeles in the 1970s, where a psychopathic father kept his daughter tied to a potty chair in a small room for twelve years. She was fed and clothed, but no one played with her or even spoke to her except to yell at her and beat her if she made any sounds. When she was discovered, she was brought to a hospital and subsequently to foster care for therapy and study. The book *An Abused Child's Flight from Silence* and the documentary movie made about the girl, named Genie, are heart-wrenching; one sees footage of her hesitant gait and bewildered look and hears the faint vocalizations she made in the early days after her rescue. As for her language development, at first her speech appeared to develop. Her voice quality remained strained and unnatural and her articulation was poor, but her vocabulary reached several hundred words. However, despite intensive efforts to train her, she was never able to master even the rudiments of grammar, so her "sentences" were just strings of words, like "Man man bicycle have" and "Want Curtiss piano play." Tests of her brain activity showed only right hemisphere activation when she spoke. In an exceptional case like this, one never knows if she was perhaps mentally retarded before being so abused or whether her failure to develop language fully was a consequence of the abuse. Subjective impressions of her in the first year of therapy showed her actually to be a quick learner in many instances. Her general mental acuity lends weight to the argument that the language areas in her brain received no stimulation at the proper time, so no amount of stimulation later could create the necessary circuits in the "grammar" part of her brain.

Another case of language deprivation was reported around the same time in northern California. The circumstances were more humane, but the outcome was similar. Chelsea had been born deaf and was cared for lovingly in a large family until adulthood, but she never learned to speak or use sign language. She was in her early thirties when someone realized that she was not mentally retarded but deaf, and she was fitted with hearing aids. Like Genie's, her vocabulary became quite large, but the concept of grammar remained completely absent, as in, "Breakfast banana eating girl." Many children born deaf in hearing families do not receive any usable language stimulation until later in childhood. They are generally of normal intelligence but don't achieve age-appropriate levels of language development. Their signing is reported to lack the polish and complexity of signers who learn early. These cases illustrate the strong role of age constraints in first language learning.

CHILDREN ARE ALSO BETTER FORGETTERS

The other side of the critical period coin is considering how old a person has to be *not* to lose a first language when a second, majority language is introduced. This becomes a crucial question in bilingual children, because as easily as children seem to learn a language, they seem prone to losing it at the same speed. Research on children's first language showed that immigrant children over age nine generally do not lose their first language when they began to acquire a new one, whereas the children investigated who were younger than nine switched their *preferred* language after just one year in English. Within three years, for most of the younger children, the new language became their stronger language.

The Iranian linguists Jamshidiha and Marefat recently investigated subtle grammar points where Farsi and English contrast. One example is whether you can say a sentence without a subject pronoun. (Spanish and Italian are the same as Farsi for this structure.) In Spanish, you can say, "Vi una rana" ("[I] saw a frog"), and the fact that it is "I" speaking is communicated in the form of the verb, so you don't have to begin the sentence with "Yo" ("I"). By contrast, in English, "Saw a frog" is not a correct sentence. It needs the "I." In Farsi and Spanish, the sentence is not incorrect with the pronoun, but sounds strange ("nonnative"). The linguists tested people's preference for Farsi sentences with and without the pronoun. They found that younger Farsi speakers learning English began to regard the explicit pronoun as sounding less strange (under the influence of English "I saw"), but older speakers did not. The cutoff age for retaining a preference for the Farsi structure was around nine.

Arguments Against a "Critical Period"

Genie and Chelsea are extreme cases. In general, the critical period analogy from the animal world applies less strongly to humans because of the greater "plasticity" of the human brain, or at least of the outer portion of the brain, the cerebral cortex, where the most human learning takes place. Language in particular—but also mathematical ability, judgment, spatial perception, planning, and reasoning—develops in the cortex. Other species, even chimpanzees, whose brain structure resembles ours in many ways, have a cortex one-sixth the size of ours, with many fewer neurons and less "uncommitted" space. Our cortex undergoes development up through puberty (and in some areas of judgment, well into our twenties). It is the uncommitted part of the brain that makes us *need* to learn and it also gives us the space to do it. That is, human brains do not come preprogrammed, because the key to human intelligence is adaptability. We need to be able to learn whatever skills are demanded by the environment. Instead of preloading the infant with a lot of software, the child comes instead with lots of "capacity." Instead of embedding the survival skills in the infant's brain, the parents are endowed with hormonal and cultural responses to protect the infant until that learning has taken place (far longer than other species).

This is not to say that the child is a "blank slate" that parents "write on." Just because the infant isn't born with his permanent teeth doesn't mean it's up to the parents to put them there. Children's "language organ" is not preloaded with English or Chinese software, nor do parents teach the child the language. But the language organ comes ready with a more general, universal program and is "wired" with a grammatical analyzer that can detect structure within utterances, abstract the patterns, and apply them to different content. The LAD (Language Acquisition Device) includes rules or structures of the type that all languages use, and the child's task is to find evidence for the structures required by the language he is hearing.

A flexible cortex is more crucial early, before children have survival skills. It is less crucial for adults, who have already been trained on their local conditions. It appears that the child's language cortex is still capable of training, whereas the adult cortex is much less so. If a portion of the cortex is damaged during early childhood, developing functions like language can be relocated to other undamaged tissue. Recovery is perhaps not 100%, but the relocated language is more than enough to function in daily life and in school. The stories of Genie and Chelsea are often contrasted with the story of Isabelle, who was kept in an attic and never spoken to but was rescued at age six. At the time of her rescue, she had no speech and was at the cognitive level of a two-year-old. Apparently, though, she caught up with other children in both speech and cognition within a year. Further evidence of children's "neural flexibility" comes from a treatment for severe epilepsy that involves surgically removing the cortex from one whole half of the brain. Such a therapy shows the surgeons' confidence that the child's brain would recruit space on the other side of the brain, the one not generally associated with language. (Although it generally worked, this approach is not used anymore, now that less radical alternatives have been devised.)

By contrast, when adults suffer damage to one of the brain areas devoted to language, chances for recovery are slim. There may be some recovery early on—for example, when swelling recedes in nearby areas and they begin to function again. But the damaged functions do not regenerate, and the impairment is permanent. Like the starfish that can grow a new arm if one is lost to an accident or a predator, until puberty, the child appears to "grow language" all over again. Adults do not. (When teenagers suffer brain damage, you don't know in advance—you have to wait and see.)

So the time constraints for learning a first grammar seem very strong, like a critical period. But the time frame for learning a second language is less critical. Children are better at it than adults, but an adult who was not exposed to a second language early can still nonetheless achieve a measure of fluency and skill in using the syntax of a second language.

How to Learn Two Languages as Easily as One: What Makes It Possible?

The timetable in chapter 2 for monolingual children's language milestones resembles the time frame for bilingual development, although often a bilingual child will be roughly comparable to a monolingual in the development of only one of his languages, not both. There is considerable concern over whether learning two languages will slow children down in attaining their milestones, so I devote an entire chapter to it (chapter 7).

One reason we say the mental effort of learning two languages adds up to less than twice the effort of one is that the elements of two key language components—sound and syntax—are quite finite in number and learned relatively quickly by the child. The other two major components—words and texts—are learned much more slowly over a longer period of time, whether the child is learning one language or more.

The Effects of Exposure on Language Learning

THE FINITE SYSTEMS: SOUNDS AND SYNTAX

To learn the sound system of a language, children have to figure out which small number of contrasts to listen to and which large number to ignore. As we saw in chapter 2, that usually takes infants the better part of a year to do. Then it takes another couple of years of vocal practice for them to train their mouths to make the sounds in such a way that other speakers of their language can recognize them. As children become more expert, they get faster and more consistent at recognizing sound contrasts within speech. Both hearing and speaking become more automatic: they take less time and energy. Except for a few of the rarer and more difficult sounds, like *r* or *th*, children do a creditable job of pronunciation by age three. Kansas researcher Betty Hart's records indicate that most children reach the halfway mark—where one-half of their utterances are intelligible to people other than their parents—between nineteen and twenty-six months. The other half of their utterances take a more variable length of time, but once the children master the set of crucial sound contrasts—forty or so in English—phonetic learning is complete. The children do not get better and better over time.

The story for syntax is similar, in that almost the whole grammar is learned within the first five years (but this topic is much more hotly contested). Without taking any side in the debate, we can observe that children's language behavior from age three, or even before, can be described, in what is now old-fashioned terminology from early works by Chomsky, as a "generative grammar," a processing mechanism much more complicated than children are otherwise capable of, where innate factors appear to play a large role. This innate mechanism seems effective for more than one language if the proper input is provided.

Developing Texts in Two Languages

In general, children's development of discourse or text-forming abilities in two languages is shown to be largely "interdependent": much of what the child learns in one language serves him in the other as well. In our University of Miami study of bilingual children's language and literacy, we devote two chapters to the extent to which the approximately 700 bilingual children's skills in reading, writing, and storytelling were interdependent. (There is a discussion of the study in chapter 7 of this book.)

Vocabulary

Unlike the phonology and syntax of a language, which are finite, and texts, which are infinite, but where growth in two languages is interdependent, the words in a language are both potentially infinite and not interdependent. Fortunately, children's lexical abilities are quite elastic. Although there is no limit to the number of words in a language and new words are being coined all the time, monolingual adults generally learn and use only between twenty thousand and one hundred thousand words. Words might compete for "storage space" in the brain if a second language doubled the number of words that a person has. We saw above, and we will see in chapter 7, that it is unlikely that the bilingual vocabulary needs to actually double that of a single language. In any event, the huge variability between twenty thousand and one hundred thousand leaves enough space that most bilingual people could double their vocabulary and still not exceed normal "storage" limits.

Words are learned more or less one at a time by an act of association for each one. The process of learning words is more sensitive to differences in the amount of exposure or overall time spent in each language than are the processes of learning grammar and phonology, where age of exposure matters more than time spent. As we will see in chapter 7, bilinguals typically have receptive vocabularies that are much larger than monolinguals', so the storage capacity is there. However, the effort to retrieve and then produce words appears to be more costly, so bilingual children's expressive vocabularies in the two languages combined are generally not larger than a monolingual's. Thus, depending on the dominance pattern of the child, the expressive vocabulary of one or the other language may be lower than monolingual children's vocabularies in that language.

We already saw above how the brain "grows." It does not add cells—it adds *connections* between the cells it has, and it does so in response to stimulation. No stimulation means no new connections and potentially even the loss of old connections. More stimulation means more connections. So it is likely that, relative to the monolingual, extra resources are recruited by the extra language.

Going back to our metaphors for the brain, we see that from a real estate point of view, the child's double-language vocabulary might run into a space problem, but the larger receptive vocabularies convince us that space is not necessarily an issue. In fact, if we look at the vocabulary question from the software point of view, we see that handling a doubled vocabulary wouldn't exceed the processing capacity. Just as you can have separate programs that run on a single computer at once, the mind can "run" separate language programs at once and has many ways to handle increases in the amount of stored data.

"COMPLEX WORDS," OR MORPHOSYNTAX

In discussing vocabulary, so far I have not distinguished words in general from complex words, by which I mean those that incorporate "grammatical bits." "Boys" is "boy" (male child) + "-s," which means more than one. "Walk" names an activity, and "-ed" adds the meaning that the activity took place in the past. I have avoided the linguistic terminology for the "grammatical bits" found in complex words because the word for them is itself complex and unfamiliar: "morphosyntax." "Morpho" means "form," so these are the forms relating to syntax.

Morphosyntax is a border zone between syntax and the lexicon (or vocabulary), and for language learners of any age—monolingual or bilingual—it is a very challenging part of language learning. Furthermore, there does not appear to be a specialized processor to help. In some morphosyntactic usages, there are rules that take up little mental storage: to make a plural, add "-s"; to make a past tense, add "-ed." But alongside the forms that are generated by the rules are the exceptions. Exceptions are about the same cost to store as individual vocabulary items, but they are more costly to *acquire*.

Linguist Steven Pinker has used past tense forms to illustrate some of the complexities involved in the morphosyntax domain. As we saw above, for the majority of verbs in English, there is a simple ("transparent") rule for forming the past tense. In addition, there are also a few hundred irregular past tense forms that survive in modern English, like "sang" or "bought." These forms are learned one by one, just like vocabulary. Because they are generally quite frequent in speech, children learn many of them early. But they may, for example, use "went" for quite a while before they realize that it's related to "go." A child who had been previously using "went" in correct environments may briefly entertain "go-ed" as the past-tense candidate. However, because these forms occur with enough frequency and in uncomplicated situations, the "go-ed" phase is usually quite short.

These "vocabulary items" (that is, exceptions in morphosyntax) are actually much harder than plain vocabulary. With "celery," for example, I learn the name and note whether there are any irregularities, and that's it for its morphosyntax. By contrast, when I learn the noun "fish," I also have to learn that it has an exceptional plural; it doesn't take an "-s." But hold on: there will be some instances when it does (as in "coral reef fishes," where it means "kinds of fish"). So that is two extra things I have to learn to know the morphosyntax of fish. I can't just memorize them; I have to figure them out. For syntax, we have the LAD, and the LAD seems to help us find the broad principles that govern the morphosyntax of a language, like how it forms the past tense or changes an adjective to an adverb (like "mad" to "madly"). The rules seem to be part of the syntax, but the exceptions are part of the lexicon.

For vocabulary, time of exposure to a language translates into how many times you might hear the word in a variety of different sentence contexts. I will probably need to see a new word more than once but less than five times in order to learn it. If I spend a summer in France, will I hear the French word for "spearmint" enough to learn it? How many times does someone who already knows "fish" as plural need to hear "fishes" before being able to figure out that it's not a mistake? I don't know of any studies that determine the answer to this kind of question, but common sense tells us it will take more exposures to plural "fish/fishes" than to "spearmint" to learn it. However, because the words have different frequencies of use, we can't really predict whether you'll get to the point of learning "spearmint" before you can learn "fishes."

"Enough input" in a language must be an amount sufficient to accommodate learning these "opaque" forms without being told what they are. We can be told them (or taught them explicitly), but knowing them on a conscious level does not translate directly into having access to them at a subconscious level in order to use them when we are speaking.

CRITICAL MASS OR THRESHOLD

The number of times you have to see a morphosyntactic construction in order to figure it out has been called a "critical mass." The amount of exposure one needs to arrive at a critical mass differs for each of the levels of the language: that is, it is different for syntax and phonology and vocabulary and discourse. Within vocabulary—including the specialized subset of vocabulary consisting of the morphosyntactic exceptions—the amount of exposure needed will vary greatly. Thus, there is not always a direct relationship between amount of exposure and amount of learning in either a first or second language. Rather, we observe what appears to be a *threshold*. There is a direct relationship up to a certain point, what is called above a "critical mass" or a threshold. After that point, more exposure does not matter. If the critical mass required is, for illustration's sake, ten exposures, then five exposures will be less helpful than ten, but if the word is learned at ten exposures, fifteen will not be better than ten.

If there were not a threshold (or a similar mechanism), then bilingual learning would indeed be subtractive—that is, one language would take resources away from the other. Children with 100% of their language experience in one language would then have twice as much knowledge of that language as children with only 50% of their language-learning time devoted to it. This is not what is observed to happen. Rather, we see the phenomenon of the threshold or critical mass in many domains of language learning.

Psycholinguist Virginia Gathercole at the University of Wales has provided us with several clear examples of critical mass in the way that children master the complexity associated with specific grammatical constructions. She has found that all children go through the same progression but that different bilingual learning groups take a shorter or longer time to work out all the details. Those with more input from home and school in the target language matched the monolinguals in their judgments sooner than those with less, roughly in proportion to the quantitative differences in their input. In all of her studies, there has been a time when the groups with less daily input catch up—when more input ceases to show an effect on grammar learning.

How Much Exposure Is Enough?

This leads us to consider how much input on a "percentage basis" is *enough* for multilinguals—whose input is split between two or more languages—to achieve the same level as monolinguals in morphosyntactic correctness (e.g., "flew"—not "flied"—for birds, but "flied out" in baseball) and for comfortable use of a language. These are questions without a precise answer. It takes monolinguals two to three years to learn the basics of a language enough to use it fluently. The added time requirement for a second language does not seem to be significant for phonology and syntax, while there does seem to be more time required for vocabulary and morphosyntax in two languages compared to one. However, the difference between the needs of an individual for learning two languages and those of an individual learning one language is generally not greater than the already great difference between individuals in the range of normal development for learning a single language.

We will see in chapter 4 that as a rough guideline, many research studies use around 20% of a person's waking hours as a minimum for exposure to each language when deciding who can be counted as bilingual. In our University of Miami Infant Study, informal learning of a language took place at almost every level of input, from 10% to 90%, but enough proficiency for functional and willing use of a given language seemed to require at least 20% of one's input per day, week, or month in that language. For one language not to overpower the other(s), a 30/70 split, with 70% of the child's waking hours in the minority language, seems ideal, and 80/20, with only 20% in the minority language, a bare minimum.

What Are the Limits? How Many Languages Can a Person Learn?

People are fascinated by the question of how many languages a person is capable of learning. Field linguist Ken Hale of MIT was said to be able to speak twenty languages, and the obituary of Charles Berlitz of the famous language schools says he spoke thirty-two. Apparently, as a young child, he was spoken to in a different language by everyone in the household, so he was fluent in four languages by age three and in eight languages by adolescence. As a toddler, he thought everyone had his or her own language and that he was supposed to have his own language, too.

The recent discovery of a polyglot savant in Britain has rekindled this discussion. "C" is a very impaired individual—he cannot tie his shoes or use a key to open a door, but he appears capable of mastering the lexicon, syntax, and morphosyntax of a language with almost no exposure to it. He has had no formal language teaching but begins speaking and understanding by just picking up a book in the language. Unfortunately, his limited mental capacity means he has very little to say in any of his twenty languages. Still, like Hale and Berlitz, "C" shows that, in principle, it's possible to speak as many languages as you have access to.

Unlike a savant, we and our children need consistent and prolonged exposure to be able to learn a language. So the limiting factors are time and access to meaningful interactions in more than four or five languages. Two is more common than three. Beyond three, people sometimes report difficulty in retrieval when they know several languages (but that is a problem we can also encounter with a single language). From a parent's point of view, as we will see in several places later in this book, it may be difficult to arrange the interactions for your child and sustain them past the time when the child would forget them. However, if the logistics are feasible, the mind seems capable of any number of languages.

How Long Should You Wait?

A major decision for parents contemplating bilingual child-rearing is whether it is better to let a child learn only one language first and then introduce another language later or to introduce the languages simultaneously. There is not a single answer to that question. Infants are well adapted to learning language as soon as it's possible, so parents promoting two or more languages may want to capitalize on their heightened readiness. On the other hand, children seem to retain their language-learning talents for a few years before they let their "uncommitted cortex" be taken over by other functions.

Hidden in the question of how long parents should wait until they introduce the second language is the opposite question: "When can you stop training the first language without suffering loss in it?" My opinion, based on observations like those above, is that you need to go through elementary school with the child supporting the first language. You can (and should) introduce the second language earlier rather than later but if at all possible should continue the first language when you do so.

In the European Union, there are more elementary schools being established on a foreign language teaching model, where children are schooled in several languages at once. Few schools in the U.S. (outside of the dual immersion programs I recommend later in the book) teach foreign languages in elementary school. One important exception is the Waldorf Schools, based on the teachings of Rudolf Steiner. They teach second and third languages from the early grades, but they are adamant about using living situations—songs, stories, skits, and games—rather than grammar drills for doing it.

As we will see in chapters 4, 5, and 8, there are sometimes reasons to wait before introducing a second language. I hope to convince you not to wait too long. Children have a special talent for learning languages—but the talent does go away, and the task becomes harder for them.

CHAPTER 4

Establishing a Bilingual Environment

IN CHAPTER 2, I DISCUSSED the issues involved in language development in general. Everything you learned for learning one language holds just as true for learning two or more languages. You see that, as parents, you do not teach children language, but you create better or worse environments in which your children's language develops. In this chapter, we explore special strategies for creating enriching environments within your household so that your child can learn a second (or third) language.

The key to raising bilingual children is for parents (or less often, the school) to establish the minority language. The language of the broader community—the language of school, commerce, government, and the mass media—is a given. In every culture, all healthy children learn the majority language, even when their parents do not. But families must make a special effort to "grow" both a majority language and another one. The minority language may be a heritage language that parents or grandparents have brought from another country, or it could be another language chosen by the parents for any of a variety of reasons. For example, it might be a second official language that children are expected to learn, as in Canada, Switzerland, or Hong Kong. Sometimes speakers of a country's majority language opt to educate their children in a language that they believe will have strategic importance later in the child's life, such as Spanish in the United States. Or it could be that the individual seeks to communicate in another modality, as with a spoken and a signed language.

For any given person being raised in a bilingual situation, we cannot know whether she will become actively bilingual or not. But we can be aware of trends. We can compare groups who are bilingual to others who seem to have the potential for bilingualism, but did not pursue it or did not achieve it. With my colleagues in the University of Miami Bilingualism Study Group, I explored the practices and ideas bilingual groups have in common. From these studies, I pinpoint the key ingredients in their experiences for fostering the second language. At the end of this chapter, I explore ways to take advantage of this knowledge in your families. Then, in chapter 5, you will hear from parents who have used these principles, and together we will evaluate how their strategies worked for them and how they might work for you.

I emphasize ways to strengthen the minority language because that is the more difficult case. However, the same principles are effective for a child who is learning a new community language, such as an expatriate or a recent immigrant. Parents wishing to encourage or reinforce the use of the community, or majority, language can also employ these strategies.

As you read this chapter, I'd like you to consider where your child will hear and use her languages and what other resources are available to give the child's languages a broader context than just your nuclear family.

The Foundation for a Bilingual Family

If you do not buy a lottery ticket, you will not win. Similarly, if you do not maintain a bilingual environment, you will not have bilingual children. Luckily, the odds of children becoming bilingual are not like the odds of winning a lottery. If two languages loom large in your life, chances are they will be part of your child's life as well. But if you, the parents, are not actively using two languages daily, then bilingual upbringing must be a conscious construction on your part. Having access to meaningful interactions in two language environments gives you the ticket to play. The stage is set for your family to become bilingual. But then you must actively seize the opportunity. You must want to make it happen, and you must believe that your actions can have an impact on whether it will happen.

Beliefs and Attitudes

Annick de Houwer, a psycholinguist in Belgium, suggests that these two beliefs on the part of the parents are the best predictors of whether children will learn two languages: Parents must have

- a positive attitude toward bilingualism and

- an "impact belief"—a belief that their own language practices have an impact on the child's practices.

It is crucial for you, as parents, to have an awareness of how your own language practices affect your child's learning, and you must use your knowledge of your role to insure the quality and quantity of your child's language exposure. These two beliefs usually go together, but either one can be absent. You probably know a parent with an impact belief but without a positive attitude toward bilingualism. For example, someone who has been speaking a minority language with his child— and witnessing that she learns it—has an impact belief. He sees that his language behavior shapes his child's language behavior. But suppose that the child's teacher convinces this parent that his child's intellectual growth will be hampered if he continues to raise her with two languages. Now he no longer has a positive attitude toward bilingualism. He has replaced it with a negative one, and the child, who had been on her way to becoming bilingual, loses the second language (amazingly quickly, it turns out).

The opposite situation is also all too common. One example comes from an intensive study of the Taiap people of Papua, New Guinea. In interviews with researcher Don Kulik, almost all the parents expressed satisfaction with their own bilingualism and a desire that their children also become bilingual in the local Taiap language and Tok Pisin, one of the important languages of the wider society. However, they were not aware of how their own language use affected their children's language learning. They thought that it would happen outside the home and that what they spoke to the child made no difference.

We do not have to travel to New Guinea to find people with similar ideas. Many parents I heard from were like the Taiap speakers. As Mark and Cindy, an international couple living in Paris, said, "We just thought if we were in the countries where the other languages were spoken, it would happen on its own." But despite the fact that they spent long periods of time in France and Italy, their children heard primarily English addressed to them, and so far, at ages four and one, they have learned primarily English. The parents did not see what role they needed to play in order to capitalize on the opportunity that their living abroad presented to them.

So, neither belief is sufficient by itself. If parents lack one belief or the other, the environment they provide for their children will likely lead to weak or nonexistent learning of one of the languages. With both a positive attitude toward bilingualism *and* an "impact belief" that their own language use shapes their child's language use, parents will be motivated to take the practical steps that foster both first- and second-language learning.

Practical Considerations
In police lingo, parents must establish "motive and opportunity" for the minority language. They need to find ways to give children

- enough reasons for them to *want* to use the minority language and

- opportunities for enough exposure to it for them to be *able* to learn it.

Where will the "input," the interactions that provide the raw material for children to learn the minority language, come from? Who will speak it with them, and in what situations? Parents must specifically consider where speakers are found who can use the other language. If you, yourselves, are to be major sources of the second language, it may be useful for you to record your interactions for a week or keep a diary that will give you an idea of what your language practices are actually like.

You also need to take the child's perspective, not your own, on the value of the second language. You cannot assume that your own desire to use the language will translate automatically into the same desire in your child. Although it is usual for children to adopt parents' attitudes and for them to want to please their parents, the use of the language must have value in the child's world, from the child's point of view. How will you make the language attractive and indispensable for your child, so that, with time, mastering it will evolve into the child's own goal?

The Odds That a Child Will Become Bilingual

Some small studies from these last decades have indicated that not every family that embarks on bilingual upbringing ends up with children who can use their two languages comfortably. Until very recently, we did not have any evidence from large-scale studies about bilingual "success rates" in large, *unselected* populations. Early accounts of child bilinguals were often case studies of linguists' children (for example, Leopold, Vihman, and Deuchar)—children whose parents were knowledgeable about language and cared deeply enough about it to make it their life's work. I am not suggesting that all children of linguists will become bilingual and all others will not, but there may be more attention to language in the households of linguists than in the average home. Thus, they would not serve as a model for most families. More importantly, if a linguist's child did not become bilingual, the parent did not write about it, so we do not know how many books about incomplete bilingual learning never got written.

A relatively large survey of bilingual outcomes is reported by Suzanne Barron-Hauwaert, a parent and member of the editorial board of the *Bilingual Family Newsletter*. She surveyed more than one hundred families, readers of the *Newsletter* and participants in a bilingual family chat-list, about four-fifths of them living in Europe. Even in this self-selected group, the overall percentage of children whose parents described them as passive bilinguals was about 20%, and even higher among the seven- to eleven-year-olds, for whom the percentage was closer to 40%.

In a larger, less selective study, Annick de Houwer and colleagues found that approximately 25% of children of bilinguals were not active bilinguals. The researchers contacted 18,000 Flemish families in Belgium, a country with two official languages, each in its monolingual region, and asked parents to list the language(s) spoken at home by each individual in the home. Of the 2,250 households where parents reported speaking more than one language at home, 75% had children who were also bilingual.

The Belgian results provide a "half-empty/half-full" perspective on parents' expectations. We can look at the half-full glass and say, "That's good; three out of four children in bilingual households become active bilinguals." Or we can take the half-empty viewpoint and say, "One-fourth of the children in bilingual households do not become bilingual. Why not?!" Because 75% of the children in de Houwer's survey were reported to be bilingual, we see that it does not take an exceptional family to raise a bilingual child: it was the majority outcome in this sample. By the same token, though, we see that it is not an exceptional case when a child in a bilingual context does not become bilingual.

Factors Affecting Whether the Child Becomes Bilingual

Exposure, Exposure, Exposure: The Input Cycle
Of all the relevant factors for enhancing language development in general that we discuss in this chapter—for example, positive attitude, frequent use, or official status—quantity of input is the most important for learning a second language. Without interacting with people using the language, no learning takes place. Without enough interaction, learning can take place, but the children do not reach enough of a comfort level in the language that they will willingly use it. In our University of Miami infant study, we found that the children with too little time in such interactions—less than about 20% of their waking hours—learned words and phrases but did not make their own sentences in the language.

When the child uses a minority language, she invites more input in that language, so the cycle is self-reinforcing, as in Figure 7. A greater amount of language input leads to greater proficiency in the language, which leads to more use, which invites more input, and the cycle starts again. On the other hand, if the child does not use the minority language, it stands to reason that she is using a different language and getting less exposure to the minority language, so she develops less proficiency, which leads to using the minority language even less, and that leads to getting even less input in that language.

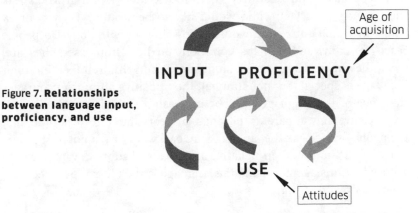

Figure 7. Relationships between language input, proficiency, and use

Other Factors
Still, this system does not exist in a vacuum. Other factors play a role in how much input is delivered and how much is taken up by the child.

THE CONNECTION BETWEEN PROFICIENCY AND USE
It is common sense that children will not use a language if they experience too much difficulty getting their ideas across in it. So, short of grammar drills, parents must do all they can to boost children's facility with the language. Here, again, amount of exposure is critical, but the age at which the child begins hearing the language is also important. A child with an earlier exposure to a language will have an easier time learning it than the child with a later exposure to it, even if the quantity of language input is the same for both. So the younger child will use the language more and acquire greater fluency in it. But as the arrows in Figure 7 indicate, this is a two-way street. Greater proficiency leads

to more use. More use leads to greater proficiency. But less proficiency leads to less use and eventually to even lower proficiency.

THE CONNECTION BETWEEN ATTITUDES AND USE

Similarly, positive attitudes of parents, siblings, and peers toward a language can add value to the language and make it more attractive to the child. A language in and of itself is generally interesting only to linguists. What makes a language interesting to the average person is who speaks it and what they say in it. Are there children who speak the language that your child would like to be around? Do you know songs in it that your child would enjoy singing with you? Do people react favorably, and perhaps comment on how impressed they are, when they hear you speak the language? When children feel that their language is special (but not strange), their positive attitude encourages their use of the language, thereby increasing the effectiveness of the cycle. Conversely, if parents, siblings, or peers think, for example, that the people who speak the language are backward or stupid, or if others make jokes about it, their negative attitudes will subtract value, lead to reduced enthusiasm for using the language, attract less input, decrease proficiency, and so on.

In some cases, the amount of input alone will make the difference between learning two languages or not, but attitudes affect how eager one is to find the input. In a study of trilinguals by de Houwer, parental language patterns accounted for 84% of the variation in the children's language patterns. That is a very high percentage, which tells us that the children's use of the three languages reflected the parents' language patterns very closely. Still, parents' language use was not 100% of the story. Patterns of exposure to the minority language are key, but there is also room for attitudes, values, and social circumstances to influence children's language choices.

In practical terms, the amount of input available is more crucial for the minority language. We and others have found that children need more exposure to the minority language than to the community language for the same measure of learning. Part of this asymmetry may stem from the background presence of the dominant language in the environment through television, neighbors, advertisements, etc. But also very powerful is the natural attraction of the majority language culture for the child.

The majority language has especially high instrumental value for the child. For adults, the instrumental value of a language has to do with getting jobs or better access to government services and health care. For children, the majority language is their social lifeline; it is their link to their peer group and to the popular culture that helps them fit in with this peer group. In France and Canada, French is an official language. It is supported by the educational system, and used in movies, music, TV, and advertising jingles. Signs everywhere you look proclaim the importance of French. By contrast, the French Canadian communities in New England and the French- and Creole-speaking Haitian-American community in Florida have relatively little political and economic power or cultural influence, so the utility of French or French-Creole is much narrower, and the language has less visibility to the child. In such a context, there is also less pressure from the community to learn French, so more of the child's motivation must come from the home.

WHEN THE CYCLE IS WEAKENED
What factors can tip the scales toward the minority language? What influences how much time the child will spend speaking the language, and how much value the child will attach to it in her daily life?

The link between proficiency and use of a language (in the input cycle in Figure 7) seems like common sense: if one does not speak a language well, one will not use it. If one reports using a language often, we can infer that the person has some skill in that language. In fact, though, this dynamic works better for minority languages than for the majority language. The extreme social desirability of the majority language can overwhelm the other factors—here, input and proficiency—and cancel out their effect. For example, California researchers Hakuta and d'Andrea found, among a large group of Mexican teenagers in California, that skill in Spanish predicted use of Spanish, but the same was not true of English. The teenagers' use of English was better predicted by their *attitude* toward English than by their objectively measured skill in it. In fact, most of them tended to overestimate their skill in English, which may partially account for their motivation to use a language that they did not speak very well.

All Children Can Learn More Than One Language

In my review of the literature, I found no evidence that the characteristics of the child make any difference for bilingual first-language acquisition (BFLA) beyond those that affect monolingual first-language acquisition, too, like poor hearing, mental retardation, autism, and so on. Personality traits are largely irrelevant. Children who are fast learners or not, who are painfully shy or not, or who have a talent for word games or not, all become native speakers of their first language. Individual differences may become relevant as the bilingual candidates become older, but by then they are no longer childhood bilinguals. Just as we have universal learning of one first language, I know of no cases of a healthy child being incapable of learning two or more first languages when both are indispensable.

Even a second language—that is, a language learned after the first language is firmly in place—always gets learned if the stakes are high enough. We saw in chapter 3 that second-language acquisition is not always as easy and automatic for small children as we are used to thinking. But I have not heard of children with "motive and opportunity"—even children with special needs—failing to acquire a second language.

For example, in the University of Miami Infant Vocalizations study, two of the children in the Down syndrome group were growing up with two languages in the home. Having Down syndrome definitely affects children's language development. Their articulation is much poorer, their vocabulary smaller, and their grammar simpler than that of typically-developing children. They are generally several years behind norms for their age and may never reach full acquisition. But in their homes, these children with Down syndrome were learning two languages, each at the rate of development and level of proficiency that we would expect for them in learning one language; thus, they could interact with both Spanish-speaking and English-speaking relatives and friends of their families.

I consider in chapter 6 how to evaluate whether dropping a second language could improve a difficult situation for a child with special needs, but so far, we have not found any conditions that automatically preclude a child from learning a second language.

No Language Is Harder or Easier Than Another

Language Type

There is nothing that makes one language or another easier or harder for any individual or group to acquire as a *first* language. A child born to Chinese parents is not better suited physically to learn Chinese than a child born to Mexican parents. If that Chinese child is adopted by Australian parents soon after birth and raised in Australia, she is as well suited to English as she would have been to Chinese and no less so than other Australian children. We have seen that children start learning about the language around them while they are in the womb but that learning remains flexible for several years and can be easily modified by new experience.

Similarly, there are no pairs of languages that cannot be learned as first languages as easily as any other pairs by a bilingual-learning child. It seems likely that adult second-language learning can be easier or harder depending on the language pairs, but the extent to which two languages are similar or different will probably not make a difference to a child. Very young children may not be aware of the linguistic relationships that adults can notice. So, for example, the fact that the vocabularies in some language pairs (like Spanish and English) have many cognates, or words with similar sound and meanings, would not necessarily mean it will be easier for the child to learn those languages than a pair (like Spanish and Japanese) without many words that have common roots.

Social Status

There is nothing in a language itself that makes it more or less learnable for a young child, but its status matters very much in determining how much input in the language is available. Using the example of French again, in most areas of the U.S., French is not associated with a specific immigrant group but enjoys high status as an international language and as one of the languages of the United Nations. People who speak French can identify with a well-known culture and enjoy a sense of pride in it. There are many speakers, possibly even young native speakers, that you can find. Less abstractly, there is a large body of literature in that language, and children's books and videos are available (at least on the internet or through outlets in France or Canada, if not locally).

MEDIA SUPPORT

Some languages are easier to learn because they are easier to find. Readily available children's materials, for example, provide families with "text backup" and give the language more value for the child. Tintin in France, Monica in Brazil, and other giants of children's popular culture are strong allies for minority languages. Children are more excited to remember what Winnie the Pooh says—and sings—than the words of routine admonitions to clean their room or brush their teeth. They look forward eagerly to the next adventure of Babar and beg to have the books read to them until they can read the books themselves. With colorful pictures and wording that is easy to understand, these stories draw the child into the language. Some of the characters are associated specifically with the language they were created in: Asterix or Le Petit Prince in French, or Pocket Monsters in Japanese, can create interest in that language, but international storybook characters can help interest a child in *any* language—provided the works have been translated and published or filmed in that language. *Sesame Street* is produced in several languages other than English, and you might find, as my colleagues Hans and Anna did, that you prefer the German version. They report that the pacing of *Sesamstrasse* is slower and calmer. Children reading about or watching Big Bird or Mickey Mouse and other Sesame Street or Disney characters may not even notice that the book is written in Spanish, or they will accept that these characters, like themselves, may speak English sometimes and Swahili at other times. Thus, the characters also become bilingual models for children. (A survey of media resources is found in the appendix.)

For slightly older children, reading leads to both greater proficiency in and retention of a language. People who are readers of a language are less likely to lose it later. In Miami, our research group kept an ongoing survey of our subjects' language profiles, and the importance of reading for the minority language skills was demonstrated by our results. We always asked students their language history and which language they preferred for various activities. The answers differed according to the activity at hand. For church, for example, our students would be more likely to choose Spanish (or Chinese or whatever their family language was), while for school activities and music, they were more likely to choose English. Not even the popular Latin salsa music won out over American pop music. (There were some interesting asymmetries in the languages people preferred to use for arguing, swearing, or telling jokes.) More to the point, the only people in our surveys who said that they preferred to speak the minority language in most situations were those who had not come to the U.S. until well into elementary school— after they had learned to read in their first language. We do not know if this happened because those bilinguals who did not begin to acquire their second language until they were old enough to have learned to read had spent a longer amount of time immersed in their first language, so their skills became consolidated, or whether the reading itself played a role in consolidating their skills. (This is a good topic for a research project, and perhaps an enterprising student will soon take it up.)

Books provide both additional exposure to a language and more motivation for language learning. Whether reading knowledge is the cause or the result of greater language use does not change the utility of books as carriers of language and culture. Literacy is not a necessary part of knowing a language—people across centuries and around the world can speak very well in languages they do not read—but it is a good example of one way in which the value of a language can be enhanced for the child so that the child will seek more input through that medium.

Songs in the language are even better than books and videos. Songs are an excellent way for children to practice a language in a non-stressful situation with a lot of repetition. They are also an effective "hook" for pulling a child back into the minority language. You can strike up a song almost anytime!

Family Factors
With respect to learning a minority language, older siblings are sometimes helpful and sometimes not. Bilingual author George Saunders (see Case Study 5 in chapter 5) reports that in his family, the older siblings set a good example for the younger children. The younger ones were less likely to question why they were speaking

German to their father, who was also an English speaker. As far as they knew, that was the normal state of affairs. More commonly, though, older siblings bring more of the majority language into the house. They have majority-language friends who come to play, and they know about TV shows, comics, and movies in the majority language that you might prefer to avoid. When children are small, you are the major source of outside materials for your children, but as they get older, the children themselves play a larger role in selecting what they read or view on TV and whom they will play with.

Children in the same family share many characteristics that typically have an influence on language learning: socioeconomic status, literacy levels of the parents, etc. But the family dynamic shifts with each child, and the family's fortunes may have changed between births. Sometimes new babies are a chance to start fresh. In some families we met, older children who were somewhat less willing to speak the minority language became convinced that the new baby in their household understood only the minority language. For example, in Case Study 4 in chapter 5, older siblings who were reluctant to speak the minority language with their parents nonetheless spoke it to the infant without prompting from the parents.

Community Factors

Finally, bilingual families do best when they do not have to do all the work of maintaining the minority language by themselves. A cohesive community of heritage-language speakers can make a big difference in the vigor of that language. By "community," we can mean a formal structure like the Welsh Language Board, which recognizes a role for government intervention to help ensure the perpetuation of a Welsh national identity through the heritage language. Or we can mean a single parish church or social agency that provides services to minority-language speakers in the minority language and in many ways keeps the culture of the home country alive and vibrant. By creating an ethnic enclave, they create a context for maintaining the minority language and culture. In her 2005 study for the Welsh Language Board, Gathercole found that the level of Welsh use was higher among parents with Welsh-speaking friends. When parents had friends who wanted to socialize informally in the minority language, they were more likely to use Welsh themselves. A social network with religious or community activities and sports in the medium of the second language makes the minority language still more useful.

The most obvious tool that communities have to bolster the minority language is the schools. We found in our research in Miami elementary schools that the effect of teaching half of the subjects at school in Spanish could more than counterbalance the effect on the children's Spanish scores of using less Spanish in the home. All of the Spanish-speaking children's scores—in all combinations of high or low socioeconomic status and bilingual Spanish-English or Spanish-only households— were much better in Spanish when they attended schools where half of the subjects each day were taught in Spanish. Avoiding the use of English in the home was somewhat less crucial to maintaining Spanish skills when children could be schooled in Spanish as well as in English. (Note that in this study, the presence of English in the home had almost no effect on the children's English scores because English was already favored by virtue of being the community language. This study is discussed in more detail in chapter 7.)

Globalization of English Makes It Harder

Language shift is a phenomenon in which a speech community of one language shifts to speaking another language. A global trend like language shift can have an effect on household language practices, too. Globalization, which contributed to the spread of English, makes the "smaller" languages harder to maintain now than they might have been even a generation ago. The days of the British Empire may be over, but still, "the sun never sets on the English language." Well-financed mass media and the internet give English even greater strength. Although internet content is being developed in Chinese, Spanish, and Arabic, for example, the overwhelming value of English internationally is well entrenched even in cyberspace, where 80% of the content is estimated to be in English, giving it an advantage over other languages. So it is not only the public rhetoric in the U.S. against languages other than English, but also international commercial, cultural, and political forces that make English one of the easiest second languages for others to learn and one of the hardest first languages to get children to set aside long enough to learn another language.

Although the number of different languages in the world is over six thousand, there are relatively few languages spoken widely. Eighty percent of the world's population speaks one (or more) of eighty-three major languages; forty percent (half of the 80%) speak one (or more) of only eight major languages. So the shift to the major languages is very strong (and not of recent origin). The pace of language shift, which has been well-documented by language geographers, compounds the difficulty for would-be bilingual families in many parts of the world.

The process is not always evident to the nonprofessional. We found, for example, that language shift in Miami is masked by ongoing immigration. Spanish appears to be a growing community language, but study after study shows that the children of immigrants there (the second generation) are *less* likely to become fluent in Spanish than were the children of previous generations of immigrants. The unequal weights of two languages cannot be attributed solely to globalization. In any given region of the world, even a relatively "small" language, like Italian in the Veneto region of Italy, can be dominant. Until a generation ago, a local Venetian dialect, not Italian, was spoken in most homes. Now, Italian is used more in public spheres, but it also holds sway in the home. So, places where two languages are used interchangeably may be finding that the more local language is losing ground.

Organizing Your Home for Your Child's Bilingual Language Development

Whatever the language combinations involved, the child must have adequate exposure to the minority language. In this next section, we consider specific ways to provide "motive and opportunity" for the minority language in the child's daily life.

Your choice of strategies for your home will depend on what your goals are and what language resources you have. I will present the major household language strategies here and describe how they work. Then, a self-evaluation survey will enable you to see where you have strengths. Where you find weak points in your current situation, you will need to find extra strategies to compensate for them. After we see from the testimonials in chapter 5 how people have used these strategies in their lives, I will offer some evaluations of the strategies. I can tell you ahead of time, though, that no one method works better or worse than the others—in general. They only work better or worse in a given situation.

The four major strategies are described below. The shorthand names for them are:

- One Parent–One Language (OPOL)
- Minority Language at Home (mL@H)
- "Time and Place" (T&P)
- Mixed Language Policy (MLP)

(We will see that there are some subcategories of these strategies. The strategies can be subdivided in various ways, and they are often combined, but overall, they represent the major dimensions of the logical alternatives.)

Note that the guidelines presented here are to be followed flexibly. While consistency is considered a key element in one's day-to-day language behaviors, rigidity is not. It is not at all uncommon for families to switch strategies from time to time, especially when circumstances change or when they perceive that things are not going as they wish. In fact, in Barron-Hauwaert's survey (mentioned above) of more than one hundred bilingual families, 20% reported switching strategies. In chapter 5, we will see that the proportion of families I consulted who changed to adapt to changing circumstances is at least that high.

One Parent–One Language (OPOL)

In families that have adopted the One Parent–One Language strategy (OPOL), each parent always addresses the child in a language different from the other parent. Most often, the parents both speak their native languages, but OPOL, like any of the other household strategies discussed here, can be implemented with a nonnative speaker as a language model. (See Cases 5, 6, 7, and 8 in chapter 5 and a special section below for advice for nonnative-speaker parents.) In one common version of OPOL, either parent can speak the minority language, while the other uses the community language with the child. If the parents each speak a different minority language, the child can hear two minority languages in the home, plus a third, majority language in the community. In 1902, in the first printed advice that we are aware of on how to raise a bilingual child, Grammont proposed OPOL. It has continued to be the favored strategy in many parts of the world, especially in Europe and Canada. (See Cases 1 to 8 in chapter 5.)

Minority Language at Home

The Minority Language at Home strategy (mL@H) involves a situation where both parents (whether both are native speakers of the minority language or not) speak only the minority language in the home. If parents are bilingual, they most often choose to speak the majority language outside of home. This plan, of course, is an option only if both parents are capable of speaking the minority language relatively fluently. It was for many years "out of favor," but is gaining ground as a recommendation, as it provides more of the minority language for the child than OPOL generally does. One of the rationales for OPOL has been the claim by its proponents that it is easiest for the child to separate the use of the languages by person: French is "Daddy's language"; Vietnamese is "Mommy's language." We certainly observe that children accept that principle very well, applying it sometimes more consistently than the parents. There is no research to my knowledge, however, that specifically compares the OPOL approach to other approaches, like mL@H. When linguist Margaret Deuchar's book, a case study of her older daughter's bilingual language development, was published in 2000, mL@H was uncommon enough that Deuchar felt she needed to explain it and argue for its legitimacy as a choice for elite bilinguals. She and others who have used mL@H report that children are also quite capable of using "place" (instead of "person") to regulate their language choice. With mL@H, they seem quite comfortable speaking the different languages to the same person in two different contexts.

"Time and Place" (T&P)

The third strategy is sometimes called the "Time and Place" (T&P) method. Bilingual school programs are often organized along these lines to vary which language is used both by time and by place: mornings in the minority language and afternoons in the majority language, or social studies in English one week and in Spanish the next, usually in a different classroom, so both time and place alternate. T&P is a grab-bag of "non-person" strategies that sounds like the "place" strategy of mL@H except that it is less a description of the family's daily routine and more a description of fairly regular departures from it. Families who use OPOL, for example, may decide to do so only during the week and switch to mL@H on the weekend, often with a trip to another area or a visit from a monolingual speaker of the minority language. Other families report a yearly cycle: mL@H for nine months of the year followed by a complete switch to the minority language, inside and outside the home, for three months, often during a trip to a country where that language is spoken.

When parents are contemplating changing their strategy, a complete upheaval of the household routines can be an excellent device for carrying out the transition. For example, an OPOL family may spend a year in another country and switch to mL@H when they come back.

Mixed Language Policy (MLP)

Use of the Mixed Language Policy (MLP) is reported in a number of geographic areas (for example, Miami and Singapore). I have seen MLP described and know many people who practice it, but I have never seen "directions" for it—perhaps because there are no special techniques associated with it. Parents use the language that suits the topic or situation. Some go back and forth between monolingual modes for different topics. They may talk with children about school in the school language, then switch to the family language to discuss an upcoming wedding, and then switch back to the community language to discuss a parade in their town. Others consistently use both languages in all utterances, and their children are encouraged to use the "bilingual mode" from the outset. Linguist Anthea Fraser Gupta says that MLP is the preferred strategy for bilingual and multilingual families in the areas of Asia that she is most familiar with, Singapore and India. Parents would not be "behaving naturally," she contends, if they stopped switching languages for their children. People from those countries find it odd that so many writers, "the experts," have proscriptions against it.

In the implementation of MLP, language choice is dictated by topic or situation and is set by the speakers: you answer in the language that you were addressed in. As in bilingual discourse in general (see chapter

3), "trigger words" switch the language. If you are responding to a code-switched utterance, you respond in the language that it ended in. Or, you can initiate a new topic in either language.

I found no parents to talk to me about it, although several said they found themselves "code-switching madly," whatever the strategy. In Barron-Hauwaert's survey, a few parents said they ended up using MLP after starting in another system. I am sure that MLP is the basis of many more bilingual exchanges, if not bilingual households, than are typically discussed.

However, I do not recommend this strategy for families who are making a conscious choice to raise their children bilingually. As we saw above in the discussion of language shift, "free market" forces lead to a bias toward English (or another local majority language). MLP does not specifically carve out space for the minority language. If it were up to me and there were a particular language that meant a lot to me, I would not leave it to chance. I would be sure to make the time and the space for it and give every advantage to the minority language. I would want to know that I did everything I knew how to do in order to overcome the "linguistic inertia" that leads inevitably toward exclusive use of the majority language. I would make it an explicit goal to help my child achieve a comfort level in the minority language—and we will see in chapter 7 that the majority language will flourish just fine, especially if children are schooled in it at for least part of the day from the time they enter kindergarten.

General Considerations for Bilingual Families

How Much of the Time Will Each Language Be Spoken?
If one parent will be the source of the minority language, how much time will that parent be at home, and how much interaction with the children can be expected of the parent during that time? We mentioned earlier that, as a general rule, research groups like ours have found that around 20% of the child's waking hours, or approximately fifteen hours a week, in the minority language would be a bare minimum. Some researchers specify that children participants in their studies must spend 30% or more of their time in the minority language (approximately twenty-five hours a week).

If the number of hours is less than twenty, what other sources of the language can you supplement the child's minority language exposure with? Can any of the child's exposure come from people who are monolingual in the minority language, rather than from bilinguals who share the majority language with the child?

What Language Will the Parents Speak with Each Other?

In deciding which language to speak with each other, the easiest thing to do is to continue with whatever strategy you had been using before, but the birth of a child is also an opportunity to reconsider. Has the proficiency balance in your family shifted? Perhaps you originally spoke Finnish together because your Finnish wife did not speak Swedish comfortably, but now, after several years together in Sweden, her Swedish is better than your Finnish. Or, you may want to consider changing to the minority language together if the amount of the minority language the child would otherwise hear is at the bottom end of the spectrum.

My respondents report that it took about four to six weeks for a conscious language switch to be accomplished. During those weeks, they found they had to remind themselves of which language to use and persevere when it felt awkward. But after about six weeks (if they got that far), they forgot that they had ever used a different language together. (Note that these were people with pretty much equal skill in both languages.)

How Well Does Each Parent Understand the Other's Language?

Is the spouse who does not understand a language willing to learn some of it along with the child? In many situations, it happens automatically, but, for example, the aforementioned survey by Barron-Hauwaert shows that monolingual fathers were less likely to do so. If one parent does not understand one of the languages, what provisions can you make in order to ensure that he or she is not excluded?

For example, Aviva is a native English speaker living in Israel who is married to Marc, a Hebrew speaker with just a rudimentary knowledge of English. He was reluctant to have his children raised speaking English as well as Hebrew because he would not understand them when they spoke English. Aviva made a pact with him that she and the children would never use English as a "secret language" to specifically exclude him. She speaks English with their four children more when he is not present, but if he is present, she tries to have one person translate for him to keep him abreast of what is going on. It has more or less worked out over time—and Marc's English has also improved. It is a little harder when Aviva's relatives from the U.S. are visiting; because they tend to speak fast and all together, Marc finds their English conversation more difficult to follow. Note that this situation can arise even when there is no language difference! (In my household, my Southern husband finds the pace of my New York relatives' after-dinner discussions hard to follow, too.)

What Language Will the Minority Language Parent(s) Speak Outside the Home and with Others?

How Will You Handle Three-Way Conversations?

When children consistently use a different language with each parent, it is hard to imagine how the child will address them both without explicitly addressing either one. Each family evolves its own plan. George Saunders (whose story I report in chapter 5) details the plan adopted by his German- and English-learning children to handle exactly that situation. They would address one parent by name and speak in the language of that parent, letting the other parent overhear. If a question needed to be addressed to the other parent, the child would switch languages for the question.

One consequence of OPOL is that in three-way conversations, there will be "non-converging dialogue"—that is, a conversation where the speakers respond to each other in a different language from the one in which they were addressed. Many people have described the facility with which even small children go back and forth between languages within one conversation, especially when the language pattern is fixed by person, as it is in OPOL. Each individual is in "monolingual mode" for speaking but "bilingual mode" for listening. OPOL takes advantage of this capability to allow three-way conversations. For instance, the father in an OPOL household may say something in French, and the mother may add something in English to the father's comment.

The child could then respond in either language. As many families report to be the usual case, the father continues in French, so that two people are talking to one another each using a different language, not the one they are addressed in.

My friend Odette reports that a common practice in bilingual households in her area of western Canada is for the parents to stick with their respective languages but insert key terms from the other language for the topic under consideration. So, in a bilingual conversation about a skating rink, for example, the English speaker might insert "patins," the French word for "skates," in an otherwise English response to a French question. Then, in the mostly French continuation of this sentence, the speaker might substitute the word "rink" for the French "patinoire." In general, she says, both adults and children in two-parent households tend to switch languages more when both parents are present with the child than when the child is alone with just one parent.

As I discuss in chapter 3, non-converging dialogues are one manifestation of a bilingual mode of speech and are not unique to OPOL. They sound difficult to monolinguals, and some bilinguals are adamant about avoiding them, especially in conversations with just one other person, but large numbers of bilinguals are not shy about using this bilingual mode and, in fact, profess to prefer it. There is an interesting literary genre developing where bilingual authors revel in the luxury of flowing lyrically into and out of each language. (See chapter 8.) Similarly, several of my respondents spoke of the happy chatter in two languages that they revert to in the company of childhood friends. In many families where the parents use the minority language with each other and in addressing the child, the child responds in English. That may not be the pattern you are aiming for, but it assures us that children—and you—can handle it.

Which Language(s) Will You Speak Outside the Home?

Some families opt to use the majority language with each other when they are outside the home. The threshold of the house is the cue to switch languages. Other families (like the Sundarramans, Case Study 9 in chapter 5) use the minority language with the family regardless of physical location. They use it in the home, outside the home, in the U.S., and abroad—whenever they are together.

Some people switch to the community language so as not to stand out. Other parents continue to address the child in "their" language for one-on-one exchanges with the child as long as it is not specifically impolite to someone present. (Of course, standards of politeness vary in different countries and need to be negotiated in a manner appropriate to wherever you find yourself.)

The key is to take the temperature of the environment where you are. Are you in a situation where speaking another language will be received warmly? Your use of a different language may make others feel uncomfortable. It is very common for people in the presence of conversations in a language they don't understand to assume that bad things are being said about them. One mother also recounted that she got worse service outside the home when people heard her talking a minority language with her children.

School-age children, in particular, are likely to express their embarrassment when you speak another language to them in front of their friends, or children who they hope will be their friends. They do not want to appear different in any way. If your child asks you directly or indirectly not to address her in your language in public, I think the best thing to do is go along with it without any fuss. This may also be a signal, though, that you have not been reinforcing your child's self-esteem as a bilingual enough. So, not in response to the child at the time she asks, but soon and often, praise the child's bilingualism. You might praise her to a third person in the child's hearing, or in other ways build her pride in speaking two languages.

How Will You Handle Having Guests in the House?

This decision generally depends on the language resources of the guest, on whose guest it is, and also on how long the guest is staying. As much as possible, parents like to stick with the "proper" language for the child. Minority language guests are a great boon.

You may be tempted to switch to a monolingual guest's majority language when speaking to your children in front of the guest because the switch is only for a short time. But remember, some out-of-town guests stay for a long while. Even local guests may end up being regular visitors, so the policy you decide on should work for the long term as well as the short term.

Parents may accommodate their guests in one language, but, as in OPOL, address the children in the usual language. The children can end up overhearing the guest's language, but unless they are to be involved in extensive conversation, they can continue to respect their "other-language" policy. Children can answer the guest politely in the guest's language but continue to address short comments to their parents in the minority language. If a parent and child have something lengthy to discuss that cannot wait, they can excuse themselves to take care of the matter.

Will the Language Policy Be the Same in the Presence of Other Children?

When other majority-language-speaking children are visiting, parents and children are both likely to be tempted to switch to the majority language, but it is generally not necessary. Aned, a parent of two Spanish- and English-learning children in Miami, feels comfortable sticking with Spanish with her children when English-speaking friends of the children are visiting. She speaks to her children in Spanish, but translates, or has a child translate, for the friend. (Another parent reports doing this, too. She points out that it's the same dynamic that she uses with her husband.) On the other hand, the Guerlins in Santa Fe (Case 2 in chapter 5) made a point of having the father address the son (in middle childhood) in English when the son was with his friends to be more inclusive of the friends.

For the most part, you will see that children (like adults) are capable of setting their conversational "response-meters" to monolingual mode and producing responses in the language that they had been addressed in. In mL@H, the family uses two monolingual mode settings: monolingual in the minority language in the home, and monolingual in the community language outside the home. But they may need to hear in bilingual mode in the home when there is someone in their midst who can speak only the majority language. Some members of the family use the majority language with guests, leaving other family members to continue in the minority language. As we see below with the Mixed Language Policy (MLP), bilingual mode is an alternative for speaking as well as for hearing.

Can Parents Who Are Nonnative Speakers Be Adequate Language Models for Their Children?

In my opinion, the stories in this book from parents of bilingual children demonstrate that parents do not have to be bilingual themselves. (See Case Studies 13, 16, 22–25.) The stories in Case Studies 5–8 and 21 also make it clear that using a nonnative language with your child can work. Parents should not refrain from speaking the second language just because it is not their native tongue and they fear transmitting their errors and their foreign accent in it. As long as you have a desire to do it, and have reasonable fluency in the language, in most cases the extra opportunity you provide for your children to practice the language outweighs the potential inconvenience of their picking up your errors. You can use this opportunity to improve your skills, too, through contact with other speakers, records, CDs, or videos. Even reading aloud from children's books will provide standard grammar and authentic idioms for parent and child to learn from together.

That said, majority language parents with skills in other languages may feel the same motivations as minority language speakers—that they want their children to grow up knowing their parents in the parents' "own" language. The emotional arguments for the native language that we heard in chapter 1 are as valid of course for the majority language speaker as for the minority language speaker. If you feel you want to relate to your child in the language you spoke as a child, no one can argue with those strong feelings. As we see in chapter 5, you do not have to be the source of the minority language for your child. There are other ways to provide exposure to it. A parent is one of the most convenient and reliable sources of speech in a minority language but is by no means the only possible one.

The key point, however, is that if you *desire* to use your nonnative language, your nonnative status is not a reason to hold back. Several of the parents who contributed to this book were nonnative speakers of the language they used with their child. They were hesitant at the outset. They questioned: Will I know enough words? Will I be able to pull it off? Will it ever feel natural? They all answered "yes." In fact, Martin, one of our parent-respondents, embarked on teaching his newborn son Yiddish on the basis of a couple of years of study in college, several years of genealogical research, and membership in a Yiddish book group. He says that now, after ten years, it feels funny to speak to *any* child—not just his own—in a language other than Yiddish. Author Jane Merrill hesitated, too. For a year after her twins were born, she says she stewed about whether she could speak a nonnative language with them. At that point, a friend cautioned her that if she was going to do it, she shouldn't wait any longer. She went home that afternoon and said, "Bonjour, les bébés," and never looked back. It is ideal to start at birth, well before the child's first attempts at speaking, but if you didn't start then, you haven't lost the opportunity. The message is, "Start now. Now is better than later, and also better than never."

There are published accounts that we have referred to of parents who spoke a nonnative language with their children: Jane Merrill, an American who spoke French to her twins on the outskirts of New York City; George Saunders, an Australian who taught his three children German; Margaret Deuchar, a British mother who joined her Cuban husband in speaking Spanish with their children; and Jameelah Muhammed, an American in Washington, D.C., who speaks Spanish to her two children. The skill levels of the people I heard from ranged from more than ten years living abroad to Martin's two years of college Yiddish. As Janette in Wisconsin said, "You're not going to have to deliver an academic paper in the language. You have to tell your child to put on his socks and drink his juice." This is not too much different from the situations of the many foreign-born parents who speak an accented version of the community language with their children with no harm done.

The nonnative-speaking parents I consulted had these three habits in common: They had excellent dictionaries for the target language, both a bilingual one to find the words or phrases they were looking for and an unabridged monolingual dictionary with which they could learn about the new words in their own context, not through the lens of the other language. They had native speakers whom they could consult; many traveled with their children to a country where the language was spoken more widely or sought out expatriates in their own country. George Saunders, in the days before the Internet, used short-wave radio to keep up with German news and maintain contact with German speakers around the world. If the parents were still learners themselves, they used the children's materials—songs, rhymes, and simple stories— as learning materials for themselves, too, and they sought out other places to improve their language. Martin, whom I mentioned above in connection with Yiddish, attends a language camp every year with the whole family—and all of them participate both in classes and in recreational activities in an immersion situation, where the daily life of the camp takes place only in Yiddish. He and his family also meet regularly throughout the year with other families whose Yiddish, at least in the beginning, was better than his own.

There is no indication that children's language suffers because of their parents' nonnative status. The key to language development for the children of nonnative speakers—as for all children—is to have a language-rich environment with varied stimulation and an accepting atmosphere where they are encouraged to express themselves and where their verbal exchanges are valued.

Troubleshooting: General Ways to Supplement Minority Language Input

Given the odds mentioned above of children becoming active and balanced bilinguals, it clearly takes some ingenuity to create a bilingual atmosphere that can compete with a global language or with the local majority languages. No matter what household strategies people use, there may come a time when their children need more encouragement than was previously necessary to keep using the minority language. Children may just refuse to answer in the minority language at all, despite reminders, or the refusal may take other forms. They might give only single word responses or answer nonverbally. They may leave the room if the minority language is being used, either subtly or with their hands over their ears. Or they may just ignore the flow of the conversation and interrupt to initiate a conversation in the other language.

In fact, it is a common refrain. One or more of these tactics on the part of children are reported by almost every parent at some point or another in the process of their "bilingual project." Whether you use OPOL, mL@H, or any other strategy, we know that the minority language is vulnerable. You might find there will be too little input from a single parent who travels extensively without the family or even from both parents when the child spends more time outside of the home than in it.

Also, parents need to evaluate whether they themselves are using a bilingual mode (code-switching) or whether their own speech is drifting heavily toward the majority language. They must consider ways to make the minority language more useful or attractive to the child and provide more people the child will want to use it with, either within the home or through travel to a country where the language is the community language. (I talk more about this at the end of chapter 5.)

Parents' Own Actions

WHEN THE CHILD USES THE "WRONG" LANGUAGE
When the child begins using more of the "wrong" language, the first thing to examine is your own behavior to see what changes on your part may be needed in order to rectify the situation. How you respond to your children when they use the "wrong" language sends a strong message to them about what you expect of them. Studies show that children pick up on these messages—which you may not be aware of sending—and that their language behavior follows closely from those messages. No single exchange turns the tide, but many small messages can build up a habit over time.

Elizabeth Lanza, a psycholinguist and mother of two Norwegian- and English-speaking children, has proposed a spectrum of parental responses that signal to your child whether you want a monolingual mode for your conversation or whether you are willing to tolerate a bilingual mode (code-switching or non-converging dialogue).

Lanza identifies five points on the spectrum of parental responses (Table 7), going from 1) incomprehension of the wrong language to 5) code-switching yourself to follow the child. In between are 2) questioning some aspect of the child's statement, 3) repeating the child's statement in the desired language and possibly asking for a restatement by the child, and 4) moving on in your own language, without comment.

Table 7. Parents' response strategies

1	2	3	4	5
I don't understand (in minority language)	Did you say *x*? (in minority language)	repeating child's utterance (in minority language)	moving on (in minority language) with no comment	code-switching to follow the child to the majority language

Parents can, of course, stop the conversation to ask explicitly that the child proceed in "their" language, and sometimes, such a discussion in "I-messages" can be very effective: "I feel so good when you answer me in my language," or "I understand so much better when you speak my language," as opposed to "you-messages": "You should speak only Russian to me," or "You know better than to speak English when your grandfather is visiting." Mostly, however, it is recommended that you make the request implicitly as much as possible, without interrupting the flow of the conversation. Conversations are by nature give and take. They are full of requests for clarification of a term or of something said too softly. So it is not unusual to say, "What?" or "I don't get that, can you tell me again?" In a bilingual conversation, such repetition can be asked for in the other language, the one the parent would like the child to switch to. A slightly more subtle request is number 2, above. For example, if the child says in German that his class went to a concert that afternoon, the parent can say in Turkish, "You went where?"

Studies show that children at age twenty-six months are sensitive to which language the other person is speaking. They may not be able to articulate it, but they speak less Turkish with the German-speaking parent and less German with the Turkish-speaking parent. Even if the children's skills are unbalanced in favor of German, so that they are more likely to have the vocabulary they need in that language, it has been shown statistically that their patterns follow the patterns set by their parents remarkably well. That is not to say that they will never mix the two languages—that is a well-attested stage of bilingual development—but their behavior follows the expected patterns well enough to show that their mixing is not just random. They are not as likely to use one language as the other in monolingual mode, and in bilingual mode, they use the two languages in proportion to how they are used by the parents.

If you can redirect the child subtly, so much the better. You can try it—and it may work. Sometimes, though, the child will say, "I want you to speak Japanese" (or English or whatever the majority language is). Jason, at age four, (Case 4 in chapter 5) said, "Don't talk like that. Talk like I'm talking now." You may have to insist, or at least insist on continuing to speak yourself in the language you prefer. I find it analogous to music lessons. Many children hate practicing and insist on quitting piano as teenagers and then reproach their parents later for letting them quit. Parents must take a child's refusal to speak the minority language seriously, but it does not mean the end of your bilingual project.

THE CURIOUS SUCCESS OF THE "I-DON'T-UNDERSTAND" FICTION

A weird illogic occurs irrespective of the household strategy used—and it works to your benefit. Quite often a parent successfully feigns noncomprehension of the child's other language to encourage the child to use the right language. It seems like it would be hard to convince the child that the parent does not understand the other language. Several of our parent-respondents, who speak the majority language with their spouse in front of the children every day, have reported—with some amazement—that the children still appear to accept the fiction that the parent does not understand it, and they act as if the parent could not speak the other language. This may be akin to the often reported habit among children of being more categorical about who speaks which language than the parents are. One family reported that despite the parents using (and modeling) a mixed policy between themselves, the child still addressed them each in only "their" language, regardless of which language the parent was using with the other parent.

A NOTE OF REALISM ABOUT SIBLING SPEECH

In my experience, when children are left to their own devices, they almost always use the majority language (or code-switch heavily) with their siblings. Even very bilingual children, like Olga and Pia, two of our survey respondents, report that they spoke Spanish with everyone else in the household, but not with their sisters. Pia's mother was apparently very uncomfortable with the children doing that and continually admonished the girls to speak Spanish with each other. The compromise they reached was that they would speak Spanish with each other in her presence because they could see that it meant so much to her, but by themselves, they used English.

Frankly, that's all you can do. The encouraging part is that children can be very strong in the minority language but still not use it among themselves. In our University of Miami surveys of college students, we found that only those who had come to the U.S. after age ten or so preferred to speak the minority language with their siblings.

All of the others reported using the majority language with siblings. In a study of one hundred and ten junior high school children, University of Miami graduate student Arlene McGee and I found that even first-generation children switched to English among themselves within a very short time of arriving in this country. In our study of Miami elementary schools, we also found a strong preference for English among young bilinguals. While children in dual-immersion schools cooperated excellently with the policies on language choice in the classroom curriculum, they overwhelmingly preferred to use English, the language of the wider community, with each other in the halls and on the way to the bus.

Enlisting Help from Others

Whether parents opt for OPOL or mL@H, it is important to consider the extra help available for the minority language through bringing monolingual speakers into one's household or through travel and schooling, especially immersion schooling. Almost everyone I met in the research for this book, especially those in the U.S. and the U.K., supplemented their efforts in the home with one or more of these additional strategies.

MONOLINGUAL SPEAKERS

Contact with monolingual speakers is a great asset for developing skill in the language the monolingual speaks. With bilingual speakers, one is often not sure which language will be used, but that issue is not in doubt when one speaker is monolingual. If possible, I prefer either older or very young monolingual speakers to teens and young adults for this minority presence, as they are less likely to be actively learning the majority language themselves. What with relatives, friends, and hired household help, other language speakers may not be too hard to find. Of the three major supports we will consider, however, hired household help is perhaps the least reliable language resource. This does not mean that this resource should be avoided, just that parents should not count on it as their only strategy for the long term.

Household Help

In general, hiring household helpers of the target language background is worthwhile for those who can afford it, but such arrangements usually do not last throughout the whole duration of the children's growing up. People's experience with household helpers is spotty. Our friends Bryan and Elizabeth's au pair (Case Study 8 in chapter 5), for example, worked harder at learning English for herself than she did at speaking Spanish to their children. Chris and Ellen's household helper (Case Study 7 in chapter 5) remained monolingual, but in the course of four years had picked up enough English to understand their daily routines, so their daughter, Sophia, judged correctly that it was no longer necessary for her to respond to her in Spanish if she preferred not to.

Many people working as nannies are balancing commitments to their own families, so, for example, in the Lopez household, the nanny, Mariella, spends only eight months a year with them and takes two-month leaves twice a year to go back home to Venezuela. Beyond her purpose to reconnect with her own family, these trips are also helpful to keep Mariella's Spanish more "monolingual" than the English-influenced Spanish spoken in Miami, where the Lopez family lives. When she returns, the children are excited to see her again and appreciate her more even than if she had never left. Still, during her absences, new (non-Spanish) habits take root and become more firmly entrenched as the children get older and more and more drawn to the English in the outside world.

Jane Merrill reminds us that we cannot assume that an au pair is a natural teacher just because he or she knows the target language. Merrill spent time training the au pairs she hired over the years, and she set out activities for them to do with the children in what she calls an "informal curriculum." An afternoon's activity, she would remind her helpers, should include outdoor play or a walk; reading, writing, or easel painting; and listening to songs or singing, as well as a snack time. Of course, you would need to make sure that books and CDs of stories and songs in their language were available. Merrill was specific about which books to read—for example, a book about trains if there had been a recent trip on a train, or *Petit Tom découvre les couleurs* (Little Tom Discovers the Colors) if painting was on the agenda. Taking a page from Maria Montessori, Merrill encouraged the au pairs to involve the children in light housework with them. She recommends polishing wood, scouring sinks, or other jobs that use tools, and especially, tasks that show results. She praises those activities for the concentrated mood they engender and their action vocabulary. Once an au pair gets used to the rhythm of activities you expect, Merrill observes, he or she will not need you to leave a specific list on the refrigerator any longer.

Grandparents

Many, many families spoke of the grandparents as a positive force in their bilingual efforts. Parents most often cited their desire for continuity from their own parents (and grandparents) to their children as their motivation for raising children bilingually in the first place. Visits back to one's country of origin are facilitated by having grandparents to see there. Even if one's family is too large to stay at their home, the grandparents provide an anchor that makes the visit abroad more feasible.

By the same token, one cannot encourage visits *from* grandparents enough, especially from the point of view of the children (as well as that of the grandparents!). Grandparents from another country typically come for a month or more at a time—long enough to reinforce the use of the minority language in the home, but not long enough to assimilate to the new country. Grandparents have an emotional bond with their grandchildren and a stake, often as fierce as the parents', in the children's healthy development. In this vein, you do not want to ignore the value of aunts and uncles. If your siblings are single, they may fit flexibly into your household and can be of enormous help. Siblings with children often bring the cousins in tow. Cousins from a country where the minority language is the community language—when they click with your children—are possibly the best language teachers there are for them: they combine the best attributes of family and friends.

Even though all of these tactics may be rather temporary, they act as booster shots to remind children *why* the second language is worth the effort. In visits of a month or two, relatives and close friends may help children reach a new level in their language ability that may make using the minority language more satisfying for them.

SCHOOLS

While dual language schooling enjoys extensive research support, the educational trend, at least in the U.S., is in the opposite direction. Parents of child bilinguals here need to make their plans for their children's language models without the expectation of help from the government or the schools. They need the confidence to work their plans around the schools to keep them from sabotaging the family's efforts.

But when they are available, bilingual schools are a big help. During the research for this book, I was fortunate to hear from many parents with children in bilingual schools in Massachusetts, Michigan, Wisconsin, Oregon, and Florida. Several respondents went to international schools in Latin America and Asia. These are hugely successful. When schooling in the minority language is not available, parents do well to create social cohesiveness through play groups for the children and support groups for themselves (as in the ads one sees for peers in *The Bilingual Family Newsletter* and on websites like *multilingualchildren.org* or *www.biculturalfamily.org*). (Information about these and other resources can be found in the appendix.)

Strategies to Promote Your Child's Bilingual Language Development

In chapter 2, we considered ways for parents to help their children learn language, whether it is one or many. The guidelines I provided in chapter 2 show ways to enhance your normal interactions to make them especially supportive of the child's attempts to communicate. In chapter 3, we saw that for young children, the second language is, in most ways, like the first. The difference is that, unlike for the second language, children will speak the first language to some extent whether you encourage them to or not.

The following set of additional guidelines overlaps somewhat with that original set given in chapter 2. For example, one should never ridicule a child's efforts to speak—in any language. I put this here again because children's mistakes mixing the languages are even cuter and funnier than the ones they make in one language, so the temptation to laugh or tease may be greater. Similarly, covert correction through recasts and expansions on what the child has said is more effective than explicit teaching of the grammar point in first language learning, too—but somehow, explicit teaching is more tempting for the adult in the second language. Because children are often at a lower level in one of their languages, they may seem temporarily to be speaking like a younger child, making mistakes you don't expect of someone their age, so you may be more aware of and impatient with mistakes that you would not notice if the child were younger.

Other guidelines are specific to learning two languages. They have to do with how to establish language habits that will accommodate two languages more or less equally and how to encourage greater use of one or the other of them. In a U.S. context, they are more specifically aimed at preserving a heritage language, but they are equally useful—and perhaps even easier—for parents who want to give the majority language an extra boost. Recent immigrants or parents of internationally adopted children may want to review the discussion of childhood second language acquisition (early SLA) in chapter 3 so that they do not misinterpret their children's behavior. Still, there is nothing in these guidelines that is incompatible with promoting a majority language. No matter what household organization you decide on for your home, you will need to keep these in mind. So here's some advice regarding the child's weaker language (for everyone).

Table 8. **Twelve steps that promote bilingual language development**

Step 1: Be consistent.   Choose one language pattern and stick with it. Make changes cautiously.
Step 2: Be gently insistent.   Remind the children often and in different ways how good it is that they are learning two languages.
Step 3: Make the second language especially rewarding.   Take pains to make it fun to use the second language. Use song and active movement to the hilt. Use tangible rewards, like new books, a favorite outing, or food treats—but sparingly. Remember: Praise, praise, praise. And repetition, repetition, repetition.

Step 4: Beware of being punitive.
You may want to try gentle threats—for example, taking away TV privileges or saying, "You can't bring your friend Joey to the picnic tomorrow if you do not speak Finnish tonight with your aunt." But beware of overdoing it. Threats usually backfire in the long run and make the language less attractive to the child.

Step 5: Use lots of media.
Use media both as primary sources of entertainment for the children (books, videos, or CDs—bilingual or in the target language) and as encouragement for yourself (websites, email lists, or manuals [like this one]).

Step 6: Direct interaction is the key.
Use media, but only as a backup. Concentrate on real live interaction.

Step 7: Don't make fun of your child's mistakes.
Never ridicule a child's efforts to speak. It is also a bad idea to laugh at how cute it is when the child makes mistakes.

Step 8: Don't ask children to "perform" in front of others. Many childhood bilinguals report that as their least favorite part of being bilingual. They also may (rightly) question your sanity when you ask them to speak a language to someone who does not speak it.

Step 9: Do not correct overtly.
Use covert correction techniques. Go for fluency. But do correct; children have to keep getting better. The expansions and recasts that work for one language (see chapter 2) work just as well for two.

Step 10: Take advantage of bilingual education.
Seek out and/or support schooling in two languages.

Step 11: Use secondary supports.
Look for family language camps, heritage-language Saturday schools, play groups, or music or art programs in the minority language. Take advantage of secondary supports, but don't make these the only focus of your efforts.

Step 12: Give the language a broader context than just your nuclear family.
Cultivate bilingual friends (and relatives) with children who share your goals.

Travel.

Encourage visits from monolingual speakers of the target language. Hire other-language household helpers. Lay out plans for how you would like them to interact with your children as part of their responsibilities.

Go out of your way to find younger speakers of the language to play with your child—monolinguals, if possible. If you find other bilingual children, structure their interactions with your child to encourage monolingual conversations in the minority language. Start meetings off with a greeting ritual in the minority language, and use songs and games to set the tone for the children to communicate in it. You may have to be the "monolingual" in the situation.

Don't ignore older speakers as potential sources. Retirees often welcome the opportunity to interact with "adopted grandchildren."

Finally, you need to be open to calling for outside help. We will discuss in chapter 6 the warning signs of language-learning problems—in one or two languages—and what to ask language professionals.

Your Bilingual Goals–Evaluating Your Strengths

I hope I have conveyed that bringing up children bilingually is normal, natural, and eminently doable. But I think it is also possible to be too self-confident, especially if English is your community language, so I presented the Belgian and Barron-Hauwaert studies about the percentage of children growing up in bilingual families who actually become active bilinguals earlier in the chapter as a caution.

However, if I give a figure suggesting that about three out of four children in bilingual environments become bilingual and one does not, it does not translate directly into a three-fourths chance that *your* child will become bilingual. Among those children who do not learn two languages are some whose parents did not want to transmit their heritage language: it might trigger painful memories, they may be estranged from their families, or they may have lost everything in an earthquake and have negative associations with the country and its language. As the studies mentioned above make clear, living in a bilingual environment is not a guarantee that a person, even a child, will become a comfortable bilingual. But the law of averages is one thing; your own determination is another.

Making Your Decisions

Now it is time for you to look at your own situation. What resources do you have for making a bilingual home? The following self-evaluation questionnaire for your family will help you see what you have in your favor and where you need to seek out allies.

Fill out the different parts of the table for the minority language. In general, marks to the left are assets, and marks to the right are liabilities.

Table 9. **Understanding your language resources: Self-evaluation questionnaire**

1. Language Resources in the Home					
	Native speaker	Monolingual	Bilingual	Nonnative speaker	Does not speak it
Mother					
Father					
Siblings					
Grandparent(s)					
Household help					
Potential visitor(s)					
Other					

	Abundant	Hard to get	Nonexistent
Print and media			

2. Language Resources Outside of the Home				
Day care	○ Yes ○ No	Ties to people abroad	○ Yes ○ No	
Elementary school	○ Yes ○ No	Language camp	○ Yes ○ No	
High school	○ Yes ○ No	Saturday schools	○ Yes ○ No	
Family nearby	○ Yes ○ No	Playgroups	○ Yes ○ No	
Friends for child	○ Yes ○ No	Electronic network	○ Yes ○ No	
Friends for self	○ Yes ○ No			

3. Likelihood of Travel Opportunities			
Long-term	Recurring	Short-term	None in sight

4. Attitudes				
	Emotional commitment	Intellectual commitment	Neutral	Hostile
Mother				
Father				
Grandparent(s)				
Professionals				
Wider community				

5. Confidence		
Personally know others who have done it	Have heard or read of others who have done it	Personally know someone who has tried it but didn't succeed

Now you can summarize your pros, cons, strengths, and weak points using the chart below.

In the next chapter, you'll see which of the testimonials—most with the summary chart that follows—is closest to your situation.

Table 10. **Minority language resources summary chart**

	STRENGTHS	WEAK POINTS
Input		
Extended family		
Community		
Print materials		
Travel options		
Attitudes and experience		
Level of commitment		
Secondary resources		

CHAPTER

How-To Testimonials

IN THIS CHAPTER AND THE NEXT, YOU'LL SEE our household strategies in action. You'll meet thirty-six of the more than one hundred families I contacted in the research for this book. They come from all over the globe, from New York to Hong Kong and many places in between. Most have some experience in the U.S. All of them have raised bilingual children, are doing it now, or thought seriously about it and then did not do it. The stories follow the order of the discussion of bilingual family household strategies in chapter 4, with the following subcategories:

- One Parent–One Language (OPOL): Case Studies 1–8

  International couples, Case Studies 1–4

  Nonnative speakers, Case Studies 5–8

- Minority Language at Home (mL@H): Case Studies 9–10

- "Time and Place" (T&P): Case Studies 11–17

  "Accidental bilinguals," Case Studies 11–13, 16

  Language moves, Case Studies 14–15, 17

- Combinations, Case Studies 18–20

- Language travel, Case Study 21

- Different bilingual schooling alternatives, Case Studies 22–27

In all cases, I tried to probe for information about the families' circumstances and their attitudes, and also to elicit anecdotes to share with you. These personal accounts do not all lead to the storybook image of a perfectly bilingual child. After all, people have different goals, and they achieve different ends. The stories are chosen to illustrate different ways parents have managed to organize their routines to increase the amount of language input to their children. As you read these stories, look for factors that make the parent's job easier or harder. Can you anticipate what people are going to do? With the benefit of your hindsight, do you see where they could have made other choices than the ones they did? After the testimonials, I will try to draw some general conclusions about them and also gather a grab-bag of tricks and techniques from these parents and others whose full stories are not included.

Selecting Your Strategy

You will see several "proven" ways to grow a bilingual child, so you do yourself a favor to listen to the voices of experience. But that does not mean you cannot improvise for yourself. You may get some encouragement from family and friends, but there is no magic formula for you to apply. The choice of home language policy is entirely in your own hands.

Children's language skills are amazingly flexible and dynamic: they change over time. Circumstances change, and children's language patterns follow the changes. Still, "as the twig is bent, so grows the tree." Smaller differences early on have larger effects than larger differences later. So here we focus on parents' strategies with younger children—at the twig stage—and what parents can do for their children's bilingual language development. We see that there is no single way to do it. Different systems suit different families in different circumstances, and nothing is fixed in stone. Families can always change course—and often do.

The thirty-six families you will meet have incorporated the use of more than one language into the fabric of their daily lives. So as their children are growing, they are learning more than one language. Without diminishing their accomplishment, it is important to point out that these are all typical parents. Many are bilingual themselves, but not all. Some live in communities with schools that promote more than one language, but most do not. Most of their children are typically developing, but several have special needs. Everyone I spoke to decided to devote some of their child-rearing energy toward providing their children with two or more languages. They do not do more or less parenting than monolingual families, but they do their parenting in more than one language. They do not instruct their children with language lessons, but they guide them through life lessons that take place in two languages.

As we will see, what all of these families share is a strong conviction that knowing two languages is good for their children. They follow three basic rules so that they provide enough opportunity for the children to hear the language in use and take steps to ensure that the children will *want* to speak it.

There is no mystery about it. Experienced speakers must

- talk to the children in a given language and

- listen when the children try to talk to them.

Also, families should

- establish routines in each language (as in the household strategies in chapter 4) so that it is known ahead of time which language to use, and it is not up for negotiation with every exchange.

(As I say this, I am aware that there are some communities of mature speakers that do not follow this guideline. Some families operate in a completely bilingual mode, as is common in Miami or Singapore, for example, with no fixed prescription for which language to use in a particular situation or with a particular person. I am sure that in a completely bilingual community where the community as a whole is not shifting away from the minority language, children can learn their languages in this manner if that is how they are hearing them. However, language shift *is* taking place in every corner of the world, developed and developing countries alike, and the process is perhaps working the fastest in the U.S. Therefore, I recommend that parents take a more proactive role in structuring their daily routines and feel that this recommendation is essential.)

These thirty-six stories are just a small selection of the more than one thousand permutations the three main strategies above can give rise to in individual families. I calculated that if we just select ten dimensions that families can vary on, like those in the chart at the end of chapter 4, and regard them as "either/or"—either the father speaks the minority language or not; either the mother speaks it or not; children's books are available or they are not, etc.—that would be 2^{10} (or 1,024) different scenarios to cover. We barely scratch the surface, but I have picked typical examples that should be useful to people in many different circumstances.

The Classic Pattern: One Parent–One Language (OPOL)

In this section, we present four case studies.

CASE STUDY	PARENTS' NAMES	COUNTRY OF RESIDENCE
CS-1	Rosalie and Jean-Paul	Switzerland
CS-2	Karine and Jacques Guerlin	Sante Fe, NM, U.S.
CS-3	Radha and John	IN, U.S.
CS-4	Olga	Tampa, FL, U.S.

Note that the lists of languages at the top of each story below are in the order in which they were learned. The language in boldface type is the one used with the child by that person. The table at the beginning of each testimonial summarizes the strengths and weaknesses the family had to work with and around.

Case Study 1: Textbook Case of OPOL–Rosalie and Jean-Paul

MOTHER'S LANGUAGES: **Italian**, English, French (late learner)
FATHER'S LANGUAGES: **French**/German (infant bilingual), English
PARENTS TOGETHER: English, then French
COMMUNITY LANGUAGE: French (multilingual)
SCHOOL LANGUAGE: French
CHILDREN: French, Italian

CS-1	STRENGTHS	WEAK POINTS
Input	native speaker mother; late learner of the majority language	father does not speak the minority language (mL)
Extended family	within 5-hour drive; 3 or 4 visits a year	
Community	multilingualism the norm; Italians living nearby	no schooling in Italian
Print materials	ample; popular culture figures	
Travel options	many	
Attitudes and experience	both parents positive; father was a childhood bilingual	
Level of commitment	emotional and intellectual level	

OPOL feels very natural for Rosalie and her husband, Jean-Paul. Both are trilingual. Rosalie's native language is Italian, and Jean-Paul's strongest language is French. When their first child, Lucas, was born, they were living in the U.S. and had been speaking English with each other, but they decided they would each speak their mother tongue to the baby. Rosalie says, "It was accepted by both of us from the beginning that our children would have to understand their parents' native languages, whatever country we were going to live in." So Lucas heard Italian from his mother, French from his father, and a smattering of English from sitters and neighbors, plus what he overheard from his parents when they were not addressing him.

They moved to Switzerland when Lucas was ten months old, and the language of the community switched to French. This also meant that, at age thirty-five, Rosalie had to quickly learn French, but she kept up Italian with Lucas, and subsequently with his sister, Marina. She always preferred to speak to babies and small children in Italian. "I don't think it was a considered decision," she says, "I just cannot talk with my kids in another language than my own."

To help Rosalie learn more French, Jean-Paul decided to speak French with her most of the time, but they kept English as their "secret language." So the children were addressed in Italian and French, each by one of their parents, and in French outside the home. The children are now ten and eight years old, and they prefer to speak French with each other. Still, Rosalie is happy with the children's level of Italian. "Our children can communicate perfectly with the rest of my family in Italy, can follow Swiss-Italian TV, and they know Italian songs and games." They read about storybook characters like La Pimpa. The children recognize Italian as a special language that not everyone in Switzerland shares, and they will sometimes let a best friend in on a few words of it, like a secret code in a game between them.

Difficulties: Rosalie and Jean-Paul's family has experienced some aspects of a bilingual home that others might perceive as problems, but they considered them minor. Lucas, the older child, whose first year was trilingual, was saying only a few words in each language before he was two, although he could understand all three languages—English, French, and Italian—much earlier. Both children mixed their languages, perhaps even more than usual because Italian and French are quite close. This was a source of amusement for the family, and some of the children's invented words are now part of the family lore. Rosalie also reports that it is hard for her to help the children with their homework because French is a language she learned as an adult, so her husband steps in to take up that duty. (That would have been the same whether Rosalie was speaking Italian with the children or not.)

Facilitating Factors: Rosalie reports that, on the whole, it has not been difficult at all to maintain the two languages. The children have never felt forced in their language choices. Childhood bilingualism is taken for granted in Switzerland, where they are living. Several other children in the children's classes are bilingual. The father had been raised as a French-German bilingual, so they knew from his experience to be especially vigilant when the children started school. As it happened, both children had been in French medium day care for several years and were dominant in French by the time they started school in French. Also, they lived near Italy, so they could see Rosalie's family three or four times a year, and there were many Italians living in their region. At one point, Lucas noticed that something was different, and he asked his mother in French, "Why don't you speak French to me like you do with everybody else?" He readily accepted her answer that Italian was the language of her family and she wanted him to know it. That was that. He did not try to get her to switch.

So this family reads like a textbook case for raising bilingual children through OPOL. We might easily say, though, it is very well for them; they live in Europe in a multilingual city. The extra richness in history, culture, art, and music that bilingualism can bring with it is right at hand and is felt in their daily life. But could they have done as well in the U.S., where childhood bilingualism is not so common or well accepted and where there are fewer visible bilingual or multilingual models for families to follow?

Case Study 2: OPOL in the U.S.–Karine and Jacques

MOTHER:	Polish, French, **English**
FATHER:	**French**, English (late learner)
PARENTS TOGETHER:	English
COMMUNITY:	English (some travel to Belgium for French)
CHILD:	English/French (now Spanish and Chinese as well)

CS-2	STRENGTHS	WEAK POINTS
Input	native speaker father; late learner of the majority language; other parent speaks mL as well	father works outside the home
Extended family	in Belgium, available for yearly visits; visits in U.S. from the French-speaking grandmother yearly	
Community		no schooling in French until high school; few French speakers in area; multilingualism the exception
Print materials	ample; popular culture figures	
Travel options	moderate	
Attitudes and experience	both parents positive; mother was a childhood bilingual	
Level of commitment	emotional and intellectual level	

The Guerlins will tell us that, yes, OPOL can work very well in the U.S. Jacques, a French-speaking Belgian doctor living in Santa Fe, raised bilingual children in two families. He writes, "I raised all three kids speaking only French to them, while my two wives spoke only English to them." We know about the "second family" better, because I heard from all three members. The Guerlins had few other people who spoke French in their circle of friends, and they knew only one other French-speaking child in Santa Fe. There was no schooling in French available until high school. While their son Paul's elementary school teachers generally saw his bilingualism as a special skill, they mostly ignored it, especially because he was perfectly fluent (and bright and academically-inclined) in English.

So, here is an OPOL situation in a monolingual neighborhood in the U.S. The children have only one source of French, and it is not a stay-at-home parent but one who works long hours as a radiologist. There is little help outside the home to reinforce the parents' efforts. Objectively, it does not look propitious for promoting active bilingualism in the children, but it turns out that there are several factors that worked in Paul's favor.

Facilitating Factors: The family had a close-knit set of relatives and friends in Brussels. There were monolingual children Paul's age whom they visited yearly and a "grandmaman" who came for extended stays in Santa Fe. Paul had good motivation to learn French. Furthermore, the other spouse understood the minority language, so no one was left out in three-way conversations that took place in two languages: English between the parents and between mother and son, and French between father and son. (Three-way conversations were harder to do on the phone, so when Paul was old enough for three-way phone calls, the calls were conducted entirely in English.)

Father, mother, and child had an absolute expectation that the child would learn both languages. As Karine says, "Raising a bilingual child came kind of automatically." She does not remember specifically discussing it before Paul was born, but notes that they chose a name that would work in French as well as English, "so we must have thought about it." Both parents considered it a golden opportunity for the child and appreciate the close bond it created between father and son. Everyone found Paul's bilingualism "comfortable and worthwhile," and they had no anxiety about it. Jacques says, "I always spoke to Paul in French, and he never answered me in English." In fact, Paul was so clear about people's fixed "language identity" that at one point when he was very little, he wanted to tell his father something that he didn't know how to say in French. So he asked his mother to tell his father, as if it were *impossible* for father and son to speak English to each other.

Finally, the family made a specific decision not to explicitly correct the child's grammar. They felt the interruptions were potentially more frustrating than helpful for the child (and I couldn't agree more).

Difficulties: The Guerlins did not escape all of the potential disadvantages of OPOL. Paul had only one consistent source of French when he was growing up. His French is not as developed as his English. His father calls it "good, but not perfect." Paul says of himself that he has some "bad habits" in his French that he would like to correct. He spent six months in Belgium after high school and took some French classes in high school and college in an effort to consolidate the knowledge he had learned informally.

Overall, by reports from all three of them, the Guerlins are very happy with the result, although Paul, who is now an adult, wishes that he had learned even more languages when he was young. In France and Belgium, Paul enjoys evoking "shocked looks on people's faces" when they see an American speaking their language. He is very receptive to other languages, having studied Spanish in high school and college and even Chinese. He is very curious about different cultures and has traveled extensively in French- and Spanish-speaking countries as well as China. He reports that he can switch back and forth between languages without getting confused (although he once shook up his friends when he spoke in his sleep in three languages at once).

In Case Study 2 we have seen that OPOL can work in the U.S., but many, many people have reported that OPOL does not provide enough exposure to the minority language to counteract the powerful pull of English in this country. Radha and Olga, in Case Studies 3 and 4, are young mothers who are perfectly bilingual themselves. They were raised in the U.S. speaking a minority language, and now they are married to husbands who do not share their heritage languages. They are trying very hard, but feel that the task is harder than they thought it would be.

Case Study 3: Trouble with OPOL–Radha and John

MOTHER:	English, **Tamil**
FATHER:	**English**
PARENTS TOGETHER:	English
COMMUNITY:	English
CHILD:	English/Tamil

CS-3	STRENGTHS	WEAK POINTS
Input	bilingual mother, native or very near native	father doesn't speak the mL; mother English-dominant
Extended family	grandparents in distant city, available for twice yearly visits	

Community		no schooling in Tamil; few Tamil speakers in area; multilingualism the exception
Print materials		limited
Travel options	every third year to India for visit	
Attitudes and experience	both parents positive; mother was a childhood bilingual	
Level of commitment	mother has emotional commitment	father has intellectual commitment, but not an emotional one

Radha lives in a university town in the Midwest. There is a lot of acceptance of different languages, but little actual support for her native language, Tamil. Her family is far away, and none of their friends or playmates for her son speaks Tamil. "There is only so much I can do," she says. She finds that it takes work to speak to the baby only in Tamil, especially when they are with other people. It is particularly hard when she sees him understanding so much more in English. She says, "I think there are a number of things I say to him in Tamil that he doesn't understand, but if I said them in English he would."

When Radha's husband, John, suggested they teach their son Baby Sign, she resisted it. She prefers to concentrate her efforts on Tamil, the language that has deep emotional meaning for her. She is his sole source of Tamil, and although she tries to speak only Tamil with him, he also hears her speak in English with his father, with her friends, and at work when she takes him with her. Because she works full-time, she estimates that she is with her son, Ravi, only four or five hours a day when he is awake. Even if she manages to talk with him in Tamil 90% of the time that he is with her, it is still so much less than he hears of English. "It's hard to say how dedicated I would be about speaking only in Tamil with him if I didn't feel so strongly about Tamil itself." Even so, she feels that, realistically, Ravi will probably not learn Tamil as well as she did in her parents' household in Georgia. (Radha's parents' story is included later in the chapter, CS-9.)

COMPARING CASE STUDIES 2 AND 3

Why is it so hard for Radha to be the sole source of Tamil, while Jacques was able to be effective as the major source of French? I can only speculate: 1) French is a better-known language than Tamil, at least in the U.S., so there is more acceptance of the language by relatives and friends; 2) Radha's husband does not understand Tamil. Even though he encourages Radha to use Tamil, she cannot do it without excluding him. By contrast, Jacques's wife speaks French, although not with him or the child, so she is not excluded. 3) Radha is a childhood bilingual, having learned Tamil as a minority language, whereas Jacques learned English later in life; French is his "majority" language. Radha more readily switches to English than Jacques does. Finally, 4) Jacques is more emphatic and categorical about the use of the minority language. Radha wants it very much, but hesitates to impose her language. Jacques has no hesitations. He sees it only as an opportunity for the child.

Case Study 4: Another Difficult Case of OPOL–Olga in Florida

MOTHER: **Spanish**/English
FATHER: **English**, some Spanish
PARENTS TOGETHER: English
COMMUNITY: English, Spanish (Tampa, FL)
CHILDREN: English, some Spanish

CS-4	STRENGTHS	WEAK POINTS
Input	native speaker mother; mother literate in mL; other parent understands mL	mother is English-dominant
Extended family	bilingual grandparents in same city; monolingual great-grandparents in the same city	mother-in-law uncomfortable with the mL
Community	50% of city Latino; several bilingual schooling options	slight stigma to mL
Print materials	ample; popular culture figures	
Travel options		none planned

| Attitudes and experience | both parents positive; mother was a childhood bilingual | |
| Level of commitment | | intellectual commitment; moderate level of emotional commitment |

Olga voices the same sentiment as Radha toward her efforts to bring up her child bilingually. Even though she lives in a bilingual community—Tampa, Florida—she calls it a struggle. Because her husband can use a little Spanish and does so when called upon in his profession, he can understand Spanish when Olga speaks it to the children. He is not left out of Spanish conversations, but does not join in at home. After all, he is the "English-parent," so, as the "Spanish-parent," Olga finds that it is up to her to provide exposure to Spanish. At first, she was surprised when she realized that she had never spoken to a baby in Spanish, and it felt strange to do so. With lullabies and children's books in Spanish, it got easier very quickly. Ironically, it is harder for her now in Tampa than it was in Virginia, where their first child Jason was born. There, Olga recalls, being bilingual was considered something really special. Jason's first ten words were in Spanish, and her friends there were very excited to hear her speaking Spanish with Jason and to hear him answer back. Also, when a baby is very young, she points out, you have more control over his environment.

So, in Virginia, where there were very few Latinos, the child's bilingualism was highly respected and under the mother's control. It all seemed pretty easy there. But when the family moved back to Tampa, Jason started preschool in English, they went to "Mommy and Me" classes in English, and pretty soon Jason and then his younger brother Matthew were answering in English—or worse, not understanding what their mother told them in Spanish, so Olga would say it to them in English. Each time she caught herself in English and switched back to Spanish, it was just a little harder to get them to follow. If she tried to read a story in Spanish, Jason would object. Before he knew the names of the languages, he would say, "Don't read it like that; read it like I'm talking now."

Moving back to Tampa also meant more access to the father's monolingual English-speaking parents. His mother, in particular, acts offended when Olga uses Spanish in her presence. There was never a question of the children not being able to communicate with their grandparents in English, but the mother-in-law's reaction creates one more obstacle for Olga—in her own home—to maintaining the habit of speaking Spanish with her children.

Olga feels she might have been lulled into complacency by her early success in Virginia and also by overestimating how much of a source of support the community language in Tampa would be. There are several Latino children in their neighborhood and at their school, but those children are eager to speak English with Jason and Matthew. Her own parents are helpful with the children, but they came to the States as teenagers and have been here for forty years, so English is now very natural for them, too. Only Olga's grandparents are still essentially monolingual Spanish speakers. To Olga, seeing the children interact with her grandparents has been one of the nicest rewards for her efforts. Her grandmother basically cannot talk to the children unless they talk to her in Spanish. When Jason sings the little songs he has learned at school, his grandmother's pleasure is immense, and of course, Jason likes all the praise he gets for it. But when Olga tries to remind him that he needs to talk to her in Spanish more so that he can learn it more, he resists, saying, "I already know Spanish."

In retrospect, Olga thinks it might be easier now if she had been more vigilant at the outset when they returned to Tampa. Bilingual preschools are hard to find in the neighborhood where she lives, but without going too far, she could have found a "Mommy and Me" program in Spanish, a La Leche breastfeeding support group in Spanish (where older children also come with their moms and younger siblings), and Spanish story times at several libraries. Spanish books, magazines, and records are not hard to find. Olga remembers that when she was young, the television was always tuned to one of the big Cuban stations. Now, she could try to have that same backdrop in her own house. She also could have had the standard Disney and Muppets films in their Spanish versions just as easily as in English if she had thought about it.

As it is, Jason, at age six, can get his point across in Spanish, but his grammar is like that of a younger child. Matthew, at four, very often cannot get his point across and sometimes does not understand Olga's simple statements and directions. (When Olga translates for him, though, during a visit with her grandmother, for example, he is quick to notice even tiny changes and complain, "That's not what I said.")

Olga is frustrated but not defeated. She knows that the situation is not static. It may be that her family is getting a second chance to establish OPOL. There is a new baby in the house, a little girl. By now, Olga is over her awkwardness in talking to babies, and she showers the little one with Spanish. Taking their cue from their mom, Jason and Matthew have decided that the baby speaks only Spanish, and they are more likely to go along with Olga when she encourages them to use Spanish "for the baby." They often speak it to her without being prompted. The children get some Spanish every day in the public school, and with that help, plus some conscious efforts on Olga's part, and more help from her parents, the family culture seems to be changing toward more use of Spanish.

"Elective" Bilingualism with OPOL

Even given the difficulties we've discussed, Radha, Olga, and other parents like them might be considered to be in a stronger situation than families using OPOL in which one or both of the parents are speaking a nonnative language to their children. Of course, it is common for parents to use a nonnative language for their family life, but we are most familiar with such arrangements when people have moved from one country to another and adopt the language of their new country. We all have friends whose parents spoke English as a second language imperfectly but used it nonetheless as their everyday language with no ill effects for the children. It is more unusual for someone to choose to speak what is a foreign language for him or her in a country where this language is not the community language. In the literature, this is often called "artificial," "nonnative," or "elective" bilingualism. It is less well-known, but we have many examples to show us that it can be done.

CASE STUDY	PARENTS' NAMES	COUNTRY OF RESIDENCE
CS-5	George Saunders (published case)	Australia
CS-6	Ellen and Chris	Boston, MA, U.S.

CS-7	Bryan and Elizabeth	Central PA, U.S.
CS-8	Rosemary	Albany, NY, U.S.

Case Study 5: George Saunders—German in an English Household (Published Example)

MOTHER:	**English**, some German
FATHER:	English, **German** (as a second language)
PARENTS TOGETHER:	English
COMMUNITY:	English
CHILDREN:	English, German

CS-5	STRENGTHS	WEAK POINTS
Input	other parent speaks mL as well	father nonnative speaker of mL
Extended family		none
Community	father uses shortwave radio to stay in contact with native speakers	no schooling in German until high school; few German speakers in area; multilingualism the exception
Print materials	available (with effort)	
Attitudes and experience	both parents positive	
Level of commitment	high emotional commitment; high intellectual commitment	

A well-documented example of elective bilingualism is provided by George Saunders, a teacher of German in Australia who raised three German-English bilingual children. He was a native English speaker who had studied German linguistics in Germany as a university student. His wife lived briefly in Germany, too, but was less comfortable in the language. Saunders chronicled his family's adventure in two books published in the 1980s. They are still interesting reading today. He explains his rationale—that he wanted his children to help him keep up his German, both because he really liked speaking German and also because he harbored a desire for them all to return to Germany one day. At the very least, he wanted to keep the possibility open. His wife had also studied German but was happy to be the "English-parent." Still, it was very helpful in such an arrangement that she understood the language and was not left out of the German exchanges between the children and their father. She came along happily when they finally did visit Germany some ten years into the process.

It was also somewhat of an experiment for Saunders. As a reader of Joshua Fishman, the international expert on reversing language shift, he realized that the future of many languages depends on people improving the way they transmit multiple languages to young children. Languages with diminishing numbers of speakers may not survive unless nonnative speakers are able to grow new generations of native speakers. That solution is generally dismissed as not being feasible for individual families, so Saunders wanted to see how hard or easy it would be, though he was prepared to abandon the experiment if the children showed any ill effects. To his delight, the children did well with it, and he enjoyed the experience as much as he anticipated he would.

Saunders's method was no different from what it would have been had he been a native speaker of German. He carried out the routines of daily life—in German. It helped, I think, that he was a very engaged parent who seemed to genuinely enjoy playing with his children, and thus he may have spent more time than the average parent engaging in "cops and robbers" and other children's pursuits. The many small transcripts of conversations throughout the book taken from his tape recordings reveal affectionate give-and-take between father and child. It is easy to understand his children's desire to please their father and speak his preferred language. He coaxed them and encouraged them, but never forced them. It must have been a satisfying experience for the children, because they also expressed great pleasure with the arrangement. In many statements over the years, they showed how natural they thought it was to be speaking German with him and how unnatural and unfortunate it would be if he started speaking English. "What would you do," he asked his middle son (in German), "if I spoke English to you?" The child responded without hesitation, "I'd speak German to you."

Saunders's books have practical advice on some problems that might be unique to the second-language speaker parent. For example, when Saunders and his children did not know a word they needed, they would agree on a paraphrase to use until they could check it out in a dictionary or with a native speaker. Then, if necessary, Saunders would use a conscious teaching strategy to correct the wrong word. He was also very concerned with monitoring the children's progress in German and carried out regular assessments in a game-like atmosphere with a tape recorder running in the background a lot of the time. Those who follow his model do not need to be as focused on outcome measures as he was, but it is encouraging to know that his children made above average progress in English and also achieved a reasonable level of proficiency in German.

Case Study 6: Ellen and Chris—Saunders in the U.S.

I have met American parents with similar motivations who have had equal success with "elective" multilingualism like Saunders.

MOTHER:	English, **American Sign Language (ASL)** (late learner), Tagalog, some Spanish
FATHER:	English, **Spanish**, some ASL
SISTER:	ASL
COMMUNITY:	English
CHILD:	English, ASL, Spanish (now picking up Chinese)

CS-6	STRENGTHS	WEAK POINTS
Input	sister monolingual speaker of one of the languages	father and mother nonnative speakers of different mLs
Extended family		none
Community	dual immersion school for one mL; informal classes for other mL	
Print materials	available	
Attitudes and experience	both parents positive	
Level of commitment	high intellectual commitment; moved to live near school with a bilingual program	

Ellen and Chris had typical American—that is, monolingual—childhoods, but both had opportunities to travel abroad as teenagers and young adults—Ellen to Latin America, Israel, and an island in the Philippines for three years, and Chris to Spain and Latin America. Ellen had also become fascinated with American Sign Language in middle school, learned it, and eventually became a sign language interpreter. They both enjoyed the connection to others that they achieved through the different languages they learned and want to avoid the stereotypical

American ethnocentricism for their children. They see no reason for a child to grow up learning only English. They want their children to know other languages in order to help them identify with other groups outside their own and be more sensitive to all kinds of differences—racial, ethnic, socioeconomic, ability, etc. Because they knew that young children learn languages relatively painlessly, they were determined to make a language-rich environment from early on in their children's lives. Looking ahead, they moved to a town that had a dual-immersion bilingual program in the public school. Soon after their daughter was born, they took steps to adopt a deaf child, and they wanted everyone in the family to be able to communicate with her as well.

When Sophia was born, Ellen and Chris used OPOL; Ellen spoke American Sign Language (ASL) to her, and Chris used exclusively Spanish. Ellen and Chris both understood the other's language but focused on their own strongest language. They also hired a Spanish-speaking housekeeper to reinforce Chris's nonnative Spanish. Sophia learned English in the neighborhood, outside of the home. Ellen points out that it is very tricky to use ASL with an infant that you have in your arms, but by the time Sophia was a toddler, when her speech sounded like "one big babble," she could use ASL to communicate with her parents. Her next words were in Spanish, then English. When the adoption of the deaf child came through, although the girl was older than Sophia, she had not yet acquired a first language and began learning ASL with the family. So Ellen and now the sister made an authentic environment for the development of Sophia's third language, ASL.

At about age three, Sophia realized that Chris understood English, and although Chris continued to address her in Spanish, Sophia responded in English. By four, she was also using English with the housekeeper, but Ellen and Chris were not too worried, because they knew that she would start at the bilingual school the next year. As expected, when Sophia started kindergarten at the bilingual school, her Spanish did take off and has not stopped. In addition to the 50% of the school day in Spanish, Sophia has Spanish-speaking friends and has also traveled to Ecuador. At age eleven, she is comfortably trilingual, and when given the choice of an elective in middle school, she chose yet another language, Chinese.

The lack of native skill on the part of her parents has had little effect on Sophia's language development. If anything, it has made the parents more willing to make the effort to find other language experts. OPOL (without English) was the foundation, creating an environment in which all of the members of the household used different languages for different purposes at different times. That was the normal state of affairs, as far as Sophia knew. They also found household help that could reinforce one parent's language. By choosing a bilingual school district, they got both instruction and peers for Sophia in one of the minority languages. Her sister attends a school for the deaf that emphasizes ASL and also has classes for siblings, so Sophia's ASL has had the benefit of both informal and formal instruction.

Case Study 7: For the Father—Bryan and Elizabeth

Some nonnative second language speakers I am acquainted with have more modest goals for their use of a non-English language with their children. They want their children to be able to function eventually in another language, but for now, they are happy for them to understand another language, and they use a second language in the home to help the children grow into better world citizens, aware of and sensitive to other languages and cultures. Like Saunders, for many of them the "other language" has emotional value, but unlike Saunders, "success" does not require active bilingualism from the child.

MOTHER: **English, some Spanish**
FATHER: English, **Spanish** (late learner)
PARENTS TOGETHER: English, some Spanish
COMMUNITY: English
CHILDREN: English, some Spanish

CS-7	STRENGTHS	WEAK POINTS
Input		father and mother nonnative
Extended family		Catalan speakers, reluctant to use Spanish
Community		few prospects for schooling
Print materials	available	

Attitudes and experience	both parents positive	
Level of commitment	father has emotional commitment	mother has high intellectual commitment

For Bryan, speaking Spanish to his children is a way to recapture his father's heritage, even though he did not learn it in the States in an all-English household. He visited his father's homestead near Barcelona during several summers when growing up, but he says the visits were not conducive to his learning Spanish there. It was in a remote area, there were no cousins his age, and just about everyone could speak English with him. (One of the old farmers he spent a lot of time with was not very verbal in any language, so Bryan's lack of Spanish or Catalan was not an issue for him either.) Furthermore, all the relatives spoke both Catalan and Spanish, but Catalan was an article of pride for them. Although Spanish would have been more useful for Bryan in the U.S., his relatives were not eager to speak (or teach) Spanish. Whatever Spanish Bryan learned, he learned in school.

So Bryan wishes he had grown up speaking another language, and he and his wife Elizabeth want to help their children do so—as much as they can. Their first child, Edward, was born in Spain, where his babysitter was a Catalan speaker, and the child's first words were in Catalan. When they moved back to the States around Edward's first birthday, they made a conscious decision to have only Spanish in the house. They hired a Mexican au pair, and they themselves spoke Spanish with each other. The au pair, however, wanted to speak English. By the time she left to go home the following year, Edward's Spanish was already slipping.

Soon after, Bryan and Elizabeth had twins, and the family now lives in a small college town in central Pennsylvania that has an appreciation of different languages and some foreign couples with children learning two languages. Still, there is no bilingual schooling for miles around. Bryan and Elizabeth try to speak Spanish as much as they can with each other and the children. They are working to get more early foreign language instruction introduced in the schools.

When I first saw Bryan, he was leading games at an outing involving several families. He was speaking English to the group, but addressed his own children in Spanish. They understand when they are spoken to, and they also understand that this other language means a lot to their father, but the amount of Spanish they hear is well below the threshold for creating an active command of the language.

Case Study 8: International Adoption—Rosemary

Another increasingly common circumstance that encourages people to try to raise children bilingually is international adoption. Many parents who would not have thought of raising a child born in the U.S. bilingually feel a sense of responsibility to the foreign-born child to maintain ties to the country she or he comes from.

MOTHER: English, **Spanish** (late learner)
FATHER: **English**
PARENTS TOGETHER: English
COMMUNITY: English
CHILD: English, Spanish

CS-8	STRENGTHS	WEAK POINTS
Input		mother is nonnative speaker
Extended family	(eventually, child will identify as Latina ethnically)	
Community	other family with adopted daughter; email list; supportive friends; Spanish as a school subject in child's elementary school	
Print materials	available	
Travel options	summer trips to Guatemala	
Attitudes and experience	parents are positive	
Level of commitment		strong intellectual commitment only for the mother

In Rosemary's words, "We want our daughter [adopted from Guatemala] to have a Latina identity and be able to connect with other Latin Americans." She and her spouse want Caridad to be able to speak to people from her country, and maybe with her birth family some day.

Rosemary has spoken exclusively Spanish to Cari from the day she met her in Guatemala when Cari was ten months old. Her own parents warned her that the child would not learn English well enough if she spoke Spanish with her all the time, but she did not foresee that becoming a problem and she has been right. Because Rosemary is fluent, but not a native speaker of Spanish, she worried at first that she would be passing her grammar mistakes on to the child, or that she would not have enough vocabulary to carry it off. She thought she might "run out of words." One solution has been to have a Spanish-English dictionary on her PDA. She has also made sure to have other sources of Spanish for Cari. They became friends with another family that adopted an older child who came to the U.S. speaking Spanish. Cari's school teaches Spanish from the first grade, and the family visits Guatemala every year.

Rosemary is also very effective in gathering a support group around them. She had talked her plan over with a bilingual friend beforehand. It was she who had provided the initial encouragement to "just do it!" Then Rosemary read a book on bilingual families, found a website about them, and joined an e-mail list of parents who are speaking a nonnative language with their children.

At thirteen, Cari is dominant in English. In fact, she rarely responds to Rosemary in Spanish, but she understands and can communicate with Spanish-speaking people. She also slips into Spanish when she doesn't want someone else to understand. Cari and her mom share an interest in Latin music and swap songs all the time, more and more as Cari gets older and knows a wider range of songs than her mother. Overall, Rosemary says it has been easier than she thought. She never thought she'd be able to continue for so long.

Minority Language at Home (mL@H)

As in Europe, our Canadian neighbors generally find OPOL to be very satisfactory, especially in areas like Quebec where English is the minority language. The French presence is strong, but the international prestige of English, its majority status in the rest of Canada and the closeness of the United States prevent it from being completely overshadowed. In other areas where the majority language is overwhelming, as English is in the U.S., we saw in chapter 4 that it takes a larger commitment and more exposure to learn the minority language. Put another way, it takes relatively more time in the "language other than English" for an equal amount of learning. To give greater weight to the other language, many families decide to use only the minority language at home, so the child hears it from two parents, instead of just one, as in many OPOL situations. There are basically two levels of mL@H:

- Majority Language Outside of the Home: Some parents speak the minority language in the home, but when family members are outside of the house, these same individuals speak only the community language. For example, social scientist and linguist Einar Haugen said that the threshold of his parents' home became his cue to switch from English to Norwegian.

- Minority Language Immersion: Others speak the minority language with family members all the time, inside or outside of the home, except in the presence of non-speakers.

We will look at two case studies in this section.

CASE STUDY	CHILDREN'S NAMES	COUNTRY OF RESIDENCE
CS-9	Radha (also CS-3 as parent)	GA, U.S.
CS-10	Olga (also CS-4 as parent)	Tampa, FL, U.S.

When Radha and Olga, whose experiences as parents were described in the previous section, compare their current situations using OPOL to the mL@H strategy their parents used when they were raising them, it is astounding how much more exposure they got as children to the non-English language with both of their parents using it, than they are in a position to provide now on their own for their children.

Case Study 9: Radha's Tamil-Speaking Childhood in Georgia

MOTHER: **Tamil**, some English
FATHER: **Tamil**, English
PARENTS TOGETHER: Tamil
COMMUNITY: English
CHILDREN: English, Tamil

CS-9	STRENGTHS	WEAK POINTS
Input	bilingual, but Tamil dominant for mother and father	

Extended family	grandparents visited for long periods of time; large family welcomed them on trips back to India	
Community		no schooling in Tamil; few Tamil speakers in area
Print materials	some written materials	limited; different script
Travel options	long summer visits to India every other year; sabbatical year in India in 2nd grade	
Attitudes and experience	both parents positive; never doubted children would learn Tamil	
Level of commitment	both mother and father had emotional and intellectual commitment	

Radha's family used a Minority Language Immersion strategy: "two-parents-one-language-minority-language-everywhere." Radha's father was a professor and her mother a housewife in northern Georgia. The parents concentrated on Tamil and let their daughter's English come from school, babysitters, and the neighborhood. At the time Radha was born, her parents were not sure whether the family would stay in the U.S. or return to India, so there was no question that she and her older brother would learn Tamil. In addition to the parents' own use of Tamil with each other and with the children, they had long visits from their maternal grandmother, trips to India every other summer for four months at a time, and a full school year there when Radha was in the second grade and her brother was in the sixth grade. They had a large family in India, including many cousins their age, and they looked forward eagerly to the trips. Their father also spent some time teaching them the rudiments of reading and writing Tamil, a whole new alphabet for them.

Although there were no Tamil-speaking institutions in her hometown—no Saturday school, no library materials, no houses of worship—those would have been only tiny additions to the substantial amount of Tamil that Radha and her brother heard on a daily, monthly, and yearly basis.

Radha's family had almost all of the elements that add value to increase children's motivation to learn a second language: monolingual relatives, travels to the home country, young speakers to play with, and the status of a major language. (From a worldwide perspective, although not the official language of India, Tamil is still a major language with almost a hundred million speakers.) The children identified with the culture—the foods, the celebrations, and the epic stories that they could recite by heart. In many ways, as young children, they were citizens of India who just happened to live in the U.S., so it is not surprising that their Tamil developed as well as it did. Importantly, their English was also excellent, and both have continued beyond college in the U.S. educational system.

Case Study 10: Olga's Bilingual Childhood

MOTHER: **Spanish**, English (late learner)
FATHER: **Spanish**, English (late learner)
PARENTS TOGETHER: Spanish
COMMUNITY: English, (Spanish)
CHILDREN: Spanish, English

CS-10	STRENGTHS	WEAK POINTS
Input	bilingual parents, learned English as teenagers	
Extended family	grandparents lived in same house with them until child was 8, then moved nearby	
Community	large (positive) presence of Spanish in community	no bilingual schools in mL; exempted from Spanish classes that were too elementary; took Spanish in high school
Print materials	available (also Spanish TV on constantly)	
Travel options	none	
Attitudes and experience	parents both positive	
Level of commitment	high emotional level; never in doubt; strong intellectual level as well	

Olga is also a full "ambilingual," that is, equally strong in English and Spanish, perhaps even more than Radha, because she is also literate in both languages at a level that makes her employable for tasks requiring writing in both languages. Her daily life as a child in Tampa also included much more Spanish than does her current language environment in the same city. She lived exclusively in the U.S., but her grandparents lived in the same house with her family until Olga was eight years old. Everyone spoke only Spanish at home. There was never any discussion about it—that's the way it was. Her parents took no steps to teach Olga English, but according to her parents, she "picked it up in the neighborhood," so when she started school, she went into regular classes, not the English as a Second Language (ESL) program.

The importance of Olga's *early* exposure is apparent when she compares her experience with that of her sister Maria, six years younger than she, who had a harder time with Spanish than Olga did. Maria had the same Spanish-speaking parents who were more comfortable in Spanish—but the key difference between the sisters appears to be the grandparents *in* the house as opposed to down the street, where they moved when Olga was eight and Maria was two. As the girls got older, their parents became increasingly oriented toward English. The longer they remained in the U.S., the less likely it became that they would be returning to Cuba. Olga eventually became dominant in English—she is not sure when—and she generally used English with her sister, but she still always had plenty of exposure to Spanish. Today, even though Spanish plays a smaller role than English in her life, she is enjoying the fruits of being proficient and literate in both languages through her contact with her grandmother, by being the bilingual room-mother in her children's classes, and as the liaison with Spain for an international research project.

"Time and Place"/"Accidental Bilinguals"

A good percentage of ambilinguals that I have met achieved their high level of skill in two (or more) languages because of their families' transfers from one country to another—and back again. Parents' jobs change, or they are stationed abroad for several years at a time. The children did not do anything special, beyond accompanying their parents. As Marieke puts it, "People say how great it is that I speak two languages. I can't take credit for it. It's more about my upbringing than something I've done." But she and the others described below—whether on their own or not—have ended up with exceptional skills in two languages.

CASE STUDY	CHILDREN'S NAMES	COUNTRY OF RESIDENCE
CS-11	Isabel	Italy
CS-12	Carmen	Continental U.S./Puerto Rico
CS-13	Gretchen	Quebec, Canada
CS-14	Leah and Eva	Israel/Pittsburgh, PA, U.S.
CS-15	Joe Spelke (published case)	U.S./France
CS-16	Rachel	Israel/U.S.
CS-17	Marieke	U.S./the Netherlands

Case Study 11: Isabel

Isabel's American mother died when Isabel was five, and a couple of years later, Isabel moved with her father to his native Italy. Although she had learned a smattering of Italian from him as a small child, she was not equipped to enter school in the fourth grade and study alongside children who had been speaking Italian since they were born. She recalls that she had six weeks to get ready. It was the "hardest thing I ever did," she says. But in the end, she succeeded and is proud to have done it. Now she credits her bilingualism with enabling her to get her current job in international publishing.

Case Study 12: Carmen

Carmen's parents' divorce moved her from New England to Puerto Rico at age ten, in time for the fourth grade. Those next years in a strict Catholic school, in classes with cliques of children who made little effort to welcome her, are not especially happy memories for her. "At least I got Spanish out of it," she says. She completed four grades in Puerto Rico and was doing well, but then she got sent back to the States to live with her father, and she finished high school in English. Today,

English is her primary language, but Carmen's command of Spanish is much better than that of her younger brothers, who stayed in the U.S. with their father except for summer vacations in Puerto Rico. It has allowed her to obtain a job like her current one, where she uses both Spanish and English on a daily basis. She also feels very proud of her Spanish and the strong connection it has helped her forge to Puerto Rico, where her mother and grandmother live.

Case Study 13: Gretchen

Likewise, Gretchen P.'s parents emigrated from England to Canada, not particularly planning for their children to become bilingual. But the law in Quebec required that immigrants be schooled in French as a condition of their entry into the country. Gretchen had no choice but to go to French school. At the start of kindergarten, she only knew how to say "yes" and "no" in French. By the end of first grade, though, she was getting marks of 100% in reading and writing—all in French. She remembers being one of very few English speakers in the school and was sometimes teased because of her name and made to feel like an outsider. Nonetheless, she thrived and came to appreciate the French language, which she still prefers to use for certain things in her life. She recommends schooling in a new language and hopes she will be able to do it with her own children.

No one was looking out for Isabel's or Carmen's or Gretchen's language education, but in many ways, no one could have designed a more effective language training program for them. These were not elective moves. No one is going to recommend that you uproot your children in middle childhood as a preferred method for them to learn a second language, but it is encouraging to see that, when it happens (for another reason), it *can* work. Such stories can inform a parent's decision to accept a job abroad.

Case Study 14: Leah and Eva

Leah and Eva's parents, for example, came to Carnegie Mellon University from Israel for their work. One factor among the several pros and cons involved in taking the job was the opportunity it would present for their daughters to learn English. The mother's own childhood had included a language move related to her father's job. She always found it a benefit—for example, her classmates were jealous when they had to take classes in English and she was exempt. Her husband, by contrast, is still struggling to master English, which he needs for his career. Compared to the experiences of Isabel and Carmen, the dislocation was gentler for Leah and Eva, as there is a sizable Israeli community in Pittsburgh, and the girls feel like they have the best of both worlds.

Case Study 15: Joe Spelke (published case)

Harvard professor Liz Spelke reports that her family spent their summers and occasionally a full year in a small town in France. During one year-long stay when she enrolled her children in French schools, her three-year-old son, Joe, announced that he was not going to say a word all year long. For four months, he stayed off in a corner playing on his own, paying no attention, it seemed, to the class activities. Spelke was sure that the whole experience would be a disaster for him. But then, one day, he said, "I've changed my mind, Mom; I'm going to talk," and his silent period ended abruptly. He was speaking in full sentences and even had learned all the words to the songs the class had been singing when he looked like he was not paying attention.

Case Study 16: Rachel

Rachel also has a strong memory of herself as a six-year-old who had just arrived from Israel at an elementary school in the U.S., speaking no English whatsoever. She was in what she calls "absorption mode" for the first two or three months. "I could neither speak nor understand the speech around me." Nevertheless, she attended school every day, played outside during recess, and tried to make new friends. "At some point, as if magically, I started to understand and speak the language." She had no trace of a foreign accent in her speech and would correct her parents on their accents and grammatical slips. Her family spent a year or two in the States three times while she was growing up: at age two, from ages six to eight, and again at fourteen. Because they were always going back to Israel, they spoke Hebrew in the house, and Rachel learned to read and write Hebrew at home while she was in the U.S. so that she would not lag behind her peers. She still feels that Hebrew is her stronger language because she knows more slang, idioms, and song lyrics in it, but her English is completely unaccented, her vocabulary is extensive, and her grasp of syntax is comprehensive. If you spoke with her, you would think she was a very typical, educated American. You might have no idea that English was a second language for her.

Case Study 17: Marieke—Back and Forth

MOTHER:	**English, Dutch**
FATHER:	**Dutch, English** (late learner of English)
PARENTS TOGETHER:	Dutch in U.S., English in the Netherlands
COMMUNITY:	first English, then Dutch
SCHOOL:	Dutch, English-speaking high school in the Netherlands

CS-20	STRENGTHS	WEAK POINTS
Input	parents both knew both languages	
Extended family		
Community	in the Netherlands, there were many expatriates; English-speaking schooling options	in U.S., relatively few speakers of Dutch
Print materials	available in both languages	
Travel options	many	
Attitudes and experience	parents both positive	
Level of commitment	strong emotional and intellectual level	

For Marieke, too, moving back and forth from the U.S. to the Netherlands and back was a positive experience and has made her native in both languages and cultures. Her American mother and Dutch father both spoke both languages. They practiced OPOL in the U.S. for the first five years of her life, so her Dutch was already pretty strong when they moved to the Netherlands, where she started school. In the Netherlands, the family switched to mL@H in English, but twelve years in a Dutch-medium school made her a native speaker of Dutch. All the while, though, her family spoke English at home and also with the large circle of expatriate friends her mother found there. Then she went to an English-medium university in Utrecht and is in graduate school now in the U.S., so her English has caught up again with her Dutch. "When I'm speaking English, I feel American, and while I'm speaking Dutch, I feel Dutch." She says she tends to be more emotional in Dutch, or if she wants to express a strong emotion, she will probably do it in Dutch. She sounds like a native in both languages—educated in both and perfectly comfortable on either side of the ocean.

Combinations of Strategies

We look at four case studies in this section.

CASE STUDY	PARENT'S NAME	COUNTRY OF RESIDENCE
CS-18	Maya, mL@H and T&P	Chicago, IL, U.S./Croatia
CS-19	David, mL@H and T&P	U.S./France
CS-20	Viviane, OPOL and T&P	U.S./Switzerland
CS-21	Jane Merrill (published case), OPOL and Creative Travel	U.S./France

Case Study 18: Maya—mL@H and T&P

MOTHER:	**Croatian**, English (late learner)
FATHER:	**Croatian**, English (late learner)
PARENTS TOGETHER:	Croatian, later some English
COMMUNITY:	English
CHILDREN:	English, Croatian

CS-18	STRENGTHS	WEAK POINTS
Input	parents both bilingual, Croatian dominant	became more balanced over years in U.S.
Extended family	long visits from mother	
Community		school somewhat hostile to mL
Print materials		relatively little available
Travel options	summers with grandparents in Croatia	
Attitudes and experience	parents are positive	
Level of commitment	strong emotional level	sometimes too busy

Many parents say they do not think bilingualism would have "stuck" for their children if they had not made a regular habit of extended visits in the country where their minority language is spoken. Maya and her husband both came from Croatia to Chicago as adults, bringing Adam, age four, who was born in Croatia. Their daughter Tina was born here. As newcomers, speaking only Croatian at home, mL@II was "the only natural thing for us to do," Maya says. That is, they spoke their native language to each other and to the children and made it the home language. The daughter went to day care from about fifteen months, and the boy to nursery school, so they had an English environment early on, in addition to their home life in Croatian. "Our daughter especially was completely comfortable with it." Maya reports that Tina would carefully catalog out loud who spoke which language, and would be surprised when someone spoke in a language he or she was not supposed to use.

In the meantime, Maya and her husband were immersed in their jobs and their studies, also in an English environment, so their English skills improved, too—and more and more English crept into their home. It got harder and harder for the adults to avoid mixing the two languages—and of course for the children even more. By around age four, the daughter stopped speaking Croatian to her parents altogether. Neither she nor her brother saw the need for it and slowly and steadily the minority language "went out the window." This was fine with the teachers at the children's school. They were not at all impressed by the children's abilities in more than one language. They were only concerned with any tiny disfluency in English, and the parents were made to feel that if the child's English was not absolutely perfect, it could only be the fault of the other language.

The children's development of a connection to the language and cultural heritage remained a strong desire for the parents, and they were not willing to let it disappear, so they applied greater effort. When Tina was six and speaking Croatian less and less, Maya felt she had to do something dramatic. She went to Croatia with her and stayed there for several weeks. Once Maya saw that Tina was oriented to the different ways of doing things there, she felt she could send the child back in following summers for a month with her grandparents. There, she had monolinguals, she had peers, and most importantly, she had a reason to use the language. These visits turned the situation around. Maya says she seriously doubts that Tina would speak Croatian as well as she does now and would not feel as connected to that culture without those summer months with her grandparents.

Case Study 19: David–mL@H and T&P

David describes the same slide toward English and the same rescue through summer trips to France. He and his French wife speak French at home and so do their five children. David, too, finds that there comes a point—around kindergarten—when the English influence becomes much stronger. His children began by mixing up the languages, and finally, when they got to first grade, if anyone spoke to them in French, they were no longer comfortable speaking French and would answer in English. However, "as soon as we got to France," he reports, "they became fluent again within days."

Case Study 20: Viviane–Teen Bilingual, OPOL and T&P

MOTHER: **English**
FATHER: **French**, English (late learner)
PARENTS TOGETHER: English
COMMUNITY: English
CHILDREN: English, some French passively

CS-20	STRENGTHS	WEAK POINTS
Input	father native speaker of mL	father had few people to speak mL with
Extended family	relatives in Switzerland	
Community		father only spoke mL when there was an au pair speaking mL; no mL classes until junior high
Print materials	available	
Travel options	several summers in Switzerland, especially as a teenager	when she went to Switzerland with all her sisters, they would continue in English together
Attitudes and experience	parent is positive; strong emotional tie to father	
Level of commitment		parents' commitment not strong

Viviane reports a childhood of starts and stops on her path to bilingualism. She started at birth, but did not consider herself bilingual until her late teens. "It was always changing, very dynamic." Viviane is the eldest of five daughters of a French-Swiss father and an American mother who initially attempted to make a bilingual household. The father spoke French to Viviane, and they had a French au pair until she was three or four. When the French au pair was replaced by an English au pair, the balance in the household tipped away from French. Viviane and her sisters responded in English, and their father spoke French less consistently. Still, there were always French visitors and the family went to Switzerland several summers for a month and a half at a time. When Viviane was eight, the youngest sister was born, and once again the family had a French au pair. The father began speaking French to the baby and continued speaking to her in French for many years. So, there was always a lot of French in the household, but the daughters spoke English even to their father.

When Viviane got to seventh grade, she was not bilingual, but she really loved French and was "primed to learn it." She had a good basis for learning it, as well as a deep drive and an emotional attachment to her father. She began it as a school subject that year and made good progress, but does not think she really became bilingual until late teenage. She went back to Switzerland for five summers, first to a mountaineering camp, and then for two summers she worked in a French organization and lived in a dormitory. Speaking nothing but French for three months straight, two summers in a row, really brought her fluency to a high level. So, she feels, you can have minimal fluency in the early years. As long as you have the early exposure, then you can learn the language intensively later.

The value of relatives who speak other languages is great, but not everyone has them. Language travel, by contrast, is available more generally (and there may be some low-cost alternatives). Here, one can join the forces of pleasure and language contact. We can invent our own immersion travel for our children (and ourselves). When children travel, they expect a new routine and are generally more open to all activities, even the same ones they are not eager to do at home. Parents can arrange strategic immersions at particularly vulnerable times for the minority language—for example, after the start of school in the majority language, or as the children are entering adolescence. We already saw, with the Saunders children, that just the goal of going to Germany was a strong motivator for the family.

Case Study 21: Jane Merrill's "Grand Tour" of Paris, OPOL and T&P

MOTHER:	English, **French** (late learner)
FATHER:	English
PARENTS TOGETHER:	English
COMMUNITY:	English (travel to France)
CHILDREN:	English, French

Jane Merrill was discovering elective bilingualism in a suburb of New York about the same time that Saunders was carrying it out in Australia, and she writes about it in her (out-of-print) book, *Bringing Up Baby Bilingual*. On the basis of a fair amount of international travel as a child and young adult and her own imperfect French, she launched into a bilingual upbringing for her twins from age one. She had been undecided as to how to go about it when a friend told her not to wait another minute.

Merrill's mantra is to make it fun—be instructive without being pedantic or letting your purpose show. Everything has a lesson and is an occasion for language learning. The capstone of the program described in her book was a modern-day "Grand Tour," a thirty-two-day stay in Paris with her twins when they were five years old. The planning guide she provides is valuable both as a guide to travel with children generally and as a field guide to the language lessons she finds around every corner. Merrill involved the children in the planning of the trip, so she was sure she could capitalize on their interests. Besides, the time spent planning did not feel like the extended language lesson that it was.

"Go where people are talking," she admonishes, "You haven't come abroad to commune with the trees." People on foot and on the bus communicate more, so stay on foot as much as you can. Waiting in the crowd for the Tour de France to pass by was more convivial than traipsing around the Louvre. Over the course of the couple of hours it took for the cyclists to pass, the children chatted with the assembled sports fans, counting colored jerseys with one man and playing with someone else's puppy.

Merrill chose an intimate two-star hotel in the center of Paris where the staff was small and did not speak much English. One criterion was customer reviews with the key word "friendly." There was a small child-friendly salon for hanging out, as a change for the children from being in their room. The children were not intimidated and could be entrusted with small errands to the front desk, like returning a key or requesting a newspaper. The location did not have to be quaint, but Merrill wanted someplace with active life on the streets. She was careful to pick a hotel near a park where there were other children. To help her children blend in, they waited until they got to Paris before getting their hair cut and buying their last-minute accessories. The haircut was a mini-adventure in itself, and the promise of purchases encouraged the children to be observant of the other children at a very detailed level. Sailing toy boats in a small lake was a standard pastime there, so she invested in a boat that attracted the attention of the other children.

As much as possible, she would prepare the children for and then let them take over routine transactions, for example, at the post office or the bakery. One clever strategy to encourage the children to do the ordering at the restaurant was to prime the children in French to be ready for the waiter's question just before he arrived. When the waiter came to the table, he heard the children speaking in French, so he addressed them in French.

While they were in France, Merrill was more lenient than at home. The children watched TV in the lobby, they stayed up later, and they were allowed to eat "fun foods" they didn't eat at home. Merrill warns against trying to do too much and was careful to pace their days with plenty of free time. They used downtime to hang out at the hotel. Throughout the month, they made a journal of the trip as a joint project, with drawings and pictures as well as dictated stories of things that had happened or things people had said. Frugality became a game on the trip. All of Merrill's suggestions are made with an eye toward the budget: Madeline in Paris on Five Dollars a Day.

The keynote of Merrill's trip abroad was having the children lead, even the five-year-olds, and putting them in safe situations where they could do it. Her attitude contrasts with a travel story told to me by another parent. The Hollanders went to Austria one summer with their children, who had been in a German immersion program at home. At the time of the trip, the children were young teenagers, eleven and thirteen. This, of course, is a much less cooperative age in general. Whereas everything, even a trip to the bakery, is new and exciting to a five-year-old, a thirteen-year-old can make it a study of boredom. So it's not surprising that the older children were underwhelmed by the trip with their parents. But I also think that the parents failed to take advantage of opportunities the trip provided. The mother recounts one evening when the son, who had been silent up until that point, sprang into action. Apparently they were being double-charged for their dessert, and the son discovered it. Unlike his parents, he was not inclined to just overlook it. He called the waiter over, explained the problem in flawless German, and got it all sorted out. Afterwards he was very pleased with himself, as he deserved to be.

On their trip, this was an isolated incident, but it seems to me, with the luxury of hindsight, to have been a signal that the parents were doing too much of the day-to-day arranging that the children could have been handling. After seeing how quick the son was to take charge, they might have engineered a little helplessness on their part, or at least a rotating system where the children took turns being in charge. As we saw in chapter 4, families can live abroad as expatriates without taking the steps you need to get the benefit of the language opportunities around you. If people who are traveling are not proactive, they will not find the interactions with the speakers of the target language that they came for.

The Contribution of Schools

So far, we have looked at family strategies for creating bilinguals. Families can do it without the schools, and in many situations, they have to. But when it is available, formal schooling in the medium of the language—not necessarily language lessons—can add a valuable dimension to the language competence the child has developed at home. When children learn a language informally, what they learn is to communicate informally (that is, they acquire Basic Interpersonal Communication Skills [BICS]). They learn "playground-Spanish" or what a friend calls "TV-German." To move to the next step, to master more abstract language for academic purposes (or, Cognitive Academic Language Proficiency [CALP]), children need "academic" experience. They need to hear formal language in political speeches or science programs. They need poetry readings and sermons at their place of worship. Reading and writing are the most common routes to abstract language. Some gifted people can get academic experience through intensive reading independently, but most of us grow into our academic language through schooling. Joining the forces of home (for BICS) and school (for CALP) seems to me to create the most well-rounded bilinguals.

From my experience, learning the language only at home without training in school does not fully develop all facets of the language. Learning in school adds the academic level, but school alone generally does not develop minority language proficiency to the fullest extent either. School learning of a minority language is less effective alone than when it can build on the home-language base. It is as if the language foundation is missing, so the school learning has nothing to attach to.

When parents do not know another language, or when they are using their own time and energy for yet a different language, schools can promote a minority language—especially if the school learns the lesson from the home and uses an immersion method. Immersion, as the name implies, surrounds the child totally with the language. They are "dunked" in it and learn it from the inside out. They do not study it so much as use it.

Canadian schools are famous for their French immersion programs for English speakers. Children who are presumed to know little or no French come to school, and from day one, everything takes place in French. Just as for young children learning their first language, in the earliest years of an immersion program, the communicative demands are low. Language leans heavily on nonverbal context, but only the target language is used. Complexity is added slowly, and within a couple of years, the language beginners are at grade level in the new language.

Some U.S. schools have made immersion programs like Canada's, but there is another system gaining ground, called "Dual-Immersion" or "Two-Way Immersion" (TWI). TWI is especially useful where there are minority language speakers who need to learn the majority language as well as majority language speakers electing to learn the second language. Both can be accommodated in the same classrooms, and both sets of native-speaking children are enlisted as language resources for the others who are learning their language. In the ideal TWI program, half the children are experts in the minority language and half are experts in the majority language. That is the "Coral Way" TWI model, named after the school in Miami, where the idea originated in the early 1960s. It was implemented by the first wave of Cubans who had left the island and settled "temporarily" in Miami until they could return to Cuba. Although that day still hasn't come, the system of two-way immersion is a lasting legacy.

The final pattern of immersion is "sink or swim," also called "submersion." Children are thrown into the majority language with majority language learners and told to catch up. Many do learn to "swim," but given that there is no provision to rescue those who "sink," this pattern is not recommended when there are other alternatives. Isabel, Carmen, and Gretchen, whose stories appear above (Case Studies 11–13), experienced submersion. They were successful, but we do not know how many are not. I will not have heard from children who were not successful. All of these methods have their advantages and disadvantages. Importantly, they all can work.

CASE STUDY	FAMILY'S/CHILDREN'S NAMES	COUNTRY OF RESIDENCE
CS-22	Pritzker family, Immersion Schooling	Vancouver, Canada
CS-23	Louisa, Immersion Schooling	MD, U.S.
CS-24	Tessa, Dual-Immersion Schooling	Boston, MA, U.S.
CS-25	Mark and Susan, Dual-Immersion Schooling	Alabama, U.S.; Edmonton, Canada
CS-26	Acosta family, OPOL and Dual-Immersion Schooling	Guatemala
CS-27	Charles and Reiko, OPOL, Dual-Language Schooling, T&P	Hong Kong

Case Study 22: Pritzker Family–Immersion School Alone

MOTHER: **English**
FATHER: **English**
PARENTS TOGETHER: English
SCHOOL: French
CHILDREN: English, French

The Pritzker children, Josh and Julie, had the choice of two schooling alternatives in Vancouver, English-only or French immersion. Because the Pritzkers were from a monolingual English home, the English school might have been the most natural choice for them. However, those schools had large numbers of nonnative speakers, so their programs were geared toward intensive second-language training in English for Speakers of Other Languages (ESOL) and the Pritzkers did not consider them appropriate for their children. The other alternative was the French Immersion program for English speakers, which gave all its instruction in French through the fourth grade and then gradually introduced more English. French Immersion was a well-established program that had a strong parents' group advocating for it. It was the most sought-after program, and people had to get on the list for a lottery to get in. Josh won the lottery, and then both children went through the program from kindergarten through middle school and did the summer Family French Camps for two weeks almost every summer. The children did well and went happily to school, but the parents feel that their French abilities are more conversational than truly academic. They speak well and read, but they would not be mistaken for native speakers.

Case Study 23: Louisa–Immersion School in Washington, D.C.

MOTHER:	**English**
FATHER:	**English**
PARENTS TOGETHER:	English
SCHOOL:	French
CHILDREN:	English, French

Louisa grew up in Maryland near Washington, D.C., and attended a French immersion program in the public school through sixth grade. The children had all their schooling in French and did not even have English as a subject in the curriculum. Their language arts program was all in French. Louisa's parents do not speak French, so all of her exposure was through the school. Starting the immersion in kindergarten, she says, she had no other concept of what school was supposed to be like. The fact that everyone spoke a new language was no newer than standing in line, having desks, or eating in a cafeteria. The school program arranged exchange programs for the children to give them experience with French as a home language. The Maryland children went to France during the summer of the sixth grade, and French children came to Maryland and stayed with the students and their families. Louisa calls the exchange component "cool," but feels that the main reasons the immersion worked so well were the French background of most of the teachers and the fact that the program also attracted some students who were native speakers of French—children of diplomats and other foreign visitors. Through the program, they achieved a sixth-grade level of spoken and written French. Although the children had no instruction in English during elementary school, they went on without difficulty to English-language middle schools (and in Louisa's case, subsequently to an ivy league university).

Case Study 24: Tessa–Dual Immersion

Several hundred programs across the U.S. follow a dual immersion model—half of the day in English and the other half in Spanish (or Chinese or another minority language). Unlike the Canadian immersion programs, which have no native speakers of the target language, American TWI programs have something to attract native speakers of both languages. Thus there are good models for both languages from peers (which we saw in chapter 4 was a plus). Also, each child has a chance to be the expert and also the beginner, so neither half of the class is superior to the other.

MOTHER:	**English**
FATHER:	**English**
PARENTS TOGETHER:	English
SCHOOL:	Spanish and English
CHILDREN:	English, Spanish

CS-24	STRENGTHS	WEAK POINTS
Input		neither parent speaks mL
Extended family		
Community	dual-immersion school in neighborhood; summer camp program	
Print materials	available	
Travel options		
Attitudes and experience		parents positive, but they did not seek out the program
Level of commitment		strong intellectual level

Earlier we met Sophia, who was learning Spanish at home and at school, but most of the children in her dual-immersion program—like Tessa—

were getting exposure to Spanish only at school. Tessa's parents admit that they did not specifically choose a bilingual program, but consider themselves lucky that one fell into their lap, or at least across the street. Tessa has been in the junior and senior kindergartens and to a summer camp so far, so it is too early to say how learning Spanish as well as English will affect her academics. Her parents are not worried, because they know many families, whose values they trust, who rave about their children's experiences at the school. Tessa's parents do not expect the language learning to be a snap, but the children are encouraged to view it as being worth the effort (and they seem to agree). It is already a source of pride for Tessa, and her mother observes that it has given her more curiosity about other languages than she would have expected of someone so young.

Tessa's parents are already very pleased with the social and cultural immersion their child is receiving. It is not like the mother's own experience in high school, where the assimilation went in one direction: "they," the minority language children, became like "us," the majority language children, but not vice versa. Just as the experiments in chapter 1 would predict, there is a reciprocal sense of learning between cultures in the school. Even in kindergarten, the parents have noticed many examples of friendships that cross the language line, and they are pleased that Tessa describes people in the school not by the language they speak but by hair color or height—in other words, in terms she would use within her own ethnic group.

Case Study 25: Mark and Susan—Bad Timing

MOTHER: **English** (single mother)
COMMUNITY: English
SCHOOL: Mandarin, English
CHILDREN: one English; one learning both English and Mandarin

CS-25	STRENGTHS	WEAK POINTS
Input		single mother who does not speak Chinese
Extended family	ex-husband's family in Taiwan; all but great-grandfather speak English	

Community	now in city with Dual-Immersion schooling in Chinese and English, and several Chinese options as school subjects; multilingualism common	early life in city with little Chinese language presence
Print materials		some available, especially through the school, but the mother can't use them easily
Travel options	several short trips to Taiwan; a 3-month stay in Shenzhen	
Attitudes and experience	parent is positive	single parent
Level of commitment	strong intellectual level	

Dual immersion is also available in Edmonton, where Shelley moved with her children, Mark and Susan. Shelley does not speak Chinese, but both children are of Chinese descent—the older child, through Shelley's ex-husband, who is Chinese-American, and the younger one, adopted at eleven months, from being born in China—so Shelley is eager for them to have the tools to participate in Chinese culture.

Mark, like Viviane (CS-20), has had a lot of stops and starts in his language learning, and it seems to his mother Shelley that her efforts have not given him a useful command of the second language. She started by hiring a Chinese nanny three days a week for Mark's first twelve months, while they were living in Alabama. Mark's first words were in Mandarin. But then the first, grandmotherly nanny had to go back to China suddenly. Shelley got another nanny for Mark, but she was young and eager to learn English. Her comprehension of English was too good, and soon Mark realized he could speak to her in English even if she addressed him in Chinese. He also resisted staying with the nanny when Shelley went to work. He asked, "Why does Googoo [the nanny] make you go away?" and he preferred to go to regular day care.

The most successful Chinese language interlude for Mark was a three-and-a-half-month trip to Shenzhen for Shelley's work when Mark was seven. By the third month of being in school and playing in the neighborhood, Mark began really talking. At one point, he and a group of neighbor boys were waiting for a bus and Mark was the first to see it. When he announced it was coming, everyone there—including the Chinese children—looked around to see who had said it, because it sounded so much like a Chinese child. However, the family soon returned to Alabama, and it took only a month for Mark's Chinese to disappear.

Back in Alabama, they tried a number of Chinese Saturday schools, but each was wrong for a different reason. At one, the teacher was too old-fashioned; another was for children who knew more Chinese than Mark did, and a third left him working on his own at a computer for the whole session. When they finally moved to Edmonton, he was too old to start in the Dual-Immersion program. Speakers of the minority language can enter an immersion program at any point, because they will have to learn the community language in any event, and the dual immersion just makes the process that much gentler for them. Majority language speakers do not catch up as easily in learning the minority language and so they can enter only at kindergarten or first grade. Programs that might have been appropriate at another point pass them by.

At this point, Mark is fourteen years old and doing well in school, but he is not an active bilingual. He has a number of Chinese friends, some of whom have Chinese-speaking parents and grandparents, but no one to make him want to speak Chinese. Shelley is resigned to the idea that the next language-learning efforts will have to come from Mark. She is hopeful that his early exposure to the language will make it easier for him if he decides later to learn it.

Timing seems to be on his sister's side. The move to Edmonton came at exactly the right year for her, and she was able to begin kindergarten in the bilingual program. At eight and a half, she is dominant in English but doing well in the Chinese program. Her teachers do not stress conversation very much, so Susan (MeiLi) does not feel like she can actually speak the language and is experiencing it more as a school-subject than as an immersion. Although it is technically a two-way program, there are almost no native Chinese speakers in the classes, so Shelley has hired Chinese tutors to work with Susan after school. Susan is cooperative, but language is less exciting to her than figure skating, and it remains to be seen how strong her identification with the language will be.

Case Study 26: The Acosta Twins—OPOL and Bilingual Schooling in Guatemala

MOTHER: **English**, Spanish
FATHER: **Spanish**, English
PARENTS TOGETHER: Spanish
COMMUNITY: Spanish
SCHOOL: dual immersion, English and Spanish
CHILDREN: Spanish, English

CS-26	STRENGTHS	WEAK POINTS
Input	father is a native speaker; mother is a near-native speaker of mL; parents speak mL with each other	
Extended family	husband's family in same country; visits from mother's family	
Community	live in Spanish speaking country; English is the minority language; Dual-Immersion school is available; bilingualism common and expected	
Print materials	many, including school materials	
Travel options	frequent trips to the U.S.	
Attitudes and experience	parents both positive	
Level of commitment	strong emotional level	

Many Latin American cities have famous bilingual schools like the poorly named "American School" in Guatemala City. Its bilingual program worked particularly well for the Acosta twins. They have a Guatemalan dad and extended family and an English-background bilingual mother with American relatives. They were born in Guatemala City, so the family did OPOL with Spanish as the community language and English the minority language. They stayed in Guatemala until their teenage years, when political tensions sent them to the U.S. They were perfectly able to pick up their studies in an American school system and went on to college and professional schools.

Their "American" school in Guatemala was organized with half-Spanish and half-English teachers, and children rotated from classroom to classroom on a set schedule either every day or by the week. Their comfortable bilingualism also seems to be a product of it being considered absolutely normal to speak and study in two languages from the beginning of school. It also did not hurt that their minority language was in great demand. In fact, their mother confides that they were put ahead of where they would have been on the waiting list because the school was eager for children with native English.

Case Study 27: Charles and Reiko—OPOL and Bilingual Schooling in Hong Kong

MOTHER:	**Japanese,** English, Cantonese
FATHER:	**Cantonese,** English
PARENTS TOGETHER:	English
COMMUNITY:	Cantonese, English
CHILDREN:	Cantonese, Japanese, English, and now some Mandarin

CS-27	STRENGTHS	WEAK POINTS
Input	mother is a native speaker of mL, but very trilingual; father is bilingual in two of the languages (late learner of English)	
Extended family	grandparents not too far away, available for summer visits	
Community	lived in bilingual country; bilingual school; multilingualism common; access to Japanese school in summers	
Print materials	available (Japanese library open to them)	Mandarin was less available when the children were young; relatively little stress on Japanese writing
Travel options	many trips to Japan	

Attitudes and experience	parents both positive	
Level of commitment	strong emotional and intellectual level	

The international city of Hong Kong, where the community languages are Cantonese and English, was a good place for Mihoko and her husband to raise two very trilingual children. Mihoko is Japanese, and her parents are still in Japan, while her husband is Chinese from Hong Kong. The family used their own language resources to do OPOL within the home, and they found different schooling options for the children at different stages of development. Charles and Reiko, now eighteen and fifteen, are comfortably trilingual in Cantonese, Japanese, and English, and they have learned a fourth language, Mandarin, at school. Mihoko feels that the children would have learned Cantonese and English in any event because both are official languages there, and the better students in the city go to bilingual Anglo-Chinese schools. She was eager for them to learn Japanese, too, because she did not want to talk to the children in a language that they spoke better than she did, and she also wanted to ensure that her children could talk with her parents.

Three languages are spoken in their home. The parents speak English together, Mihoko speaks Japanese with the children, and her husband speaks Cantonese with them. When they are all speaking together, they use Cantonese. The children's first language was primarily Japanese because Mihoko stayed home with them when they were little, and they went to Japan many summers to spend a month with grandparents. The children are very proud of speaking Japanese as they get a lot of attention when they do. Their fondness for Japanese cartoon characters (Pocket Monsters, Dragon Ball, and Gundum) motivates them to speak Japanese at home. Among their friends, they are handy translators who can read the Japanese instructions for all their electronic gadgets and games. They are the experts on Japanese game software. Mihoko says, "I didn't push Japanese writing, but they can at least write letters to their grandparents in Japanese."

What is so unusual in the story of Mihoko's household are the many different schooling options for the children. In addition, they supplemented the offerings at the schools with tutors and travel. The children were dominant in Japanese when they started in a full-time Cantonese kindergarten. Then they went to a Cantonese elementary school, where they learned Cantonese (which is now their dominant language) and also started English. In the Cantonese school, there were ten forty-five-minute sessions of English per week and the parents hired exchange students from the U.S. to teach the children more English. Also during the summer vacations of their elementary school years (from age seven to age twelve), the children attended one month at Hong Kong's Japanese school, which operated on a slightly different schedule. Their Japanese was good enough for them to be admitted into a regular class in the Japanese school, and they could use the school's library and join in the after-school activities.

Mihoko reports that about 70% of the high schools in Hong Kong are Anglo-Chinese. (There are options for other European languages as well.) In the typical Anglo-Chinese schools, the medium of instruction is basically English, but Chinese, math, and some science subjects are taught in Cantonese. Mandarin, the major dialect of mainland China, is still relatively rare in Hong Kong, but as the political economy changes, it is becoming more important there. The older child studied Mandarin as a school subject in high school. He can communicate somewhat but is not fluent. The family chose Reiko's school for her because history, geography, Chinese, and art are taught in the medium of Mandarin, so her Mandarin is stronger.

Overall, Mihoko and her husband didn't feel that it was difficult to raise the children trilingually because there are many international people and places in town and such good schooling options. They also accepted that one language might not be as strong as the others. Their goal in Japanese was for the children to develop basic skills in order to communicate within their extended family. Only in Chinese and English did the children need to develop academic proficiency as well, which they have done.

The Scorecard: Evaluating the Strategies

So now we need to step back and make some evaluations. What works where for whom?

Mixed Language Policy, "Time and Place," Bilingual Schooling

I have already voiced my reservations about the Mixed Language Policy, based largely on Joshua Fishman's advice to those who are trying to reverse language shift. The key strategy, according to Fishman, is for communities to carve out domains for each language. When two languages inhabit the same domain—whether the home, a house of worship, or the public sphere—they are in competition with each other. Eventually, there will be a winner and a loser. Fishman's advice to communities who want to preserve or add their heritage language—just as you do—is to separate the languages. Thus, I am always pleased when I hear that a mixed language policy has worked for a family, but think it is less likely to work in the future than it has in the past.

There is no need to compare Time and Place to the other strategies, as it is a useful complement to whatever else you do. If you get an opportunity to travel or to move to a country with another language for a year or more, the immersion in the second language by itself is not enough to create bilingualism, but the immersion makes your other efforts much easier and more effective. The same is true of schooling options. Schooling in a heritage language does not replace your efforts at home, but as we saw above, they enhance what you can accomplish at home. Bilinguals who do not become readers in their minority language can still attain great fluency and will enjoy the basic communication skills that interaction with speakers of the language affords. They may achieve a level of proficiency that lets them pass for native-speakers. Certainly, they can be near-native, with a very high degree of facility and identification with the language and the culture associated with it. Non-readers will, however, experience the same limitations as "unlettered" first language speakers. Their language will be less likely to conform to language standards, and may be less useful for business or academic purposes.

OPOL versus mL@H

So, it boils down to which is better: OPOL or mL@H? Clearly both can work in a variety of circumstances—but neither is guaranteed in all circumstances. Would Paul (CS-2) have been "native" instead of "near-native" if he had had more sources of French than just his dad? Or if he had some of his early schooling in French? Or if he had been convinced to read more widely in the language? It is quite possible, but it is clear that OPOL suited the family and produced a child who is at home with both sides of his extended family and who has an unusual interest in languages.

Barron-Hauwaert reports outcomes for families using different strategies in terms of the children's reported language use at the time of the survey: monolingual, passive bilingual, active bilingual, or trilingual. Eighty percent of the families said they used the same strategy throughout, but they may have added some "T&P" reinforcement. She received the most responses from people using OPOL, which is not surprising, because that was the focus of her investigation.

The "batting average" for OPOL appears to be about 78%; 58 out of the 75 children were reported to be actively bilingual, if not trilingual. However, because more than half of those are zero to three years old, it's too early to grant them "success." Without the children under age four, the percentage drops to 63%. The survey received relatively few responses from families using mL@H, but their children tended to be older, which I take as a sign of persistence. Using the same logic, taking away the one child under four in the mL@H group, there appear to have been around five children who became at least bilingual of the eight mL@H families, or 62.5%. Percentages for both strategies rise when the passive bilinguals are added in.

So what can one cautiously conclude from this self-selected sample? To me, it says that passive and active bilingualism are achievable for our children and that no single strategy is better than another. The best strategy for you is the one that fits your family. The only wrong way to raise a bilingual child is not to do it at all.

Deciding between Strategies
The Self-Evaluation Questionnaire in chapter 4 should help you clarify your goals and identify your strengths and weaknesses. It also functions to some extent like a decision tree.

- *Your partner does not speak the minority language?*

That rules out mL@H and MLP.

- *You place a priority of 10 out of 10 on your child learning your heritage language?*

To me that rules out MLP. (See discussion in chapter 4 and in Selecting Your Strategy section at the beginning of this chapter.) It will probably work, but "probably" isn't good enough. You want to know you have done everything you could possibly do to make the two languages easy for your children to learn. It probably also means you will use mL@H if it is available to you, and will be open for opportunities to implement Time and Place, summers abroad, or a sabbatical year in a country where the language is native.

- *You are a single parent?*

You will probably choose OPOL to raise a bilingual child. Some people report that a grandparent can be the "other" parent, but like your own relationship with the child, it has to be a grandparent who sees the child consistently over a long period of time, about 20 hours a week at a minimum. Single parents can also avail themselves of the various school possibilities for other languages for their child and should try to find other support groups for themselves.

- *You want to speak a language of which you are a nonnative speaker, and your spouse speaks the majority language?*

You may be more likely to choose OPOL. It will be good for the child to have a native model in the home for one of his languages (but see Ellen and Chris, CS-6, for a counter-example).

- *You are a nonnative speaker (and your spouse speaks a minority language)?*

You may opt for mL@H, using your nonnative input to boost the amount of interaction in the minority language and can be confident that the community and schools will help your children with the majority language.

Providing Motive and Opportunity–but How?

The advice to provide children with motive and opportunity for the minority language is a little like the standard advice to succeed in the stock market: "Buy low; sell high." Easier said than done. If it were obvious to everyone which stocks to buy in order to buy low and sell high, we would all be rich. But it is not obvious, and most of the variables that make a stock a good bet are not under our control.

Likewise, it is not always obvious to us how to provide motive and opportunity to use a second language. Your children need both. In this chapter, we have seen a number of strategies that at least to some extent *are* under your control to create the opportunities for children to use the target language. The more crucial and more difficult part is to provide the motive. If children want to use the language, they will seek out the opportunities. Your task then is to plant the desire for the language in your child.

This task is difficult, but not impossible. Parents do it all the time. In fact, it is a crucial part of parents' job description to create and sustain in their children the desire to live in harmony with others, even their brothers and sisters and people in the sandbox who are intent on taking their toys. Advertisers, too, are adept at making things attractive to different segments of the population and motivating them to buy things they could live without. As a parent motivating the use of a second language, you can take typical parenting goals—and add some "Madison Avenue" techniques.

We have spoken above about how to set up one's household. Some household strategies you might use target both opportunity and motive at the same time. For example, one sure-fire way to motivate the use of a minority language is to make it the child's only language. You do not have to do anything to get healthy children to talk; in fact, it is harder to get them to be quiet. So, at least in the early stages of development, if you only have one language in the children's environment, they will speak it. But realistically, we are concerned here with a world of many choices for the child. In an OPOL household, for example, people's schedules address the question of how much opportunity a child will have to speak each parent's language: if the parent is home for only an hour when the child is awake, there will be less opportunity for using that parent's language. But even if you equalize the opportunity, you still have the question of which parent the child will prefer to talk to.

Which would you prefer to talk to, the parent who is showing you how to clean under your bed or the one who is playing a game with you? The parent who screams at you or the one who praises you? Will you go out of your way to find out how dust collects on the windows, or how rain collects in puddles? Will toddlers want to talk to the parent who talks too fast or in language too complicated for them? They won't know how to say "slow down." You have to be able to figure it out yourself.

A Bag of Tricks

While I don't suggest you adopt a commercial atmosphere in your home, you might want to take a few cues from the successful commercials you observe to heighten the appeal of the second language. A useful set of easy-to-follow strategies is listed in Table 11, below.

Table 11. **A Bag of tricks: How to encourage your child to speak the minority language**

Trick 1: KISS.   *Keep it simple* (otherwise known as "KISS") and easy to repeat.
Trick 2: Use repetition.   Learn songs with refrains that are easy to join in and hard to forget.
Trick 3: Make it stand out.   Use bright colors and attractive images to draw children's attention to materials in the minority language.
Trick 4: Associate the minority language with desirable things.   Why do car ads show the latest models with beautiful women lavishly dressed (or undressed) in the picture? The women don't make the cars drive better, but they are designed to draw the attention of at least many male consumers. Likewise, you can use a little marketing psychology to associate the minority language with comfort and fun. Use it to comfort the child, play games, or go to the movies. Say "Let's get ice cream" in the minority language, but not "Put out the trash."
Trick 5: Use monolingual mode in your own speech.   I can't emphasize enough the need to monitor your own behavior. Children are sensitive to subtle differences in adults' rate of switching between languages, and then they match their own rate with that of the adult. If you are constantly switching out of the minority language, it will not be a surprise that the child does, too.

Trick 6: Use small rewards.

Educational psychologists discourage the use of prizes to reward behaviors that are their own reward. For example, they say it is counterproductive to pay children for each book they read, as you will teach them to read only for someone else, not for themselves. That doesn't prevent using a pot of nickels as a reminder, like one family does. Each person starts dinner with a stack of five nickels. Each time someone says something in the "wrong" language, he or she puts a nickel back in the pot. You get to keep any nickels still at your place at the end of the meal. Sometimes the "bribe" is one that extends the use of the language, like offering a new book in the minority language as a reward for using it more.

Trick 7: Be especially helpful.

Help the child find the words he needs—but don't interrupt or correct. Instead, tell stories together, that is, co-construct everyday narratives, as we saw in chapter 2 with younger children.

Trick 8: Have some humorous line to arouse attention and pull the child back to the minority language.

A simple expression like "Allons les enfants!" or "Vamonos!" can be a conscious trigger to activate the minority language.

Trick 9: Be consistent.

But don't be rigid.

Trick 10: Use positive reinforcement rather than punishments.

You can learn to use more "I-messages," like "I feel so good when I hear you speaking my language." When you are looking for things to praise, your attitude automatically becomes more positive. There are parent education courses for people whose natural tendency is to use "you-messages" instead of "I-messages." Seek them out at your local library or community center.

Trick 11: Use your imagination.

A number of people have had good success with puppets who speak only the other language. Our friend Matt invented Pepe several years ago, and the character is now a member of the family. Pepe is not an elaborate puppet; in fact, he's just an old sock with some fake fur, but he's got personality. He's a grouch with a gruff old voice that invites children to try to rile him. He's always sleeping (and snoring), and when Matt's son Jamie is talking to him, Pepe may fall asleep and Jamie has to wake him up. Jamie is old enough to know that it's his father's hand in the sock, but he treats Pepe as if he were a true Mexican. Jamie sometimes tries to teach him English. Pepe goes along with it, but has a horrible accent and can't do it and ends up saying that Spanish is so much better. Just pulling Pepe out is enough to change the conversation into Spanish.

Trick 12: Be realistic.

No one learns a language overnight. Recognize steps of success when they are before you. There is no single version of success, and everything that does not fit your vision of success is not failure.

A bilingual life comes naturally to some people, but others need to be reassured and convinced by a book like this one, or by the examples all around them that they must open their eyes to see.

By now, you see that language itself is a specialized skill quite unlike other mental activities. On the other hand, language behaviors follow the general principles of human behavior that you are familiar with from other parts of your life.

It is important for you to have a positive attitude and a belief that what you are doing is possible so that you do not doubt yourself and start giving up slowly after having convinced yourself that it is not worthwhile. When you have an emotional commitment to the second language, it makes you want to overcome all hurdles. In the end, you will also be more relaxed about it because it is the only way you can imagine things to be. You certainly cannot become aggressive or punitive about using the language, as this will make your child hate it. However, your own desire does not suffice for the child. You must plant the desire for it in your child with both art and craft, making sure to keep it light and fun every step of the way.

CHAPTER

Are There Any Children Who Cannot Learn Two Languages?

SO FAR, I HAVE EMPHASIZED THE POSITIVE SIDES of learning more than one language. In this chapter I give you guidelines to help you decide when it might be less beneficial for your child to begin or continue in two (or more) languages.

In other chapters I have suggested that all children are capable of learning two (or more) languages—if provided with the right environment for it. I compared Bilingual First Language Acquisition and early Second Language Acquisition to Monolingual First language Acquisition and proposed that their development is very similar. In the early acquisition of the second language—as for the first language—individual differences in how children learn to speak are tiny compared to the overall uniformity of how children do it—in every language, in every culture, everywhere around the world. However, that is not to say that bilingual children will never have a problem with language.

Just like monolingual children, bilingual children are not immune to language impairments. Children may stutter or have difficulty pronouncing some sounds. They may suffer from another condition which can impair their language. Children with deafness, Down syndrome, or autism, for example, are often language impaired in their first language. Others exhibit a type of impairment called Specific Language Impairment (SLI). Children with SLI are typical in every respect, but they get lower scores than expected on tests of language. They process grammatical forms less well and speak in shorter and simpler sentences with more pauses, hesitations, and repetitions than their typically-developing peers.

In and of itself, language impairment, including SLI, does not mean a child should not learn two languages, but the parents' decision process is different than when there is no impairment. If you suspect that a bilingual child has a language disorder, it is important to find a clinician familiar with bilingual development. If you are not able to find a bilingual therapist, you should at least seek a second opinion. First, you should have the child's hearing checked. Then, if someone knowledgeable about dual language development determines that your bilingual child does in fact show signs of impairment, the recommended treatment will not automatically be to give up the one of the languages. The clinician should help you evaluate, given the child's social, cultural, and educational circumstances (including the use of two languages), whether or not it would be beneficial for the child to continue in two languages while being treated for whatever condition has been diagnosed.

Background

Barring some physical impediment, everyone learns to walk, and likewise, everyone learns to talk.

If learning a first language is like walking, perhaps we can compare second language learning to learning how to ride a bike. Not everyone who learns to walk goes on to ride a bike. Some of the reasons for not learning to ride have nothing to do with the child's capacity. The child may not have access to a bicycle, or the terrain where he or she lives—like a desert or a jungle—may not be suited to travel by bike. We can also imagine some characteristics of the child that would make it inadvisable to put him or her on a bike. For example, a balance problem would make it hard for the child to master the technique. Poor vision or hemophilia could make bike riding too unsafe. In those cases, the dangers of riding might outweigh the benefit the child stood to gain from it.

As with biking, there may be some conditions that would make learning two languages inadvisable for a child. We might look for potential problems with the subskills required—maybe poor memory for sounds or reduced hearing—that could make it more difficult to learn two languages. We might also consider whether there are any social situations where learning two languages would be more burdensome for the child. What would those skills and situations be, and how common are they? How will parents be able to recognize conditions where bilingual learning may be ill-advised?

In general, I recommend that your child learn a second language for its many cognitive and social benefits. These benefits are also available to children with language disorders. I recognize, though, that there is less harm to the child to be without a second language than to be without a first language—or to go without food on the table, have low self-esteem, or lack many other things that are priorities for parents and children. Learning a second language can usually be done without interfering with other goals in life. In fact, the second language can be useful in achieving many of those other goals. But everything in life is a balancing act. There will be times when it will not make sense in the bigger picture of your life, when the energy necessary to maintain a bilingual environment exceeds the benefit to be gained. You are the final judge of how the cost-benefit ratio applies to your own circumstances.

What about Language Impairment?

In the discussion that follows, I want to show that a language disorder does not necessarily rule out bilingualism. In the past, educators and psychologists were quick to lay the blame for whatever they perceived as slow or deviant language development in a bilingual child on the second language. That made it easy to "correct" the situation—just drop the second (or third) language. It might be nice if that solution worked, but there is no evidence that it does. Likewise, there are anecdotes but no research showing that language impairments either stem from or are aggravated by learning two languages.

Reading has its own syndrome, dyslexia, to describe people's difficulty learning to do it. But there is no condition called "dys-bilingua." There is no label for poor learning of second languages except *aphasia*, which applies generally to any language—first, second, or other. Selective interruptions of both languages of a bilingual are sometimes observed, most often brought on by a stroke in elderly people. Children can get aphasia, too, with rare kinds of brain damage. Occasional peculiarities are reported where one or the other language cannot be accessed, as mentioned in chapter 3, but in most cases, both languages are affected more or less equally. When there is uneven damage, the second language is as often spared as the first language. Neither language seems more "basic" than the other.

Children in bilingual circumstances are no different from their monolingual peers with respect to first language learning. All relatively healthy children become "native speakers," but despite the uniformity I mention above, there is a range of ability within what is "native." A recent study in the U.S. Midwest by speech scientist Bruce Tomblin and colleagues established that about 7% of five-year-olds qualify as having Specific Language Impairment (SLI). That is, they were typically-developing children in all their other skills but scored more than one and a half standard deviations below the mean on language tests and were receiving special language services from a speech pathologist. Children with other impairments that lead to language problems add another one or two percent to the incidence of language impairment.

One of the biggest obstacles to learning first or second languages is difficulty with hearing. If a child appears to be having difficulty with either language, the first thing to check is the child's hearing. It may be a temporary situation, like frequent earaches, and may be fixed with antibiotics or tubes in the middle ears to help them drain and let the sounds pass through to the child's brain more easily. Or it might be a more permanent condition, like deafness, or a less common condition called *auditory neuropathy*. (With neuropathy, the problem causes the nerves to deliver auditory information to the brain inconsistently.)

Three Canadian scholars active in the fields of bilingual language development and language disorders, Genesee, Paradis, and Crago, describe the relationship between bilingualism and language impairment this way:

> *Everything we know about children tells us that they are capable of acquiring more than one language, simultaneously or successively. Furthermore, our own work on bilingual French-English children with Specific Language Impairment (SLI) . . . attests to their ability to learn more than one language.*

That is, children with language problems can learn two languages. These authors go on to say that there are many gaps in our knowledge about disorders in bilingual children both for deciding whether there is a problem and for selecting a treatment to correct a problem when one is found. Therefore, they continue, the diagnosis and treatment of language disorders in bilingual children remains as much an art as a science. Each case must be evaluated in light of "scientific knowledge balanced by professional experience and judgment." In other words, there is no blanket remedy. Every case must be considered individually.

Dual Language Assessment and Intervention

According to Genesee, Paradis, and Crago, all studies to date (and there have been very few) indicate that children with SLI who are learning a second language in an immersion situation (like those recommended in this book) suffer no harm to their first language skills or their academic achievement. That is, their impairment in the first language is no different from that of children with SLI in conventional single-language academic programs. However, even children with SLI learn more of the second language than children with their profile who do not have the extra exposure to it from the immersion program.

Genesee and other authors demonstrate that most bilingual children with language impairment in one language show equivalent disorders in both languages—but different languages present different areas of vulnerability, so the actual symptoms of the disorders will be different in each language. The structures most likely to be affected depend on the structure of the language in question. For example, a very common problem for English-learning children is learning the verb inflections, especially for past tense (for example, saying "he walk" instead of "he walked"). By contrast, in languages like Spanish and Italian, where verb endings are more prominent in the grammar, typically, children learn them earlier and do fine with them even if they have SLI. However, pronoun forms are more difficult for them, and certain pronoun errors are signs of a disorder. In German, researchers have pointed to characteristic problems with word order that help them identify language disorders.

If you see problems with one of these "red flag" danger areas in a language, it is worth stepping back and getting a fuller diagnosis. According to Genesee and his coauthors, the impairments bilingual children exhibit in a given language resemble the impairments of monolingual children speaking that language (like verb endings in English, pronouns in French, and word order in German). In their studies of French- and English-learning children with SLI, they have found no impairment that is specific to bilinguals. However, they warn, there are a couple of behaviors that are typical of bilingual-learning children that are commonly mistaken for impairments.

Normal Bilingual Behaviors Often Mistaken for Impairments

The first is "mixing." Monolinguals very often see bilingual children mixing their two languages and conclude that it is a problem when it is not. We saw in chapter 3 that much of the mixing observed in children is a reflection of mixing by the bilingual adults in their community. In fact, if adult speakers generally switch between their languages within the same conversation, it would be strange for their bilingual children not to do the same. Beyond that, though, young children may show some intrusion of one language into the other that is not modeled by adults. Some of the intrusion is positive, and some is negative, but whichever it is, it should not be the only basis for a diagnosis of language impairment.

A second normal behavior that may give rise to a false diagnosis is the natural tendency for bilinguals to have a dominant and a non-dominant language. If a child is below the norms for his age in one of his languages, the reason is often insufficient exposure to that language and not impairment. Thus it is important to assess the child in both languages, or at the very least, in his dominant language. The same test should not be used in both languages, but each test should target the structures where weakness may be expected in monolingual speakers of that language.

WHEN TO SEEK HELP

The cue to seek testing is often that the child is learning verbal material at home and at school considerably more slowly than other children. One should seek help, especially if one sees the child having a problem with one of the "red flag" constructions that alert pathologists to problems for that language in monolinguals. Because there are no diagnostic measures based on bilingual children, monolingual measures need to be applied with caution, with perhaps some allowance in their scores for having less exposure to the language. This is especially important if you have no alternative than to test the child in a non-dominant language. If the child is extremely delayed, or if the delay is found in the child's dominant language, it is important not to dismiss it by saying "oh, it's because he's bilingual" and fail to provide intervention because of that.

Many delays can be overcome or at least reduced with speech therapy. Genesee, Paradis, and Crago note that therapy in one language is generally effective for both, especially if it is in the dominant language—but it is less effective than bilingual intervention. Rather than drop one of the languages, the better solution, when possible, is to use both languages for the therapy. (This strategy also circumvents the psychological disadvantages of dropping one language suddenly.)

So, when things are not going well with a child's language, and the child's hearing has been checked, parents will have two issues to respond to:

- Is the child's condition being fairly diagnosed in light of what we know about language development in bilingual children? and

- Is the second language helpful, detrimental, or neutral with respect to making sure whatever therapy is decided on will be as effective as possible?

The decision to continue with the second language hinges on both questions. In this chapter you will meet parents whose children have been diagnosed with a language impairment. With some of them, I question the diagnosis; with others I share with you the parents' evaluation of the potential benefit to be gained or lost by letting the second language go. I present examples of parents who have chosen to discontinue the second language and of others who decided to continue it, despite the child's impairment, even a hearing impairment.

Questioning the Diagnosis

I have heard from some people who regret fifteen years later that they gave up using their own language with their child because a teacher said that he or she thought it would be better if their child heard only one language. (I might add that pediatricians are not shy about giving similar language advice, although they generally have no expertise in the area.)

Case Study 28: Alicia—Lack of Confidence

One of our parent-respondents, Alicia, says, "If I could start all over, I definitely would not have listened to my daughter's elementary school teacher without getting a second opinion." Apparently, the child was still mixing her pronouns occasionally when she went to first grade, and the teacher jumped to the conclusion that she was being "confused" by also speaking Catalan. Alicia has since earned a degree in linguistics focused on language acquisition. "If I had known then, what I know

now," she says, "I would never have thrown over my whole family's language because of a small dysfluency in a five-year-old."

In a similar situation, Radha's Tamil-speaking parents (see their story in chapter 5, CS-9) had more self-confidence and counseled patience during one fall when Radha was having some language trouble. After her return from a year in India, she had not readjusted to using English again by the time school started. The teachers suggested that the parents stop using Tamil at home to hasten her transition to English. They also wanted her to repeat the year she had missed while she was away, even though she had been attending a more advanced school in India. Radha's parents asked the school to wait a little longer for her former fluency in English to return. By Thanksgiving, the problem was already forgotten.

Case Study 29: Marcia M.–Phonetics Training
Similarly, Marcia M., whose parents spoke French and Spanish to her at home, at age seven was slow to learn some of the more complex sounds in English. Rather than change the home languages, her parents sent her for phonetics training. After a short time in therapy, the problem was resolved. As an adult, Marcia credits her command of three languages with helping her get her current job in international publishing.

Case Study 30: The Kosters–Ignoring Early Warning Signs
The Kosters were speaking their two native languages, Polish and Italian, with their daughter, Elena, and they let her learn English from the school and in the neighborhood. They were advised more than once, by teachers in two schools, that their daughter's language was progressing more slowly than that of other children her age, and that they should stop speaking languages other than English with her. They dismissed the warnings, saying to themselves that the teachers had no experience with trilingual children.

Finally, when Elena was four, she was referred to a psychologist. After a series of tests, the parents were alarmed to find that, in fact, the child was behind in many domains, including language. She was having trouble organizing her thinking and planning her sentences, which made her speak less fluently, and it was harder for her to express herself and understand others. Following recommendations of the therapist, the parents made several adjustments in the way they interacted with the child—one of the hardest being to stop speaking their native languages with her. Within a year or two, the situation was completely different. The therapist worked with the child and taught the parents activities to do with her. She started going to a private school with small classes and individualized curriculum. By first grade, her parents say, the child had "blossomed."

No one will ever know if the extra languages were the key pieces of the puzzle, or whether, with different therapy resources, they could have treated the child's language difficulty and kept her extra languages as well. However, it might have proved very difficult to find a therapist in New York who could work with all of the languages.

Even if, as Genessee, Paradis, and Crago say, dropping one of the languages will rarely result in a "cure," parents have to evaluate how much effort the second language is worth to them and the child. The Kosters were sad to think that their child would not share that part of their heritage, but there was no compelling need for Elena to speak Polish and Italian in New York City. When they made short trips to visit their families in their home countries, either people spoke English to the child, or the parents translated for her. She was even able to play with local children, communicating at a very basic level with them. Now that she is nine, she feels very positive about the languages and is proud to claim that she speaks Polish and Italian, even though her abilities in both are quite basic.

Case Study 31: Kathryn and Leon—Keeping Both Languages
The circumstances were different for Kathryn and Leon's older son Kurt, age eight. Kathryn and Leon are foreign graduate students in a small New England university town. They speak German with each other and with their three children, ages eight, four, and two, and have many bilingual German friends in the area. They will probably return to Germany after they get their degrees, and the children will likely do the rest of their schooling there.

Kurt was four when they came to the U.S., and at first, no one saw any problems. He played well with other children and communicated effectively "on the playground." Then, in kindergarten, the teacher recognized that he was having more difficulty than other foreign students she had worked with, and his parents observed that his German grammar was also not as developed as it would be if he were growing up in Germany. The teacher recommended a concentrated program of English for Speakers of Other Languages (ESOL) that Kurt could do part-time in school, without leaving his class permanently. He worked in the special program for a year, going twice a week and working in a small group. The extra attention seems to have turned the situation around.

When Kathryn looked at the family history, she found that many members of her husband's family, including her husband, had had difficulty with the English and Latin courses required of German students after age ten. She would not have been surprised if Kurt had difficulties with second and third languages had they stayed in Germany. Although it was a source of frustration and an extra effort for Kurt, she feels thankful that he had the opportunity to learn English so much better than he would have if he had never come to the U.S. For him to have dropped either language would have been a hardship for the family and for Kurt himself. To have dropped German would have complicated all three children's eventual return to Germany; to have dropped English would have cut them off from the social and educational community here. With extra help in the second language, the problem was taken care of—and Kurt remains as bilingual as the rest of his family.

Case Study 32: Malcolm—Suspicions of Dyslexia

Malcolm, Gretchen P.'s younger brother, did not have as easy a time as Gretchen did when their parents immigrated to Quebec from Britain and they were required to attend French schools. (See Gretchen's profile in chapter 5, CS-13.) Malcolm had so much trouble learning his subjects in a French-medium school that he petitioned the court to be allowed to switch to an English-medium school. However, his school problems were just as severe in the English school, and in the end, he was ordered to return to the French school. To this day, as an adult, French is still a problem for him—but so is English. From Gretchen's description, it seems likely that Malcolm is dyslexic. He needed more sensitive teaching in both languages, but it sounds like he never got it in either.

Case Study 33: Lisa Potter—Successfully Treated Bilingual Dyslexia

Lisa Potter is luckier than Malcolm: she has been diagnosed with dyslexia and her bilingual program has been adjusted to use her learning strengths in both languages and compensate for her weaknesses. She is an American-background child and attends a bilingual Dual-Immersion program in Spanish and English in Boston. Her parents had been in the Peace Corps and feel strongly that children should know more than one language and culture. They also feel an extra language will open up international job opportunities. They wanted their daughter to start a second language before high school, because they knew learning would be easier and better then. However, because her father had dyslexia, they worried that the extra language could be an extra burden for Lisa, and they worried whether foreign language curricula would be flexible enough to accommodate children with different learning styles.

In fact, the Potters did have difficulty getting Lisa's specific learning disability diagnosed. Because Lisa is so well spoken and bright and loves to read, she didn't seem to be dyslexic. As they had feared, the older Spanish teachers who were trained abroad tended to be more traditional in their teaching methods. Some of them would overlook Lisa's problem and just let her read without doing her lessons. Others were very rigid and even punitive when Lisa could not answer their questions. School became very stressful, and her parents thought that Lisa might have to transfer out. However, the principal was very supportive and helped come up with a plan for Lisa, even though the school had no special program for dyslexic children. She was switched to another classroom, and a paraprofessional worked with her on a structured reading program in English during English language arts classes. She took her other classes as before. In fact, once she was getting the appropriate work (as well as the recognition that she was not just being lazy or contrary), the tension was defused and her confidence and her pleasure in school returned. Once she was back on track, she went back to the original class where her friends were.

The Potters did not feel they could afford a private school but found the services of a private therapist well worth the expense. When Lisa's problems arose, they did not want to wait for the school's special services personnel to get around to evaluating her fifteen months later. They felt she needed to be evaluated quickly, before the problem got worse. The therapist recommended a more structured, multi-sensory approach, which the school implemented for her. The parents still have not found materials in Spanish for Lisa's dyslexia, but working in the one language has given her strategies that she can apply on her own in the other. The teachers also adjusted her workload to let her use her stronger oral skills more than writing in her assignments.

So Lisa was able to continue in both the school program and the associated enrichment activities, which have also been very worthwhile for her. The after-school drama class is bilingual, as are many children in Lisa's Girl Scout troop. Mother, father, and daughter hope to participate next summer in a Spanish-language family camp run by parents at the school. The whole family has been accepted into the school community, which reflects the half-"Anglo" and half-Latino population of the classes and values both cultures equally. Lisa's mother, Mary, contrasts the spirit at the school with her own suburban high school, where the few Latino children were expected to blend in with the non-Latino children. She has enjoyed becoming friends with the parents of her daughter's schoolmates. They have encouraged her to use her Spanish at home with Lisa, even though Lisa finds Mary's accent too American and does not respond to her in Spanish. One of the nicest things about the school for the mother is that she is getting her Spanish back, too, and the whole family has gotten to participate in cultural activities they would not otherwise have access to.

Lisa is proud of her special ability, and she is very comfortable in the school's atmosphere, where she is considered a friend by all of the children in the class. Rather than let Lisa's disability end her foreign language learning, the parents did all they could to keep her in the Dual-Immersion school. That was what they wanted, and that was what Lisa wanted, too.

Case Study 34: Allegra–Abandoning the First Language
One of the families in the University of Miami Infant Study ended up abandoning their bilingual goals for their daughter at age five after she was diagnosed with a rare progressive sensory-neural deafness.

In Allegra's case, it took so long to make the diagnosis that she was already far behind in her English language development and would have to learn at four times the rate of typically-developing monolingual children in order to make up for three years of lost time.

Allegra's parents were graduate students. The father was American who had studied Spanish in school, and the mother was Cuban-American and a perfectly balanced bilingual herself. They started out speaking mostly Spanish at home, and Allegra's developing vocabulary at age two was almost entirely in Spanish. She was at about the 50th percentile on the measurement we used—average—but we considered it a little low for her, given the very high educational level of her family. Allegra was two years old when her brother was born, and her parents sent her to an English-speaking preschool. She continued to be able to speak to her parents in Spanish, but when she attempted English, it was gibberish— very fluent but with no recognizable words. Her mom had nieces and nephews who had made a much smoother transition from almost all Spanish to Spanish and English, so she knew this was not common and suspected something was wrong. She had Allegra's hearing checked, and they put tubes in Allegra's ears—still no improvement.

When we listen to the tapes of Allegra even before age two, when her hearing began to deteriorate more rapidly, we have trouble believing— in hindsight—that the problem was not more evident to us. One sign was her voice, which was very low and breathy. Also, the tapes of her with Vanessa, the research assistant, are full of admonitions to "look at Vanessa when she's talking to you" and to "say good-bye when Vanessa tells you good-bye."

Part of the difficulty in figuring out the problem was her residual Spanish. Her Spanish also had stopped developing around age two, but at least for a while she had enough hearing to use what she had already learned (but not enough to be learning more). It took another two years before she was fitted with hearing aids and began to try to make up for lost time. By the time she began learning English, her parents felt she no longer had time for the luxury of two languages. She was in a race against time to learn the language of her community with the little hearing that the hearing aids provided for her before the window for first language learning would close for her, somewhere around age ten.

Case Study 35: Javier and Corrine—Two Languages Despite Compromised Hearing

Other parents will arrive at a different answer to a similar dilemma. Javier and his wife, Corrine, feel an urgent connection to their native languages, Spanish and Dutch, and they are determined to help their daughter Sonia become trilingual despite the auditory neuropathy she was diagnosed with soon after birth. Auditory neuropathy is a relatively rare hearing disorder that affects the transmission of signals from the inner ear to the brain. The person's hearing may or may not test as normal, but even if the person can hear pure sounds, he or she will have trouble understanding speech, and sounds may seem to fade in and out. The neuropathy is a serious impairment, but not as severe as Allegra's almost total hearing loss.

Javier and Corinne recognize that Sonia's level of attainment may be lower in each of their languages—just as it will be in English when she learns it—than that of a child without her challenge, but they willingly accept the extra effort both they and the child will have to make so that Sonia will feel firsthand the bonds to her parents' native cultures. For Javier and Corinne, those cultures are much more meaningful than the more generic American culture that they feel surrounded by in the small city in New Jersey where they live. Javier was a teenager when he first began to understand and embrace his Argentine roots. He made several trips to Argentina, and was amazed how "at home" he felt there. Now, back in the States, he is very involved in the activities of the Argentine community in his city. Although he grew up in the U.S., it is his American identity that feels secondary to him.

Sonia is still young, but at age three, she speaks some words of her mother's native Dutch and is also making progress in Spanish with the use of a system her father has found, called "cued speech." It will be a challenge to find an appropriate school placement for Sonia, no matter how many languages she is learning, but the parents are dedicated to continuing their home language efforts to supplement a normal English curriculum that accommodates her need for extra hearing support. So far, it seems that her intermittent hearing is permitting her to speak with relatively normal voice quality, but it is still too early to determine how well she can remain within the normal limits for syntactic and semantic development.

Case Study 36: Sebastian—Bilateral Cochlear Implant

Sebastian's parents in Germany feel a similar passion for their children's bilingual upbringing. His parents are not native speakers of English, but they think it is important for the children's future for them to be bilingual and bicultural. They have an English au pair and sent their first son to an international preschool where the children are not taught in German until they are fluent in English. When Sebastian, their second son, got meningitis at five months, he lost his hearing. They thought he would not be able to continue learning two languages. Sebastian got two cochlear implants at eleven months, and as soon as the parents saw that he was making progress in German, they called in a speech therapist who had experience with bilingual children. They began training Sebastian in the English sounds as well as German, and, in general, did everything with Sebastian that they had done with the first child, but more carefully. They separated the language input by person (German from the parents and English from the au pair) and also sent him to the international preschool.

When I saw films that his therapist had made of him at age five, Sebastian and his two brothers were singing and imitating a rock star on an imaginary guitar and having an uproariously good time. The film was recorded in Germany, but all three boys were speaking English. Ironically, Sebastian is better in English than his normally-hearing brothers. The therapist does not know whether that is because he is a better language learner or because the parents were more meticulous in following all the "rules" for bilingual upbringing with him after the fright of his meningitis. The therapist notes that the mother had been a preschool teacher and is exceptionally good at working with children and at getting lots of responses from them (like the teacher we saw in the Burns-Hoffman study reported in chapter 2).

Making the Right Decision

Sometimes it is hard to know when you should listen to what others are telling you and when you should thank them politely for their advice and then ignore it completely. As parents, it is normal to feel insecure about whether we are doing the right thing, because we will not know the ultimate outcome of our child-rearing practices for fifteen or twenty years. There is a fine line between confidence in what you are doing and stubbornness about it. Experience tells us that, most of the time, things work out for the best, but we must be alert to signs that something might be wrong and that we need to change what we are doing.

Treatment of language and cognitive disorders in children who speak two languages is still as much an art as it is a science. Many people who consider themselves qualified to give advice about language—teachers and pediatricians in particular—usually have no special knowledge about bilingual language development and may even have misinformation about it. Clinicians with knowledge of dual language development and disorders are rare. Even they have what Genesee and his colleagues call an "insufficient knowledge base," so they do not always follow evidence-based treatments. They must rely on their clinical intuitions. At least, if those intuitions were developed through training on the outcomes of *bilingual* language-impaired children, they would be more sensitive and have more appropriate expectations for the bilingual child.

The advantages of childhood bilingualism are present even when problems arise in language or other domains. What may change is the weight of the disadvantages. Only in rare cases, as Genesee and his colleagues caution, will dropping one language, especially a first language, solve the language problem. Often, it will cut children off from their most effective sources of help. However, it may be that, with the impairment, the disadvantages outweigh the advantages and parents need to reevaluate earlier decisions and strategies.

When a child has these extra hurdles to first language learning, the parents may find, like the Kosters, that the additional effort of a second (and third) language, is more noticeable both to parent and child than if the child had no impairment. The practical value of the minority language in their daily lives could be too limited to outweigh the potential frustration the child may face, and there may be no resources available to use the heritage languages in the child's therapy. Because the parents are already integrated into their home language communities, they take on the responsibility of being the child's bridge to the extended family and their culture, more consciously, perhaps, than if the child had more language-learning facility.

In taking all factors into consideration, the total welfare of the child and the family is paramount, not the goal of achieving bilingualism.

Usually the child's general welfare and the child's bilingualism can be served by the same course of action. You can comfort a child, build her self-esteem, and guide her toward independence in two languages as easily as in one. However, if one has to choose between the second language and the child's well-being, health and welfare win out over the second language every time.

CHAPTER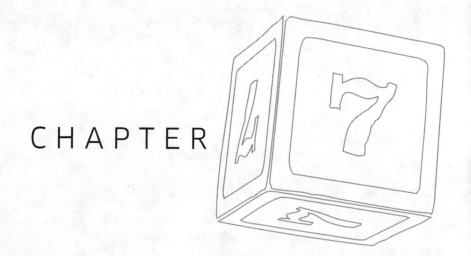

Research Comparing Monolinguals and Bilinguals

You may hear from others—or may be worried yourself—that learning two languages will harm your children. By far the most frequent concern is that learning a second language too early will take away from the first language. The second most frequent fear is that learning two languages and trying to be part of two cultures will create confusion about identity. Chapter 8 is devoted to the identity question. In this chapter, I consider different kinds of research evidence to help answer the following questions related to the advantages or disadvantages of becoming bilingual.

- Are bilinguals slower language learners? How do they compare with monolingual children on developmental language milestones?

- Is it better to start at birth with two languages? Do children do worse or better in either language if they wait until they begin school to learn the majority language?

- Can you learn two languages "additively," or does one language inevitably "subtract" from the other?

- What do standardized tests tell us about how bilinguals compare to monolinguals?

The short answers are:

- No, bilinguals are not slower in language development than monolinguals when comparisons are made carefully between groups of children. With respect to most developmental language milestones, bilinguals are either at the same level as or ahead of monolinguals.

- One need not begin with two languages at birth, but it is often desirable. Children do better in the minority language if the majority language is not begun until school, and they do no worse in the long run in the majority language if it is not introduced until school.

- Children can learn two languages additively, but we must exercise care not to allow one, usually the majority language, to subtract from the other.

- Finally, there are *no* tests standardized on bilinguals, so the use of existing standardized tests is categorically wrong for bilinguals. We can, however, examine data from the limited tests available and evaluate their results in light of what we know about bilingual development.

This chapter elaborates the research evidence behind these answers.

Is Bilinguals' Language Development Slower (or Faster or Neither)?

Lucia, one of our parent-respondents, says in exasperation:

> *"I have read everything and its opposite, and I'm quite confused. If there is a scientific study with statistics on the advantages and disadvantages of being bilingual that could allow us to decide clearly, 'yes it's good,' or 'no, it's bad,' I would be interested in such a study."*

In fact, there is no such study—and for good reason. We can never prove clearly, once and for all, that being bilingual is either good or bad in every instance. We cannot truly prove whether childhood bilinguals are slower in developing their language than they would be if they were monolingual. There are really two claims here—not just that bilinguals score higher or lower than monolinguals on a variety of linguistic and academic measures, but also that being bilingual is the cause of their being ahead or behind. Scientifically, what is required to prove both parts of either claim—that being bilingual makes children more or less advanced than monolinguals—is not available to us. The required experiment is not possible.

Showing that bilingualism is associated with slower or faster language development for some individuals or groups of children is relatively easy; we can make comparisons and relate measures of language development to the number of languages spoken. However, the second part, showing *causality*, is much harder.

Suppose we found that bilinguals were better than monolinguals on every measure we could think of. That would still not be enough to decide the question. We would not know if they were better *because* they were bilingual, or because of some other factor we had not ruled out. Bilinguals may get better schooling; they may come from families that provide more resources. It may be that parents who are imparting two languages to their children spend more time with their children than they would if they didn't feel responsible for providing the extra language. If we could arrange for a set of families with all the same background and resources to treat their children in a manner absolutely equivalent to that of bilingual families but not impart two languages, we might find that it is not the languages *per se* but the extra care that contributes to a superior outcome.

Lack of Experimental Studies

In medical research, for example, when scientists want to see if a new drug cures cancer, they must show not only that people who take it get better, but also rule out all alternative explanations. They do this by using an *experimental design*. Everything about all the subjects' backgrounds and treatments must be the same except the use of the drug being studied. The "experimental" group gets the drug, and a "control" group gets a placebo, which is a treatment that looks and feels like the experimental treatment but substitutes a sugar pill for the drug. The most crucial element of a true experimental design is random assignment. If there are other factors that might influence the results, people with those factors must be just as likely to be in the control group as in the experimental group. Subjects are assigned to groups randomly—for example, by picking a number out of a hat. Then, when one compares outcomes between the groups, if the experimental group does better, we can say that the drug *probably* caused the difference.

There have been no true experimental studies that compare monolingual to bilingual upbringing—and there never will be any. We cannot just go into a major metropolitan hospital and assign every other baby to be raised bilingually. Even if that were not completely out of the realm of possibility (and ethical behavior), it is equally improbable that, for the fifteen or twenty years it takes for a child to grow up, the only factor affecting how the children in the groups developed would be the number of languages spoken to them over the course of their lives.

Alternative Studies

We can never get around the obstacle to the experimental method presented by the fact that families choose bilingual upbringing for themselves. However, that does not mean we are completely helpless in our attempts to weigh the benefits of one course of action over another. We can make many shorter-term comparisons between groups and try very, very hard to make sure that our groups are equal in as many respects as we can, using what is called a "quasi-experimental" design.

Although we cannot attain a level of certainty beyond a shadow of a doubt, we look for evidence from as many sources as possible and see how many of the findings point in the same direction. In the following sections, we will look at the evidence that has been accumulated in the following areas:

- Developmental language milestone comparisons
- Early versus later introduction of the majority language
- Standardized tests

EVIDENCE FROM DEVELOPMENTAL LANGUAGE MILESTONES

Even some people strongly in favor of childhood bilingualism express the opinion that children make slower progress when they start out in two languages than they would if they were trying to master just one or one at a time. In fact, much of the research on early development fails to support that opinion. Early language milestones are remarkably similar everywhere around the world, regardless of which language children are learning or how many languages they are learning. As with learning to walk, all children take about the same amount of time to produce their first syllables, words, and two-word combinations. Both the average age and the wide variability around that age appear to be universal. Because parents everywhere are focused on these events, we have observations from large numbers of individuals and large numbers of different groups. Everywhere around the world, these landmarks happen at approximately six-month intervals—with mature babbling appearing at around six months of age, first words at around twelve months, and first two-word combinations at around eighteen months.

Everywhere, too, the windows around those averages are very large, approaching five months on either side of the mean for first words and six months plus or minus for first phrases and two-word sentences. So, while the figures are consistent around the world, great variation is also the rule. Therefore, within your neighborhood or your family, language development may not seem uniform at all. One average child may have a recognizable word at eight months, and another equally average child at sixteen months. I have seen a very precocious child with a word or two at only seven months and intelligent children who wait until seventeen months before they utter their first words.

Children who reach their milestones even later may still be "normal," but the timetable is consistent enough that if at ten months your baby is producing only vowels and no consonants, it is worthwhile to test his hearing. If the child is later than seventeen months in uttering a first word in any language (including sign language), you can have his hearing checked, and then you and your doctor can seek out measures of "symbolic behavior" (such as the *Communication and Symbolic Behavior Scales* of the First Words Project at Florida State University).

Given these robust behaviors and large windows of normal variation, it will be very difficult to find monolingual-bilingual differences greater than the very large differences within the monolingual or bilingual groups individually. In fact, the bilingual groups that have been examined are squarely in the middle of those norms we do have.

MATURE BABBLING

This milestone is a fairly sudden change from the primarily vowel-like vocalizations infants make before they master the coordination to make consonants and say them in sequences (such as "dada," "ada," or just "ba"). No matter what language or languages they are exposed to and will eventually speak, all children at this stage sound more or less the same. Psycholinguist Kimbrough Oller and colleagues have shown that this "canonical babbling" develops quite reliably between five and eight months in typically-developing children, and failure to babble by eleven months can be the first sign of a later-developing (or later-discovered) neurological problem.

In Oller's study comparing monolingual and bilingual babies, the average age for each group to produce mature, canonical babbling was 27.3 weeks and 26.7 weeks respectively. The bilinguals were an average of four days earlier. Four days is not a significant delay for the monolinguals, but it is also certainly not a delay on the part of the bilinguals.

FIRST WORDS

Similarly, research on first words shows that groups of bilingual babies begin to produce words at the same time as monolingual babies speaking the same languages. In both monolingual and bilingual populations, some children say their first words by ten months, while other children do not start until seventeen months or even later. The University of Miami Infant Studies, an older Canadian study by Doyle, Champagne, and Segalowitz, and more recently, Laura Petitto and her lab at Dartmouth have all found the average first word onset of their monolingual and bilingual groups to be within the same time frame.

THE BEGINNINGS OF GRAMMAR: TWO-WORD SPEECH

In early syntax, the picture is less clear because there have been no widespread statistical summaries of monolinguals in many different languages for us to compare against. The evidence we can find is specific to the children and constructions being studied. Nineteen months is the average age at which two-word combinations appear (e.g., "More cookie" or "Find Grover"), but it is not considered a danger sign until after twenty-four months if the child has not yet begun to put two words together. No studies have yet polled large numbers of parents about their bilingual toddlers' early phrases, but extensive reviews of the literature like those by de Houwer (1995) and Genesee, Paradis, and Crago (2004) conclude that both the rate of development and the stages bilingual children go through in learning various grammatical constructions are similar to monolinguals'. Based on their own work and that of a large bilingual first language acquisition research project led by linguist Jürgen Meisel, Genesee and his colleagues assert that bilinguals follow the same course and rate as monolinguals in each language in many aspects of their development, "from the sound system to grammar." Although more research needs to be done, there is no controlled comparison to my knowledge that indicates that bilinguals take longer than monolinguals to start putting words together according to the rules of their grammars.

So, "onset" measures are very robust. Despite great differences in child-rearing practices in different cultures, these language systems seem to "mature" at about the same time in all children.

EVIDENCE FROM OTHER LANGUAGE LANDMARKS

Other, smaller landmarks on the path to learning language have also been shown to be equivalent between monolinguals and bilinguals.

Recognizing the Native Language

One of the very first language skills researchers have been able to isolate in newborns is that they can recognize the language they were overhearing during their time in the womb. There are several different ways to test what infants hear, but the principle is the same—that babies get bored with one sound. When you first play a sound, babies pay attention briefly and then lose interest. If you then play the same sound again, the baby goes "ho-hum" and doesn't respond, but if you play a different sound, the infant perks up to see what's new. The babies' responses are recorded differently according to their ages. While babies are still in the uterus, researchers play two different languages for them through a microphone inserted right next to the uterine wall, and they watch for changes in heart rate. Once babies are born, researchers use different measures of the speed of their sucking or their looking preferences, as well as their heartbeat.

In the early 1990s, Moon and colleagues showed that two-day-olds can distinguish the sounds of their language from those of an unfamiliar language if the overall rhythms of the sentences are different between languages. Their tiny subjects could tell English from French and Japanese because they have different rhythmic structures, but not English from Dutch, because the rhythmic structures are very similar. By five months, English-learning babies could distinguish English from Dutch, too. At that same age, bilingual Catalan- and Spanish-learning infants could distinguish both of their languages from other languages and from each other.

Learning Phonetic Contrasts Used in Your Language

Bilingual babies also share the same timetable as monolinguals for learning the phonetic contrasts used in their languages. Recall that learning the sound system of your language is a process of learning which sound contrasts are important in your language. Once the baby knows that, she learns to ignore the sound differences that the language she is learning does not require.

According to the famous experiment by Janet Werker of the University of British Columbia, at six months, babies are all "universal listeners" and show equal interest in all sound distinctions, even many their parents do not appear to hear. By twelve months, they become more selective and ignore contrasts that they have not been hearing in the language spoken around them, while remaining responsive to the contrasts that are found in their language. So when you play pairs of sounds—for example, r followed by r, r followed by l, etc.—six-month-old Japanese babies signal that l and r sound different to them, but by twelve months, they already treat them as the same sound, because r and l are variants of one sound category in Japanese.

This test has been done in several ways with bilinguals, too. Catalan, for example, makes a distinction between two e's, roughly the difference between the vowels in "bait" and "bet," but Spanish treats them both as the same sound. Three groups—Catalan monolinguals, Spanish monolinguals, and Catalan-Spanish bilinguals—were tested on the distinction. All three groups, at four months, reacted to the two sounds as different sounds, but at twelve months, Spanish-learning babies treated them as the same sound. Only the Catalan and Catalan-Spanish bilinguals continued to be able to tell them apart.

Similarly, Canadian researchers testing French-English bilinguals found the same thing, but the story was a little more complex because the contrasts they tested were more complicated. The same sound must be interpreted differently in the two languages. For example, as we saw in chapter 3, the French p and the English b are the same sound when you measure them on a laboratory instrument, but the sound works one way in French and another way in English. In French, this sound (the French p/English b) contrasts with the French b, an easy distinction for French people to hear, but these two French sounds are both heard as b by English speakers. The same thing happens in the other direction, where this sound (the French p/English b) and the English p both sound like p to a French listener. A bilingual, therefore, has to switch his or her interpretation of that shared sound, hearing it as b when speaking English and as p when speaking French.

Like French-speaking adults, the French-learning babies at twelve months heard the English p and the English b as the same sound. Like English-speaking adults, the English-learning twelve-month-olds heard the French p and the French b as one sound. That is, both groups made the appropriate contrast for their language and ignored the other. The bilinguals as a group attended to both contrasts, but at twelve months and again at fourteen months were somewhat less successful on them than the monolinguals were. When the researchers looked at individuals within the group, they found two response patterns. Half of the bilingual babies distinguished one or the other contrast—just like the monolinguals. The other half of the bilinguals discriminated both contrasts. One type of responding cancelled out the other type, so the group average did not reflect either pattern.

Dominance patterns, which we see here may develop by the end of the child's first year, make measurement of bilingual groups difficult. It looks like a jury might say, "Bilinguals acquire this sound contrast discrimination skill later; score one against bilingual." But they do not lag behind monolinguals in acquiring the skill; it just takes longer for the skill to be measurable in bilinguals as a group. In fact, some bilinguals were doing as well as monolinguals, and others were doing better than monolinguals. However, their group results might be interpreted to mean that bilinguals are slower in contrast discrimination development if the reporter is not careful to look within the group.

We will return to the question of dominance later in the chapter.

USING CLOSE PHONETIC CONTRASTS FOR WORD LEARNING

In a new series of experiments, Janet Werker and Chris Fennell of the University of British Columbia have taken infants' phonetic learning into the realm of word learning to see when children can use their knowledge of close sound contrasts (like *b* versus *p* in "bin" versus "pin") to learn a word. They paired two objects with either a regular word or a nonsense word and taught the pairings to infants. Then they tried to see whether the babies would notice if they switched the pairing. So, in the training phase of the study, the experimenters showed the babies a short movie of a star-like object and called it a "sug." Then, in the next phase of the experiment, they showed the baby the star-like object, but this time, they sometimes called it a "sug" and sometimes called it something else—for example, a "dib." The test was to see if the infants registered surprise when the object was paired with a different, "wrong" nonsense word.

At fourteen months, the children seemed to notice when the experimenter used the wrong word for the object in the video. They could recognize it especially well with common, one-syllable real words, like "ball" or "star," and they could also do it with non-words that were very different from each other, like "dib" and "sug." When Werker and Fennell tried to teach the babies non-words that differed by just one sound, the way "bed" and "dead" do, fourteen-month-olds could not successfully perform the task—but seventeen-month-olds could. When the researchers tried the same experiment with bilingual babies at seventeen months, the babies couldn't tell the difference between these closely contrasting sounds, but they could at twenty months.

This looks like the first concrete example of a process that might slow bilinguals down in learning vocabulary. They are three months slower to use a minimal sound contrast to learn a word. This may be the earliest evidence we have of bilinguals starting to fall behind in language development relative to monolinguals. But does this really signal a disadvantage?

Will it interfere with real-world early words? Babies' words at this stage are rarely so alike as "bih" and "dih." They are learning "juice" versus "milk," "up" versus "down," and "yes" versus "no." So children can be learning words in their homes just fine without being able to do the laboratory task. It might even be helpful for bilinguals *not* to be too quick to dismiss a possible category. They may be saying, "I know that 'bih' and 'dih' are not quite the same for speaker A, but maybe they are the same for speaker B. Let me just make sure before I decide against it." So, this apparent slowness may be a useful strategy.

MAKING THE SOUNDS OF THE LANGUAGE

Young children's ability to hear and understand speech sounds is prodigious, but in their ability to reproduce what they hear, they are all rank beginners. It takes several years for them to be able to reliably make the sounds that they can hear. Direct teaching seems to be of no help. You may have tried, like I did:

Child: Pishie!

Me: Yes, those are fishies. Can you say "fishies"?

> *Child: Pishie.*
>
> *Me: Fffffff . . .*
>
> *Child: Fffff . . .*
>
> *Me: ishies.*
>
> *Child: ishie.*
>
> *Me: Fffff . . . isshies.*
>
> *Child: Ffff . . . ishie.*
>
> *Me: Good. So, what are they? What do you see?*
>
> *Child: Pishie!*

In phonology, as with first words, there are very wide ranges of normal articulation—and until age three, we really have no norms. In one of the University of Miami infant studies, we conducted a standard phonological assessment in Spanish and in English with thirty-six-month-old children and compared monolingual and bilingual groups to each other.

The monolingual children were in the average range on the assessment of their phonological development. As with word learning, there were large differences even among children who were all "typical." Some children at age three spoke almost all of their sounds in the adult manner; others produced just the most basic sounds correctly—*p*, *d*, and *t*, but not *r*, *s*, *th*, or *l*, which are notoriously hard for English-learning children, as illustrated by the cartoon sentence, "I taught I taw a putty tat" (where *t* is used for *th*, *s*, and *k*). Likewise, almost no Spanish-learning children could make the *rr* sound, as in "ferrocarril" (railroad); they were also unlikely to pronounce the consonants at the ends of words, as, for example, in the Spanish word "flor" (flower). The bilingual children were somewhat more likely than the English-only children to leave off the final consonants, but they were more likely than the Spanish-only children to use them when they were called for.

The bilingual babies' performance was equivalent to that of the monolinguals. There were no statistical differences between the monolingual Spanish toddlers and the bilingual toddlers in Spanish or between the monolingual English children and the bilingual children in English.

Becoming Intelligible Speakers

The University of Miami Infant Studies project also looked at how soon children begin to make the sounds that are unique to their languages in a recognizable way, so that listeners know what language they are hearing. For example, *p* and *t* are not unique to either language spoken by Spanish-English bilinguals (i.e., they sound rather similar in both languages). By contrast, the Spanish *r* and the English *r* are pronounced very differently.

For monolingual speakers, we found little evidence of language-specific sounds in babbling or even in early words. For her dissertation, University of Miami graduate student Ana Navarro used "blind" testing techniques to see if bilingual adult listeners could identify enough language-specific sounds in children's early words and phrases to tell which language the child was using, even if the listeners did not understand the word they were hearing. In the blind testing, listeners heard the child's taped voice alone—they did not see the child, and they did not know whether they were hearing a boy or a girl, a Spanish learner or an English learner, or a bilingual.

Navarro found that listeners could hear very few language-specific sounds in the speech of monolingual children, even that of twenty-six-month-olds. In this out-of-context presentation, listeners did fine with adult utterances, but understood less than one-quarter of the utterances of the children, regardless of whether they were spoken by a monolingual or a bilingual child. (Remember, the words were all intelligible in context, or else Navarro could not have used them in the experiment.) When the listeners did not understand a word or phrase, they also did just as poorly at identifying which language it was spoken in. They were able to correctly identify the Spanish utterances spoken by the monolingual Spanish children about 62% of the time, and they could tell which were the English utterances when they were spoken by monolingual English children at about the same rate. For four out of ten children in each monolingual group listeners were never able to tell (better than guessing) whether they were speaking English or Spanish.

Of the ten bilingual children in the experiment, seven were able to communicate to the listeners which language they were using. Three communicated intelligibly in Spanish only, and three in English only. Only one child was able to do this in both of her languages. That is, she clearly produced language-specific sounds in Spanish and language-specific sounds in English as well. Statistically, the bilingual children were neither ahead of nor behind their monolingual peers, but their equal performance was found in only one of their languages.

Navarro's experiment also illustrates that part of the subjective impression of a bilingual child's slowness may be "slowness" on the part of the parent, not the child. Even if a bilingual's first words are objectively as intelligible as a monolingual's—which they clearly were in this experiment—it may be harder for parents to find the words in what the bilingual child says to them. It will be harder for the parents to understand if they don't know in advance which language to listen for. Consider a baby-word like "apu," a fairly common child's rendition of "apple." Especially if there is an apple in the scene, one might be able to interpret an English-learning child's "apu" as "apple." But the same word is not far from "arbol," the word for "tree" in Spanish. A Spanish-learning child, especially one pointing to a picture of a tree, might say "apu" to mean "arbol." If we hear the same "apu" from a bilingual child, it will be harder for us to anticipate which one he means. One of our parent-respondents, Radha, reported that this had happened to her. She was so focused on her son's Tamil words that she missed his first English words. Another couple, also listening for the "other" language, in their case, French, realized, after hearing it for about two weeks, that the child was saying, "Wha dat?" (for "What's that?").

This may be one advantage of the OPOL and mL@Home household strategies over the MLP (Mixed Language Policy). Those household strategies help parents anticipate which language they will be hearing, so they can understand the very young child better.

THE "LEXICAL SPURT"
So, if bilinguals are not slower at the outset, do they fall behind later?

Thanks to a new assessment tool developed in the 1990s, we now have records of how many words—of a standard set—children learn at different ages between ten and thirty months. The original versions of these *Communicative Development Inventories (CDIs)* were made for Italian and English, but once people saw how useful they were, adaptations were created for many different languages. The word "inventories" implies that these are exhaustive lists, but it is not necessary to count a child's every last word to get an idea of how he compares to other children his age.

Parents are given a list of about five hundred common words that are drawn from the words babies often know—words for foods, toys, animals, body parts, etc. Parents check off whether the child, up to sixteen months, understands a word but doesn't say it, or, up to thirty months, understands *and* says a word. A database of responses from over a thousand children gives us a much better idea of which words children are most likely to know and, at each month, how many words the average child (the 50th percentile), the faster child (75th and 90th percentiles), or the slower child (25th and 10th percentiles) will know.

We see from the monolingual children who were sampled to establish the norms for the *CDI* that about two thirds of children have a "spurt" in their vocabulary growth curves around the middle of their second year. Until then, babies learn early words in isolated instances. With their first twenty-five or fifty words, they don't seem to have picked up the general principle for how to do it quickly. At a certain point, it's as if a light goes on and the baby realizes that everything has a name. They start going around asking, "What's this?" "What's this?" "What's this?" What had been slow growth up until this point turns into a spurt. They begin learning about twenty or more words a month for several months. (The growth in new words seems to slow down when they turn their attention to beginning syntax.)

Most bilinguals also experience this lexical growth spurt at the same time that monolinguals do. In one of the University of Miami infant studies, we graphed eighteen bilingual children's word learning at several points from ten to thirty months. While we found that children were growing typically in both languages, only their growth in one language or the other—or in both languages together, but not individually—showed a spurt. Martin, the child in our study with the largest and fastest-growing vocabulary, for example, added a spectacular ninety words a month in

Spanish from sixteen to twenty months of age, more than four times what we used as the cutoff for saying that there was a spurt. However, while his English was also making steady progress during that period, (at around the 50th percentile), it was not at the same explosive rate, so it did not qualify as a spurt. Over the next time period, Martin's Spanish slowed down, and his English showed a spurt.

To qualify as having a growth spurt in both languages at once, the bilingual children would have to score higher than 85% of the children who take the test, and the growth would have to be parallel in the two languages. Martin was well into the top 15%, and several other bilingual children in the study were in the top 25% of all of children for rate of word learning, but none qualified as having a spurt in two languages at the same time. Still, their growth was well within the normal limits for monolinguals.

Tracking growth rates in vocabulary is one area in which we can see important differences in children's development according to which language (or languages) they are learning. This was demonstrated in a study of French-, English-, Swedish-, and Japanese-learning babies by psycholinguists Benedicte Boysson Bardies and Marilyn Vihman. The Japanese babies in the study were slightly slower to reach the ten-word landmark than children in the other three language groups. When the authors investigated to find the reason for this apparent delay, they found that the Japanese "baby-words" were slightly longer than the baby words the other groups were learning, so the Japanese-learning babies had more to learn than the others. The difference was in the languages, not in the babies. So when we look at different language learners, we can expect that some differences in children's language development are not related to the capabilities of the children but to structural differences across languages.

The Size of Early Vocabularies

Here, too, in tracking the bilingual children's vocabulary growth in two languages, we begin to experience some of the difficulties that make comparisons on the same measures between bilinguals and monolinguals such a problem. One issue, as mentioned above, is that the same measure may have different meanings in two different languages. The second problem is that, no matter what the languages, the same measure does not represent the same amount of knowledge in a bilingual and a monolingual.

Using the Communicative Developmental Inventories, it looks like comparing a bilingual's English vocabulary to the norms for English speakers and the bilingual's Spanish vocabulary to the norms for Spanish speakers should be very easy. Counting the number of words on the child's English *CDI* and the number of words on the child's Spanish *CDI* is straightforward. But then what do we compare it to?

A word is a pairing of a consistent sound associated with a meaning, but what are we counting? The sounds? The meanings? Or the pairings? When a child associates the sounds "d-o-g" with the small animal, he is pairing one "word-form" ("d-o-g") and one meaning or concept referring to the animal. If the child associates the sounds "dog" and "perro" ("dog" in Spanish) with the same animal, there are two word-forms, but just one object in the world, or referent. Is that the same as knowing two referents for two word-forms, such as "dog" (paired with an image of a dog) and "cat" (paired with an image of a cat)? The association of "dog" and "perro" with the animal entails the same number of word-forms and the same number of pairings, but one less referent.

For the monolingual, the number of words tells you the number of word-forms, the number of referents, and the number of pairings. But for the bilingual, the number of pairings is not necessarily the same as the number of referents. If you count word forms, you may be giving the bilingual child credit for more referents than the child actually knows. If you count the number of referents, you are not taking into account enough word-forms *or* enough pairings. In addition, the bilingual has at least one additional piece of information associated with each word form—that is, a "tag" to tell which language it is (which a monolingual toddler has no inkling about).

Using a *CDI* in each of the child's languages, one of the University of Miami infant studies devised a way to count and report either concepts (referents) or word-forms to compare the bilinguals' word knowledge to the word counts for monolinguals. Practically speaking, we had two lists: the child's words in Spanish on one and the child's words in English on the other. It was useful to keep them separated for some purposes—for example, to help us gauge which language was stronger for the child at that point. But to compare the number of objects in the world that the child could name, what we called the "Total Conceptual Vocabulary," between monolinguals and bilinguals, it did not make sense to ignore the portion of the child's words in the other language. Because some of their words in each language were translation equivalents (TEs—like the "dog" and "perro" example above), the second language term for those pairs did not expand the number of concepts the child could talk about, so we were careful to count TEs only once.

The Total Conceptual Vocabulary is an improvement over making single-language comparisons, but it still underestimates bilinguals' word knowledge. There are two problems with trying to count the pairings (that is, just adding the words on the Spanish *CDI* list to the words on the English *CDI* list). First is the problem described above: you'll get the bilinguals' total word-forms right but not necessarily the right number of referents, and you are not crediting the language "tags." The other problem is that the number of words a child is credited with on the *CDI* has everything to do with how many words are on the form. The monolingual has only five hundred alternatives, whereas the bilingual has one thousand. Our solution was to get all of the information separately—word-forms or pairings (Total Vocabulary), meanings with word-forms associated with them (Total Conceptual Vocabulary), words in English, and words in Spanish. That way, we could document the complexity of bilinguals' word knowledge and make several comparisons more flexibly.

For the University of Miami Infant Studies, we started by confirming the *CDI* averages on a local monolingual population so that we could compare our bilinguals to children growing up in similar conditions and being assessed in the same way. Then we compared the Miami group's scores with the bilingual children's scores. Our research looked at receptive vocabulary in twelve bilingual children from ten to sixteen months of age and expressive vocabulary in twenty-five bilinguals from ten to thirty months of age. There were two comparison groups: one group of children learning English monolingually and another group learning Spanish monolingually. (However, because there were no norms for Spanish-learning children at that time, the Spanish monolingual group is not represented in the graphs that follow, and the comparisons in Spanish vocabulary development for the bilinguals are approximations for illustration purposes only. Note that the Spanish *CDI* norms are now available.)

The results for *receptive* vocabulary are shown in Figure 8. The bilinguals seemed well ahead of the matched monolinguals in receptive, or comprehension, vocabulary. The monolingual English learners and the bilinguals in Spanish performed at approximately the 30th percentile (based on the norms for the English *CDI*), and the bilinguals were at approximately the 25th percentile in English. The difference between monolingual English learners and bilinguals in either English or in Spanish was not statistically significant. However, when we counted the Total Conceptual Vocabulary, the bilinguals' totals were significantly higher. Thus, it appears that in *receptive* vocabulary, bilingual infants are well above monolingual levels in the number of labels they can recognize for things in the world.

Figure 8: **Receptive vocabulary comparison for bilinguals and monolinguals**

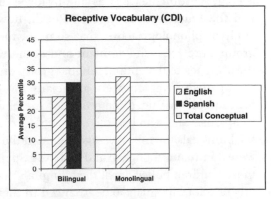

The monolinguals in each language were ahead of the bilinguals in *expressive* vocabulary in each language individually, but even the rather large difference between the groups—in Figure 9 below, the difference between the 17th (bilinguals in English) or 15th percentile (bilinguals in Spanish) and the 34th percentile (English monolinguals)—was not statistically significant. When we counted Total Conceptual Vocabulary, instead of just vocabulary in a single language, even the non-significant difference between the monolinguals and bilinguals disappeared, and the group scores were practically identical.

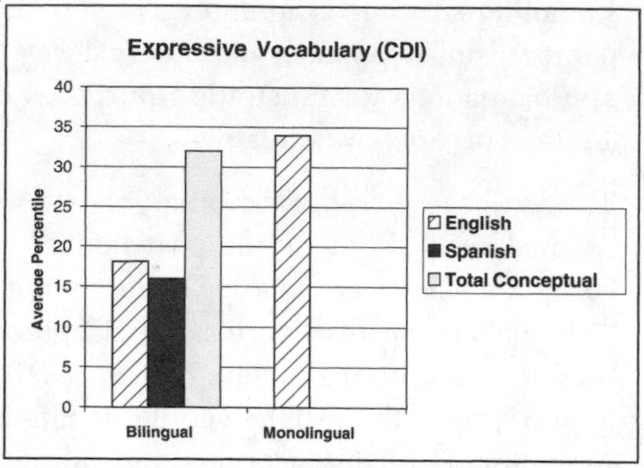

Figure 9: **Expressive vocabulary comparison for bilinguals and monolinguals**

COMPARING APPLES TO APPLES:
USING THE BILINGUAL'S DOMINANT LANGUAGE

When we compared the monolingual and bilingual vocabularies of the toddlers in the University of Miami Infant Studies, the bilinguals' average score on the *CDI* was slightly lower than that of both the Spanish and the English monolinguals. Recall, however, from Ana Navarro's study of phonology above, that some of the children in the bilingual group were Spanish-dominant and some were English-dominant, so the averages of the entire bilingual group on the English inventory and the Spanish inventory were artificially low. Their average in English, for example, included the scores of the children who were dominant in Spanish and who had relatively little exposure to English. Likewise, the bilinguals' Spanish average included the scores of the children who were dominant in English and had little Spanish. The Spanish scores of those children pulled down the bilinguals' average in Spanish. Because it is rare for bilinguals to be balanced in their two languages, counting their weaker score as well as their stronger score gives an erroneous picture of their actual skill in vocabulary. We must remember to split the bilingual group scores according to the children's dominant language before we make such comparisons. After all, the comparison is to the monolinguals' dominant language—that is, their only language, which is dominant by default. In Ana Navarro's experiment, as well as the lexical measures, splitting the bilingual group by dominant language made the difference between the monolingual and bilingual means disappear completely.

So far, we have concentrated on early development and on areas where the method of measurement is a problem. Our last two domains are areas where the focus is on the conceptual knowledge of the child—where the language is important, not for itself, but as a way to know the level of the child's *concepts*. Here, the important issue is to conduct the measurement in the language that tells you the most about the children's concepts. In these domains, bilinguals do not score lower than monolinguals, especially when they are tested in their better language.

TELLING MATURE STORIES

As we discussed in chapter 2, children up to age five are busy mastering the grammar of sentences. Much of the development that takes place after age five involves making links across sentences. Mature speakers organize information into texts or larger structures of discourse according to the conventions of their language. One of the most important of these larger structures is the narrative: a story with a beginning, a middle, and an end, which recounts events in the past and also provides some interpretation of the events for listeners. Narrative forms are both language-specific and universal; they are one of the ways that children (and adults) make sense of the world they live in.

Psychologist Jerome Bruner distinguished the "landscape of action" from the "landscape of consciousness" in narratives. Children need to master both. They have to be able to recount a chain of events or actions in a chronological order that will not confuse the listener, and if there is more than one character involved in the story, they have to progress beyond calling everyone "he," for example, so that listeners will always know who did what to whom. However, more important than recounting the actions themselves, narrators have to make listeners *care* about the actions being recounted. They do that by bringing the landscape of consciousness to life: they explain the characters' motivations and their own reactions to the events of the story. The ability to do this combines conceptual and linguistic development in fascinating ways. Children learn to understand what others are thinking when it is different from what they themselves think, and they need to be able to use and understand the complex language required to express those thoughts—for example, "She thought that there were crayons in the box, but it was really candy."

A worldwide study of how *monolingual* children learn to relate events in narrative form, based on one particular "frog" story, has been going on for the last twenty years. The story—*Frog, Where Are You?*—is a wordless picture book by children's author Mercer Mayer. Researchers Dan Slobin of the University of California, Berkeley, and Ruth Berman of Tel Aviv University coordinated studies of children ages five, seven, nine, and eleven, and adults in five languages—English, Hebrew, German, Turkish, and Spanish—all telling the frog story under similar conditions. Their primary findings were published in a book in 1994, but work with the frog story continues and has been done in at least eighty languages and with several groups of bilinguals and trilinguals. There are no standard scores here, but the Berman and Slobin studies give us a good idea of what kinds of developments one can expect at different ages. They also indicate which elements of narratives tend to be same across many different languages and which elements differ when told by speakers of different languages.

What do *bilingual* children do? In the University of Miami Language and Literacy Study of bilingual elementary school children, I used the frog story to compare bilingual children's stories in English with the same story they told on another day in Spanish. The bilingual participants had different language backgrounds that we matched to each other very carefully, and we also compared them with monolingual children of the same ages and socioeconomic status, at second grade and fifth grade. When we looked at how well the stories provided information about the "landscape of consciousness," we saw that the level of the child's story in one language matched the level of the story in the other language— even for children with unequal grammar skills in the two languages. When we compared the bilinguals' stories in their dominant language to the monolinguals' stories, we found that, on a number of elements, especially vocabulary and word endings, the bilinguals were sometimes still not up to the level of their monolingual peers. At the same time, however, they were as good as or better than the monolinguals with respect to the more demanding narrative elements: clear reference to characters, complicated time relationships between events, and descriptions of the characters' thoughts and desires.

READING

Reading, too, is a skill that is, to a large extent, independent of the language in which it takes place. There are different ages at which children growing up in different countries are expected to learn to read. In the U.S., children begin with the alphabet in preschool and kindergarten, and they are expected to learn to read in first grade, at age six. In Sweden, the schools wait until children are seven before introducing reading. Learning to read is generally more difficult than learning to speak, and reading presents specific difficulties to large numbers of children (and adults). Estimates are that approximately ten percent of young monolingual children experience dyslexia, a reading impairment.

What about bilinguals? It is not known whether the percentage of dyslexics is higher or lower for bilinguals, especially those who learn to read in two languages. However, the University of Miami Language and Literacy Study showed that by fifth grade, there were no differences in reading scores between the monolingual and bilingual groups. Significantly, this project also showed quite strongly that bilinguals were not handicapped by learning to read in two languages. In fact, they did better in both languages when they learned to read in two languages rather than only in one. (Compare this to Bialystok's results in chapter 1 as well.)

Latino children who learned to read in Spanish as well as in English did better at reading in English than those who did not learn how to read in Spanish at all. It is not too surprising that performance in Spanish of children with instruction in Spanish would be better than that of children with no instruction in Spanish; the big payoff was that the children who learned to read in Spanish as well as in English also did better at reading in English.

I see many bilingual education programs making elaborate schedules for how to stage the introduction of reading in one language with at least a year between it and another language. I have never understood why. When reading is introduced in both languages at the same time, non-English-speaking children get the benefit right away of learning to read in a language that they are already comfortable in, and they do not delay getting to English.

So, for these twelve language landmarks, there is no clear evidence that groups of bilinguals are slower at learning language than comparable groups of monolinguals.

Which Is Better—Two Languages from Birth or a Second Language Second?

Can we say whether it is better to learn two languages from birth or to wait until the child is five and let the school introduce the second language? This question has two sides, depending on whether you focus on the majority language or the minority language. Constance, one of my survey respondents, worried about the majority language:

> *If I emphasize Greek so much when the children are little, will it hurt them when they go to school and have to do everything in English, which will be a brand new language for them? Should I try to teach them English as well as Greek in my home so they will not be behind in English when they go to school?*

Pilar worried about the minority language:

> *If I introduce English in the home, will it diminish the children's abilities in Spanish? Am I better off waiting until they go to school before introducing English?*

The short answer is "no" to Constance and "yes" to Pilar. The evidence from the University of Miami Language and Literacy Project indicates that, at least in the U.S., there is almost no difference in English achievement between bilinguals who were exposed to English and Spanish equally in the home from birth and those who had been exposed to only Spanish in the home and first started to learn English when they began to attend school. For that reason, there is little motivation to have English in the home. (One may have other reasons for it, but English achievement should not be the sole motivation.)

On the other hand, there is a relatively large advantage for children's abilities in the minority language when the majority language is not spoken in the home until elementary school.

English Achievement

The University of Miami Language and Literacy Study of bilingual elementary school children was designed to address questions like those posed by Constance and Pilar. As explained above, it was not a true experimental design, because no one can manipulate who speaks English in the home and who doesn't, but although it didn't have random assignment, it had careful control groups. That is, we selected the participants so that they would differ on just one point and be as equal as possible on everything else. The children being compared were in the same schools, they lived in the same neighborhoods, and their parents had the same levels of education. The standardized mathematics scores of the groups were equivalent, and, of course, they were the same ages. In response to the questions posed in this section, I focus on the home language differences.

Half of the bilingual families reported that they spoke English and Spanish in the home, approximately half of the time each, and the other half used only Spanish in the home until the children went to school. In each home-language group, half of the children attended Two-Way Immersion bilingual schools and half were in English-only schools. The study tested kindergarten, second grade, and fifth grade children on nine standardized tests in both English and Spanish as well as on a series of probe study measures focused on more specialized skills. I report the fifth grade results first, because those represent the longer-term, more permanent results.

When overall scores for the fifth graders on the nine standardized tests in English were averaged separately for the children with only Spanish in the home versus those with English and Spanish in the home from birth, the difference was not dramatic. The English scores for the children with English as well as Spanish in the home were barely two standard score points higher than the children with no English in the home. This was not a statistically significant difference. So, there was very little gain in English scores from having English in the home.

Unlike the fifth grade results, at kindergarten, there was an early advantage in English for the children with English and Spanish at home. At the time of that testing, the only-Spanish-at-home children were still very new to English. The difference in their daily exposure was still a very great proportion of their total exposure to English. As they got more contact hours in English, the daily difference became less noticeable— just as you would miss $1 more if you only had $2 than if you had $2,000. The advantage the children with English in the home had in English was restricted to oral language tests, especially vocabulary tests. The advantage was statistically significant in kindergarten and second grade; it had disappeared by fifth grade. By then, the Spanish-at-home children had caught up. On the other hand, children with English and Spanish in the home had no advantage in English reading and writing skills, not even at kindergarten or second grade.

Spanish Advantage
The advantage to Spanish development by *not* having English in the home was significant at kindergarten (especially for expressive vocabulary), and the advantage continued through fifth grade. As in English, there was no benefit in reading and writing in Spanish from having only Spanish in the home—presumably because those skills are not particularly supported by the oral language spoken in the home. When all nine scores (both written and oral) for the fifth graders were combined, the advantage to the children's Spanish of having no English in the home was about four points—statistically significant but not dramatic.

Add the Help for the Minority Language from the School
When a similar comparison was made, this time between Latino groups with English only *in the school* versus those in the Two-Way Immersion programs, the results in English were quite shocking. The English-only advantage at fifth grade was barely one point in the standardized scores. There was a small advantage in English vocabulary at kindergarten that disappeared in three of four subtests by second grade and disappeared on *all* subtests by fifth grade.

By contrast, the two-way schools benefitted children's Spanish by an average of ten standardized points, a very significant difference. The advantage was greater than ten points for children with less Spanish at home, and it was "only" eight points—still a very strong difference—for children with only Spanish at home. Furthermore, the advantage of the two-way school in Spanish was *not* present at kindergarten, so the advantage seen at fifth grade for the two-way school in Spanish appears to be entirely due to the children's experience of the school. The benefit of the half-day taught in Spanish to children's Spanish scores was very large, while from the same program, the loss to their English scores was very small.

BILINGUAL PRESCHOOL

Thus, parents like Constance who worry about not giving their children the benefit of starting school ahead of the game by already knowing English may want to consider a bilingual preschool for the child. This will give the child a head start in English in a sheltered atmosphere but will also support continued growth in the minority language. If children start early in a monolingual preschool, they get the idea early—when their minority language is still not well established—that English is all that matters, so I do not recommend an English preschool at a time when you could be solidifying the child's command of the minority language. In a nationwide study of a thousand families, researcher Lily Wong Fillmore of the University of California, Berkeley, showed that families whose children went to English-only preschools were five times more likely to switch to English in the home than families of children who went to minority-language or bilingual preschools.

In the research for this book, I met several parents who recounted that very experience. For example, Rakhmiel and Rose spoke only Yiddish with their son Ari until the second week of English preschool. As Rakhmiel recounts twenty-five years later, he and Ari would count the steps as they came up out of the church basement where the preschool was held—"Ein, zvei, dri . . . ('One, two, three' . . .)"—until one day Ari countered with "four, five, six, seven, eight." Rakhmiel says that from then on, Ari was no longer interested in speaking Yiddish with them. I suspect that the transition was more gradual, but it is revealing that Rakhmiel's memory locates the switch so precisely in the stairwell leaving the preschool.

Meanwhile, four-year-old Marianna is currently enrolled in a bilingual preschool in Michigan. She still speaks only Spanish in her mother's household and in her father and stepmother's household, too, but she is getting an introduction to English at a bilingual preschool. Having

Spanish alongside English in the preschool sends a clear message to the child that Spanish is important, too. It is unlikely that Marianna will abandon her first language early, as Ari did. As the University of Miami Language and Literacy Study shows, it is not essential to learn English before school, but it is important not to drop the minority language when English is introduced.

Other Concerns about When to Start Two Languages

LANGUAGE FORGETTING

In this connection, I recall the diplomat who boasted that his children had learned seven languages—and forgotten six of them. Traces of the different sound systems seem to remain with young learners throughout their lives, but it is amazing how quickly the use of a language can be reduced to a few simple greetings and names for relatives and foods—if it is not continually reinforced. Even adults who have not been speaking their other language for a while will take some time to "switch their minds" back to that language when they need to. But with adults (and, I will say, children over ten), if they spoke another language well, it is like riding a bike—it comes back even after many years without practicing it. Children under three who leave one language environment for another seem to lose the language that is "out of service" completely within a short space of time. Four-year-olds lose it only a little less quickly. Besides, as Olga points out (Case Study 4 in chapter 5), parents have the greatest control over their children's language patterns when they are young. That is the time when you want to build their skills in the minority language and help them want to keep using it. If not, you may wake up and find that what you so carefully nurtured in the first three or four years of the child's life is gone.

EXAMPLE OF THE IMPERMANENCE OF THE LANGUAGE

Nancy, one of my child bilingual resource people (now grown), recounts that Spanish was her dominant language after she lived in Chile with her parents for the three years, from ages three to five. She spent most of her time there with Spanish-speaking housekeepers and their families, to the extent that recordings of her Christmas greetings to relatives in the States during those years sounded like they were from a little Chilean child. She imitates herself on those recordings in the stereotypical accent: "Dear Uncle Susie and Aunt Ralph, Santa Claus came and left me two pieces of crumb." When she returned to the U.S. and started first grade, she still had a strong Spanish accent in her English and was put in the reading group for Spanish speakers even though her family was not Spanish speaking.

From this early experience, Nancy's identification with Spanish was very strong, so she was shocked, she says, when she went to Mexico at age ten to live with a Mexican family and was not able to speak a word of Spanish. She opened her mouth to speak and nothing came out. It took more than a week for her to recover her Spanish and begin to make progress in it. The same thing happened the following summer, although this time, she did not panic about it, because she knew that the Spanish would come back. By then she was almost a teenager, and her Spanish has since remained with her.

ADDING A LANGUAGE WITHOUT SUBTRACTING FROM THE FIRST

I have encouraged additive bilingualism by continuing support for the first language when a second language is added, but I must acknowledge that my argument does not go both ways. The minority language does not take away from the majority language, but the majority language does take away from the minority language. So if you add a minority language, the majority language will not be diminished, but if you add a majority language too soon, or without specifically providing support for the minority language, the minority language may decline prematurely— before the majority language is in position to take its place.

In an ideal world, we would not want to envision either language taking the place of the other. In the world of official French and English in Canada, where Wallace Lambert coined the terms "additive bilingualism" and "subtractive bilingualism," it was easier for him to envision two languages on an equal footing. But in the United States, no minority language is on the same footing as English. None has the currency that English does. No language (alone, without English, too) will let your child earn a living in it here, get an education, or follow the presidential elections. So, parents of bilinguals in the U.S. must be careful to insure strong English skills along with the minority language.

Before rushing to English, though, it is important to remember that the first language provides the foundation for the languages that come after it. A strong foundation in the first language facilitates the development of subsequent languages.

We can imagine graphs representing subtractive and additive bilingualism like this.

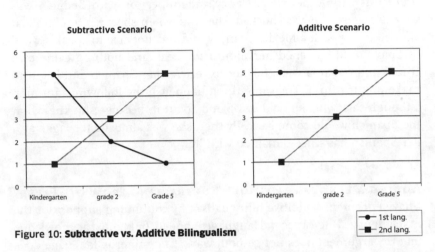

Figure 10: **Subtractive vs. Additive Bilingualism**

During the period when the first language is declining and the second is still growing, the child might essentially have no age-appropriate language. This is not such a far-fetched scenario. It is easy to imagine a child speaking a language like Romanian in the home and with the extended family until she goes to school at age five. Then, the parents, who are learning more English themselves, decide that because the child needs English at this point, they too will switch their home language to English and reserve Romanian only for special occasions, visits from abroad, and so on. In this case, the child's Romanian declines quite quickly, and her English is building quite slowly. (Canadian researcher Cummins estimates that it takes a child two to three years to develop oral language skills and five to six years to achieve age-appropriate levels of literate language.)

For a child only a few years older, the situation is quite different. The first language is more firmly established and less likely to desert the child. I have a colleague who came to the U.S. in 1956, when she was nine years old. It was a sudden transition, and she spent some time unable to participate in her classes the way she had done in her native Hungary. The school officials were going to put her back a grade, but she was ahead of her class in math. If they put her back a year, she would be even further ahead of the lower grade. So she stayed where she was, in a "sink or swim" situation. Luckily she already knew how to "swim" in Hungarian—she could read and write and had begun learning science concepts already—so she could stay afloat long enough to learn to swim in English, too. She doesn't remember how it came about, but within the first year, she could speak and understand and do most of the things she could do in Hungarian in English as well (and went on in English to get a Ph.D.).

Using this same logic, one would not wait before adding a second minority language—and would hold off on introducing the majority language until they were both well established.

STUDIES DEMONSTRATING ADDITIVE BILINGUALISM
Given a choice, everyone would opt for adding a second language to the first rather than replacing the first with it, but many people are unaware that there is a choice. They feel they have to choose between their two languages. It seems like common sense to them that if they take the time out of adding the second (majority) language to maintain the first, their child's progress in the majority language will be slowed. In fact, the logic is the opposite. If schoolchildren use the first language to learn the second, their progress in the second language will be faster.

Language researchers Hakuta and d'Andrea provide a powerful illustration of additive learning for minority language speakers learning English. These researchers studied three hundred eight Mexican teenagers in California. They gave them several tasks in both English and Spanish. In the graph in Figure 11 below, comparing English scores to Spanish scores, the children are grouped according to a system the researchers devised to capture fine-grained differences in the teenagers' backgrounds. In particular, for those born abroad (Depths 1 to 3), the key was the age at which the child arrived in the U.S. (younger than five, between five and ten, and after age ten). Among those born in the U.S.

(Depths 4 to 6), Hakuta and d'Andrea found that the critical variable was how many of their parents were born abroad. In the legend for Figure 11, I have lined up the authors' "depths" with the more common description of immigration history, by "generation."

Figure 11. Additive bilingualism in immigrant families*

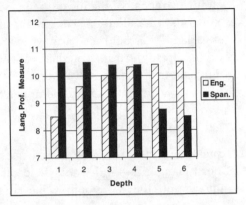

Legend:

1ST GENERATION

Depth 1—born abroad, children came to the U.S. after age 10

Depth 2—born abroad, came to the U.S. between 6 and 10

Depth 3—born abroad, came to the U.S. by age 5

2ND GENERATION

Depth 4—born in the U.S., both parents born abroad

Depth 5—born in the U.S., at least one parent born in the U.S.

3RD GENERATION

Depth 6—at least one grandparent (and parent) born in the U.S.

Figure 11 shows the scores the six groups of bilingual teenagers earned on a language task they did in English and in Spanish. The pattern of results does not follow the generations. Depth 3 (a subset of the first generation) and Depth 4 (a subset of the second generation) were the strongest bilinguals—the most balanced, with the highest scores in both languages. These are the first generation children who came to the U.S. by age five and the second-generation children who were born here but *both* of whose parents were born abroad. What do these two depths have in common? Early exposure to English (begun by age

* From Hakuta, Kenji, and D. D'Andrea. "Some Properties of Bilingual Maintenance and Loss in Mexican Background High School Students." *Applied Linguistics* 13 (1992): 72–99. By permission of Oxford University Press.

five)—in order to have strong English—and parents who speak mostly Spanish in the home—in order to have strong Spanish.

This graph makes a strong case for additive bilingualism. Depths 1, 5, and 6 seem to show that either the Spanish or the English score can be high, but not both. If we looked only at those three groups, we might want to agree with those who say one language takes away from the other. But Depths 3 and 4 strongly contradict that view. The children in Depth 3 and especially Depth 4 have identical scores in English and Spanish, and they are both high. These two groups have both the motivation and the opportunity for maintaining Spanish. When we look at the relationship between English and Spanish, we see that the children's English skills rose very quickly within the first generation, at a time when Spanish skills were still at a peak. English did not wait for Spanish to "disappear" to rise to native or near-native levels. It was well established along with high Spanish scores. The sharp decline in Spanish came *after* the rise in English: in this illustration, the decline came two "depths" later, at Depth 5. Not coincidentally, after Depth 4, Hakuta and d'Andrea found a strong shift in the *parents'* language as well from using mostly Spanish at Depth 4 to using mostly English at Depth 5. Compared to Depth 5 and 6 parents, Depth 4 parents also had stronger ties to their country of origin and went back there or had visitors from there more often.

What Do Standardized Tests Tell Us about How Bilinguals Compare to Monolinguals?

I have concentrated on arguments in favor of becoming bilingual, but you will also see studies that say bilinguals get lower scores than monolinguals on common standardized tests of student achievement. What are you to think when you see headlines declaring that bilinguals are pulling down scores for their schools on standardized tests across the nation?

Some of these headlines will be based on faulty studies. They may be making an uneven comparison, using an inappropriate measure, or in some other way reporting slanted information. Some of them, though, will be based on true differences between bilinguals and monolinguals. In those cases, I want to make you aware of yet another potential flaw in the argument. In some cases, the comparisons that they are based on may be valid, but the inferences drawn from the comparisons are not. The areas of the most persistent differences will be principally vocabulary and morphosyntax (described in chapter 3). Those focused areas relate to broader language skills and intelligence differently for bilinguals than they do for monolinguals.

Unequal Comparisons

Bad testing of bilinguals has a long history. In the sections that follow, I take up various problems with testing, especially with standardized tests that are, at present, categorically inappropriate for bilinguals.

The earliest studies comparing bilinguals' and monolinguals' language development and intelligence from the 1920s and 1930s failed to match the groups on anything but age, and there were many more differences between the children being compared than just their monolingualism or bilingualism. Most of the monolinguals were middle-class children familiar with test-taking. Most of the bilinguals were new immigrants unused to the situation of testing and not acquainted with many of the situations that were the background for the items in the test. For example, a fellow professor at the University of Miami remembers that when he came to the U.S. from Hungary, he was given a common IQ test, the Wechsler. To this day he remembers one question he missed about how to make change for a dollar. Because Hungarian children in those days were not supposed to handle money, he was not only unfamiliar with the nickels, dimes, and quarters in the pictures but also with the whole concept of making change. Despite being more advanced than most American children his age in mathematics, he missed the question. For many years, little thought was given to whether a test was culturally fair to the people taking it.

Socioeconomic Status (SES)

Since the first days of the Civil Rights movement in the U.S. in the 1960s, numerous studies, including our University of Miami Language and Literacy Study, have shown that socioeconomic status (SES) has a large effect on children's standardized scores—so much so that some people claim that the SAT score is more highly correlated with parents' income than with scholastic aptitude.

In the University of Miami Language and Literacy Study, we were able to demonstrate this strong association of SES with scores in a bilingual Latino population having a wide range of SES. The Latino population of Miami is not like other immigrant communities in a number of ways, especially in the range of social classes found there. The Latinos in Miami—Cubans and other Central and South Americans—are not predominantly of a lower socioeconomic status than the monolinguals, as is the case elsewhere in the United States. Latinos in South Florida are bankers, lawyers, politicians, doctors, and so on. A large proportion of them are politically powerful and economically well-off. Because of the wide range in the sample, we could compare Latinos of high SES to Latinos of low SES and also compare them to non-Latinos of high SES, and we could compare Latinos of low SES to non-Latinos of low SES, instead of the more usual comparison between non-Latinos of high SES and Latinos of low SES. In fact, in this Language and Literacy Study, SES was the strongest statistical effect (after age) for all the English tests (but not the Spanish tests). In many comparisons, the difference between high and low SES *within* the language groups (both bilingual and monolingual) was greater than the difference *between* the language groups.

Because most bilinguals in the U.S. are immigrants, and most immigrants have lower socioeconomic status than the leaders of the Latino community of Miami, a large proportion of studies of bilinguals are done with low-SES bilinguals. Any time a study does not specifically explain how the researchers took SES into account, it is almost certainly flawed in that respect. That is, unless the authors state otherwise, we can assume that comparisons of bilinguals and monolinguals confound language background and SES, and we can be skeptical of their findings.

LANGUAGE EXPERIENCE

To make matters worse, old-fashioned research mostly done in the 1920s and 1930s often tested the bilinguals in a language they did not know or had just started learning. I don't think my IQ would be very high if it were measured by a test I took in Russian, a language I studied in school for only two years. I would be justified in saying that the test did not measure what it was supposed to measure—or what it measures for people who speak Russian fluently. Conversely, when studies did not confuse language exposure for language ability, the comparisons of language scores were not so one-sided.

The research tide turned in the 1960s with the study done by Peal and Lambert, two Canadian researchers, comparing bilingual and monolingual children in a school in Canada. Here, bilinguals were doing better than monolinguals. They were more divergent thinkers, better problem solvers, and ahead in content in school. These studies, however, suffered from another flaw: a self-selection bias. Rather than being randomly assigned, children in the bilingual school had chosen to go there, so their motivation might have been greater, while the comparison group attended their neighborhood schools. Furthermore, the researchers chose for the study only children who were balanced bilinguals—so they may have also selected only the strongest students among those in the bilingual program. It makes sense to screen out individuals who were essentially monolingual with just a smattering of experience in a second language, but the preselection potentially invalidates the comparison.

Faulty Predictions

College Entrance Exams and Bilinguals' Academic Success

Parents in a professional family voiced to me a specific concern about how their bilingual children would do on the college entrance exams. Maya asked, "If our children do not hear sophisticated uses of English vocabulary in our dinner-table conversation with them (because we use another language), how will they do well on their college entrance exams, which depend so heavily on advanced vocabulary?" Her concern is not unfounded: college entrance exams present an unfair obstacle to bilingual students, but not just for the reason Maya feared. I will discuss below some issues related to vocabulary, but a study I did at the University of Miami illustrates how college entrance test scores made the bilingual students look weaker academically than they were.

When Spanish-English bilinguals do badly as a group on their tests, the large standardized testing companies claim to be "just the messenger." They say it is not the test's fault; it's that the bilinguals are not well prepared. This assertion was hard to accept at the University of Miami, where Latino bilinguals are among the better students. They are not poorly prepared, they do well in their classes, and they graduate on time. In fact, with the help of the Office of Institutional Research there, I was able to compare the grade point averages (GPAs) after four semesters of all the Latino bilinguals who had entered the university in a given year with those of all the monolinguals who entered the same year: 2.96 versus 2.95 (on a scale of 0 to 4). The bilingual students' GPAs were .01 higher than the monolinguals'. That's not a significant difference, of course, but it also makes it safe to say that these bilingual students were not worse students than their monolingual peers.

Then I looked at their Scholastic Aptitude Tests (SATs), both Verbal and Math. The bilinguals' average score on the SAT was 50 points lower (on a scale of 200 to 800) than the monolinguals' on both the Verbal and the Math subtests. That *was* a statistically significant difference. So what was going on? The SAT is supposed to be a predictor of how students will do in college, and, in fact, the University of Miami had a policy at that time not to accept students with SAT scores lower than 525 on each section unless there were exceptional circumstances. But here was a group of several hundred successful students who had an average SAT subtest score of 500, clearly below the cutoff. If the SAT were the only item in the students' portfolio, none of these highly successful students would have been admitted. I did a statistical test to find out whether the SAT scores and the grades were related systematically. There was indeed a statistical relationship between SAT scores and GPA for each group separately. For the monolingual students, an SAT Verbal score of 550 was shown to "predict" a GPA of 2.95. For the bilingual students, an SAT Verbal score of 500 was shown to predict a GPA of 2.96. We can only speculate as to what it is about being bilingual that made the SAT score of a successful bilingual student lower than the score of a successful monolingual student. However, in that study, it is clear that the SAT was not "just the messenger." The test was clearly giving the wrong message about the bilinguals as a group.

LACK OF A PROPER REFERENCE GROUP FOR BILINGUALS
I suspect that all standardized tests are a little off in their evaluation of what average performance for bilinguals is. I can make that statement

with a high degree of confidence because there are no standardized language or intelligence tests that are normed on bilinguals (although I'm glad to report that such tests are under development). Thus, at present, *no* standardized score quite fits a bilingual.

A standardized test score is basically just a score that expresses how the performance of the individual taking the test relates to the average score earned on that test by a group of people who were specially selected because they share characteristics with the individual you want to evaluate. The people selected for the norming sample—usually one hundred or more children at each age—take the test, and their scores are analyzed. A standardized score of 100 on a standardized test with a mean of 100, for example, means the person with that score was right in the middle: half of the people in the norming sample got a higher score and half got a lower score. A norming sample based on the general U.S. population includes in it the same percentage of white middle-class children, white working-class children, African-American middle-class children, African-American working-class children, Latino children, Asian-American children, Native American children, and so forth, as found in the last U.S. Census. The average score (50th percentile) for the norming sample is called 100, and then the test developer calculates the 80th percentile (approximately) and makes that a score of 115, the 20th percentile (approximately) becomes 85, and so on. If a child's score is lower than 85, you know that the child's performance is comparable to that of the lower-scoring children in the norming sample.

Invalid Inferences from Standardized Test Scores

Vocabulary tests make a good illustration of the consequences of having the wrong reference group to compare to. Single-language vocabulary scores even of very able bilinguals tend to be lower than those of monolinguals of a similar background. A comparison to a monolingual norming sample compares monolingual to monolingual on 100% of their vocabulary. Unlike a monolingual child, a bilingual child has words for some of the concepts he knows in one language and words for other concepts he knows in the other language. There will be some portion of his words for which the child can answer equally well in either language—those that are translation equivalents of each other.

But even the most balanced bilinguals have some words they know in one language and not the other—for both languages. In a number of studies, we found that almost all of the participants, especially children, had some vocabulary that they knew in only one language, even in their weaker language.

So, if you give a Russian-English bilingual a standardized test in English, you will give him credit for words he knows in English and not in Russian, and his standard score will be lower than what the sum total of his two languages would yield. Similarly, if you give him a standardized test in Russian, you will credit words known in Russian but not in English. That score, too, will be artificially low. Neither score counts all of the bilingual's knowledge, and neither score compares it to an average for other bilinguals of a similar background and similar language exposure. Even a balanced bilingual who has the advantage of being tested in both languages—including his stronger one—will have two slightly low scores that don't represent the totality of what he knows.

A single-language measure of vocabulary may be instructive for some purposes—for example, to plan an instructional program for a child based on his knowledge of a particular language. However, vocabulary is often used as an indicator of more general academic aptitude. With monolinguals, the inference is usually justified, but with bilinguals, we see clearly that it is not.

In a recent reanalysis of the data presented in the book *Language and Literacy in Bilingual Children*, we found what psycholinguist Kim Oller, our coauthors, and I call a "profile effect." Monolingual students with low scores in vocabulary were generally low across the board. So for monolinguals, low vocabulary scores predicted low reading and writing scores, and one has cause to worry that a limited vocabulary is a marker of limited skills generally.

You cannot make the same inference for bilinguals. Bilinguals with low scores on vocabulary tests were no less likely than bilingual children with high vocabulary test scores to do well on the other tests. The study provided clear evidence that low vocabulary test scores are not at all a marker of poor skills generally for bilinguals.

Vocabulary, as you recall from chapter 2, is the part of language that has the least specialized processing and that has no critical period. We learn it all our lives. And the specific vocabulary learned in one language will not be much help in learning vocabulary in another language (until a much later age). So vocabulary takes time, and it is directly related to the amount of exposure.

RELATION OF MORPHOSYNTACTIC ACCURACY TO OTHER LANGUAGE SKILLS

In addition to vocabulary, there is another area where persistent differences are observed in the rate of acquisition of specific structures. The other area where even careful comparisons often favor monolinguals is morphosyntax (as introduced in chapter 3). As we saw in chapter 3, morphosyntax is a level of language between the lexicon and syntax (in our "language tower" in chapter 2) that governs how words are put together and used appropriately in sentences. Morphosyntactic accuracy involves some fine points of grammar, especially word forms and word endings. Because the bilinguals have less exposure to the structures in comparison to monolinguals, they appear to take longer than monolinguals to learn those forms. One can know the general principles of how words are combined in a language but not know all of the particular lexical items that may be exceptions or where the rule may apply slightly differently. There are currently no norms for bilinguals that will assess whether a child is making satisfactory progress in morphosyntax. We do not know exactly how long it takes bilinguals, especially in their non-dominant language, to hear a particular structure enough times in enough different contexts to be able to figure it out in all its complexity. Therefore, there is a period of time when the morphosyntax of bilingual's speech may not match the maturity of the other elements of the child's language (and conceptual development).

In monolingual children, the failure to have developed key areas of morphosyntax—as we saw in the discussion of Specific Language Impairment (SLI) in chapter 6—is taken to be a sign of language delay more generally. In bilingual children, in contrast, it is often just an indication that they hadn't yet had enough time and opportunity to completely learn that aspect of the language. They have not yet reached the learning threshold for that structure. Except in cases where the bilingual child's input may be faulty (as in some communities with few monolingual speakers of the respective languages, like in some Latino neighborhoods in Miami that we observed), children's progress in the sequence of stages involved in learning different constructions is on track but slower, so the lack of some specific forms will not be an indicator of developmental delay. Bilingual children catch up faster than children with SLI.

However, these are very salient errors that can color one's impression of a person's speech generally and result in a negative response to the person out of proportion to the error. I compare it to the impact of spelling errors in formal writing. A document feels less official when it contains even one spelling error, even if it is still perfectly well worded and understandable. We once received a note from our daughter's teacher reporting some incident of her misbehaving in class. The note contained two common misspellings ("it's" for "its," and "definately" for "definitely") that kept us from taking the message as seriously as we should have. Twenty-five years later, we have forgotten the content of the message but remember the spelling. I am not advocating sloppy spelling, but its importance can be overestimated in assessing fluency, especially multiple fluency. Such absolute snap judgments and cultural biases must be tempered by consideration of other factors, as the research within the field is starting to do.

Morphosyntax Tracks Language Experience Similarly in L1 and L2

Even very advanced second-language learners report difficulty with fine points of the morphosyntax, like the endings used for different genders in languages like German or Spanish—for example, "el sapo" (toad) is masculine, and "la rana" (frog) is feminine. They can be correct 98% of the time, but one only remembers the 2% of errors. Our BSG colleague Virginia Gathercole looked at children's knowledge of exceptions to gender rules in Spanish. For example, "agua" is a feminine noun, but the article used with it is masculine—"el agua"—not, as one would expect, feminine—"la agua." This switch may be motivated by phonetic reasons, the way English changes "a" to "an" before a word beginning with a vowel: "an apple," not "a apple." But although it makes sense, it is not applied across the board, so there are other words, like "la audiencia" ("the audience") or any adjectives that begin with "a," as in "la alta muchacha," where the "la" does not change.

Another example of Gathercole's test cases is learning the "much/many" distinction in English. For this structure, like many others she has studied, Gathercole charted a learning sequence based on the stages monolingual children go through as they get more exposure to and hear more instances of the irregular patterns. In English, for example, knowing when to use "much" as opposed to "many" is difficult in ways we rarely think about. It requires children (first or second-language learners) to figure out whether the following word refers to an individual item or a substance and whether it can take a plural or not: "much water" is good, but "much trees" and "much waters" are not; likewise "many trees" is good, but not "many tree" or "many waters." Earlier work by Gathercole showed that monolingual English-learning children master the "much/many" distinction in stages. They first show that they know the basic distinction, recognizing what one can say (around age five), before they reliably reject what one cannot say. The progression is roughly first rejecting "much boy" around age five, and then rejecting "many boy" around six and a half years. At that point, children still accept "many water," which they then reject around age seven, but they still accept "much boys," which Gathercole found that many ten-year-olds would accept as okay.

Her work shows that the stages bilinguals go through in getting the different parts of the structure correct are the same as those that monolinguals go through, but the process takes bilinguals longer, approximately in proportion to the amount of exposure they have to the language where the construction is found. The bilinguals in her study did not show evidence of learning poorly, but of taking longer to get the required amount of exposure for these more advanced elements of grammar.

As a general conclusion, we see that comparisons between bilinguals and monolinguals are tricky and more often than not, downright misleading. Much of what one reads in the press, for example, uses a slanted definition of the word "bilingual." Too often in public discourse in the U.S., the term "bilingual" is used to mean "a person of a low socio-economic status with limited English skills." In many school districts, it is a synonym for "LEP," Limited English Proficiency. However, when you look carefully at comparisons of bilinguals, where bilingual truly means "speaks two languages" and all other characteristics of the individuals being compared are equivalent, you will see equivalent performance. Hopefully, for our bilingual children, one day soon the situation will change, and instead, we will see books and articles asking whether monolingualism is harmful for our children.

CHAPTER 8

About Bilingual Identity

CAN A BILINGUAL PERSON SUCCESSFULLY MERGE two cultures in one individual? In this chapter, I report on comments from people who have reflected on their bilingual upbringing and share their insight—and perhaps their hindsight. I have also consulted bilingual scholars and essayists who have written on the topic. Whether or not the argument has merit, several voices of popular culture raise the alarm about possible psychological harm from growing up bilingually, but childhood bilinguals, themselves, by and large appear to be happy with their experience.

One Culture or Two?

Nina is German, married to a Japanese man, and living in Japan with their two children. She describes their daughter, now age five, as having a "torn character" with "two souls in her little chest," and she worries whether she should have ever started her bilingual project. Like all parents, she wants her children to grow up in a secure environment that will be easy for them to understand. If the family had only one culture, she reasons, her daughter and now her daughter's younger brother would not have to worry about which culture they belong in. Nina thinks she should have waited until her daughter was about seven and had developed a stable personality before introducing a second language. She perceives that the child's personality is developing poorly because of having two languages.

Is Nina right? Would her daughter be better off with just one language? Would the children of international couples, in general, have an easier time if only one part of their heritage is recognized?

Mixed Messages from Waldorf Schools

Nina's doubts about the wisdom of bilingual upbringing for her children intensified when she enrolled her little girl in a Waldorf School in Japan. The principal told her to drop German and wait until the child was seven before starting it up again.

Waldorf Schools are among the most vocal and effective promoters in the world of early foreign language training for children. So it is somewhat ironic that a Waldorf School should discourage an early start in two languages. Their teachers' guides emphasize the importance of more than one language for intellectual development. Suggestions for classroom activities highlight an immersion setting—introducing children from first grade to two foreign languages through songs, poetry, games, and skits, all with a large component of whole-body movement. The writings of Rudolf Steiner, the founder of the Waldorf School movement, are full of eloquent claims for the benefits of early foreign language teaching—how it expands the child's mental and spiritual capacity. Waldorf websites are a treasure trove of ideas for how to make other languages come alive for children. (I have shared some of them in chapters 4 and 5.) Because Waldorf Schools are generally models of foreign language excellence, if there were an argument from its founder against infant bilingualism, I would take it very seriously.

In order to get an authoritative answer for Nina about Waldorf guidelines, I asked the Research Desk at the Rudolf Steiner Library to direct me to Steiner's teachings on the point. They were not able to find a single paragraph for me. Apparently, Steiner was silent on the question of infant bilingualism. It is modern interpreters of Steiner who have written that one should raise children in one language only until they are old enough "to say 'I' to themselves"—which I take to be around age three or four. If, as Steiner *clearly* says, foreign language is a great aid to thought and development, I am mystified as to why anyone would not want to take advantage of an obvious way to increase a child's comfort and success by providing language interactions in two languages from the beginning of life if one has the opportunity to do so.

On the other hand, there are often other practical reasons for delaying the majority language for a child that have nothing to do with the Waldorf philosophy. If one is convinced, as some Waldorf proponents argue, that the child needs a strong grounding in "the unique logic" of one language in order to support and strengthen the child's personality development, it would not be harmful to wait until age four. Many proponents of the Minority Language at Home household strategy give similar advice. Certainly, it does no harm, but as I have discussed above, it has no scientific basis for being considered the superior method for the growth of bilingual children.

One of the assertions made by the interpreters of Steiner I consulted is that when people have grown up with two languages, they "do not feel absolutely sure of either." They tell us about one such person who reports that he "dreams in Spanish, but thinks in English, and speaks whichever language is required by the situation." As we saw in chapter 1, *absolute* assurance in the unique logic of one language or another may be a formula for closed-mindedness. For me, it is a great *advantage* that the bilingual child may understand more than one language and be sympathetic toward the people who speak them.

For the reasons I gave in chapter 7, I do not think science can prove or disprove the statements of Steiner's followers. My own personal preference would be for my child to develop the appreciation of multiple cultures that frequently emerges naturally when children recognize that they are speaking two languages.

Lack of Expert Opinion

How in the world could one determine, even with hindsight, what Nina should have done? I encounter the same problem in making a judgment like this that I did in trying to answer the "better or worse" question about cognitive development in chapter 7. I cannot imagine a study that could answer the question. Certainly, the experimental method is of no help to us here. We cannot assign people in international marriages to live in one or both of their cultures for the duration of the children's growing up. Even if there could be such an improbable experiment, we will see below that there are currently no tools to judge the health of bilingual people's personalities in order to evaluate the outcomes. Therefore, we have no alternative to speculation and opinion. I think Nina and the rest of us must base our decisions on what we want to do and on the testimonials of other people who have grown up bilingually.

There is a large body of literature on personality development, but according to researcher Aneta Pavlenko of Temple University, no one has used an objective social science framework to look at bilingual development. In her effort to show that this is a neglected side of social psychology, she presents a number of horrific pronouncements about the alleged pathology of being bilingual. Nina and others with similar doubts will have no trouble finding extreme, negative statements from "experts" about the dangers of being bilingual. The following statements span the last century. From an 1899 linguist:

> *"A bilingual child's intellectual and spiritual growth would not thereby be doubled, but halved. Unity of mind and character would have great difficulty in asserting itself in such conditions."*

From the British Home Secretary in 2002:

> *"The use of English rather than the native language would help overcome the schizophrenia which bedevils generational relationships in immigrant families."*

Bilingualism has been linked to alienation, emotional vulnerability, disorientation, and rootlessness. Such pronouncements about the error of being bilingual and the virtues of being monolingual sound, frankly, intolerant, based on prejudice, even racism: "We are good; speakers of other languages (including you) are bad." There is some comfort in the fact that these dire pronouncements are all assertions, not evidence. There are no scientific studies supporting them, but neither will there be any scientific studies to refute them.

It is hard to reconcile this negativity with the optimistic statements from bilinguals themselves on their success at "playing roles in two worlds rather than one." In a playful passage, Norwegian-American linguist Einar Haugen says he does not know how he escaped—"if only by a hair's breadth"—the dire developments predicted by the experts, but he ended up with a comfortable allegiance to both his parents' heritage and their adopted country. As our Colombian respondent Ana said,

> *"My identity includes both my languages.*
> *How could I give up either one?"*

The Monoglot Myth

The myth of monolingual superiority, which we encountered in the quotations above, is quite entrenched. Cultural historian George Steiner (not related to Rudolf Steiner) attempts to understand its origin. It is very recent, he says, a by-product of the romantic nationalism of the eighteenth and nineteenth centuries. Politicians and philosophers began to proclaim the genius of their country and language over all others. Their need for purity allowed no incursion of other tongues. Similarly, Steiner sees modern monolingual rhetoric as a way to cast aside "lesser" cultures.

In his book *After Babel,* Steiner discusses the myth of Babel, which he says recurs in many cultures. In Native American lore, it is often a sacred animal that is accidentally killed, or elsewhere, a taboo that is violated in the pursuit of forbidden knowledge (as in the Garden of Eden or the Tower of Babel in Genesis). In the myth, before Babel, there was an imagined single language that was a completely faithful representation of the world—because it was used to name the world. Before Babel, people could communicate directly with God, or with the springs of being. After the fall of the tower—or when the language serpent is cut into innumerable pieces—dialogue is no longer possible, and communication with God becomes the monologue we are familiar with as prayer. After Babel, language no longer translates the world as directly as before.

Steiner himself writes and translates in three languages natively (French, German, and English) to the point that he cannot tell which is his first language. He is grateful for all of his native languages, as well as the several others he has learned as an adult. He rejects various methods people propose to discover one's "true" language: the language you dream in, the language you cry out in during an accident or in love-making, or the one in which you do mental arithmetic. Each of those activities, he says, he does in whichever language he was hearing or speaking most at the time. Steiner writes brilliantly in all three languages and cannot conceive of which ones he would give up to become monolingual.

The Physical Feeling of Being Bilingual

Subjectively, being bilingual *feels* different from being monolingual, and many are aware of it as a physical sensation. The Tamil speaker Radha said she would "switch her hat" to move from one language to the other. There is, in fact, a tiny physical realignment in the posture of one's mouth in one language as compared to another, which may be reflected in a more general whole-body sensation. For example, we can compare the neutral filler vowel in English, which is a low, lax "uh" ("I . . . uh . . . don't know") to the French pause filler, "euh," made higher in the mouth with more tension in the muscles. So the "resting position" for each language is different. Also, differences in characteristic speaking rates for different languages may give speakers a subconscious impression of more or less relaxation when speaking one or the other of their languages.

There are documented cases where the same people give slightly different responses to a questionnaire depending on the language it is presented in and the language used to answer it. Each language has different "cultural frames," the webs of memories and associations pulled up by its words. Studies show that they are switched for different tasks in different languages (hence the name "cultural frame switches"). Different cultural frames can be triggered by the different pronunciations of one's name; for example, author Julia Alvarez reports that hearing the English "Julia" prompts her to extend her arm for a handshake in greeting, while the Spanish pronunciation, "Hoolia," prompts her to proffer her cheek for a kiss.

Several of my respondents refer to the fact that they can say things in each language that they cannot say in the other. It appears to be quite common to be able to swear or talk about subjects in a second language that feel taboo in the first. Our childbirth education group in Miami hired a Panamanian nurse to teach labor and delivery classes in Spanish, only to find that she couldn't use the anatomical vocabulary she needed in Spanish—only in English. The Irish-English poet Nuala Ní Dhomhnaill reports using Irish for emotions and discussions of internal states and English as a bridge to the outside world. One language, she says, is for memory, and the other for future events.

None of this appears to be a source of distress to my respondents, nor to the bilingual authors in the anthologies I consulted (and recommend). Their titles, tellingly, are *Bilingual Writers on Identity and Creativity* and *Bilingual Games*. Many of the authors of the works in these books celebrate the "bilingual mode," like Ilan Stavans's "Love Affair with Spanglish" or Ariel Dorfman's "need to live in two dimensions, inhabited by both English and Spanish in equal measures." The authors claim that their most authentic works combine both languages fluidly. They do not complain of being fragmented but are happy to be "travelers between languages."

Is such "fragmentation" possible? Clearly, it is—but it is not restricted to bilinguals. When a monolingual person feels torn between competing influences in his or her life, bilingualism certainly cannot be blamed for the feeling. If a bilingual feels similar pressures, knowing two languages is often conveniently fingered as the likely culprit.

The Real Experts

According to philosopher of language Anna Wierzbicka, writers who have lived in two languages and two cultures are our greatest authorities on the bilingual mind. Their own explorations of the inside of their own minds are pushed further than would be permissible for another observer. Thus, we can turn to the writings of novelists and essayists who are themselves bilingual for insight into the "bilingual personality." Novelist and essayists—like the child-bilingual respondents who offered me their perspectives on their upbringing—lean more toward the pleasures than the discomforts of being bilingual. Even those who, in Wierbicka's words, refer to themselves as "crossing frontiers of identity" or as feeling split in half like "someone with two exiles and no country" are positive in their overall assessment. None of them regret the "emotional and literary enrichment that being bilingual has brought them."

The sense of exile in writings about being bilingual may be heightened for authors who are not childhood bilinguals. Eva Hoffman's memoir *Lost in Translation* eloquently portrays her struggle to adopt a new identity when she came to a new language—from Poland to Canada—at the sensitive age of thirteen. Her teenage assessment was that she could not continue to be Polish the way she had been and also become Canadian. She judges that her younger sister reached a similar conclusion for herself but, at age eight, had less Polishness to "undo," so the transition appears to have been easier for her. We have no other autobiographies of teenage language learning that are as lyrical and analytical as Hoffman's. Her teen anguish is compellingly portrayed, and the picture of her unease stays with the reader.

Hoffman recently wrote a postscript to her earlier book on language migration. This time, no longer a teenager, her reflections on language are much more comfortable, stemming from the realization that both languages can coexist. She recounts a "sudden leap," when she realized that her Polish would not dislodge her English, as she had let or made English dislodge her Polish twenty years earlier. Her Polish had since been in hiding, but now was "percolat[ing] up like an upward-pushing stream" and coexisting with English in what she calls "one sturdy structure." Her two languages have finally learned to cooperate, rather than compete, and her story is now one of bilingual wholeness, not fragmentation.

The fact is that much of the world is busy crossing borders, and more and more people *are* language migrants. Bilingual writers have discovered that the "space at the borders" of their two languages is a fertile field for creativity, a space for innovation and playfulness. In opposition to those who would purge the country of difference, they encourage stretching beyond a single language, as in bilingual punning: for example, "creative bilingual games" pronounced with a Spanish accent becomes "creative bilingual gains." One Japanese writer speaks of the electricity he feels in his head when he makes connections across great distances. The juxtaposition of familiar things in two languages makes them feel unfamiliar and fresh.

Other writers and respondents just do not feel strained by the so-called split. As Marieke says, "I feel Dutch when I speak Dutch, and I feel English when I speak English." She can be either or both at the same party, depending on who else is there. She can support more causes that are important to her and lend her voice in more debates.

Confusion or Cornucopia

The biblical Babel is generally considered a punishment or a curse, but in George Steiner's view (even when he was a child), language diversity is a great gift. In Steiner's words, "our words create our worlds." The distance between the word and the world creates the possibility for language to "free human beings from the . . . present tense"—to imagine how we want the world to be. Languages, he says, represent our adaptive power. Babel is not a confusion of languages; it is a cornucopia.

Frequently Asked Questions and Alternate Table of Contents

Do you have a specific concern? Jump straight to the appropriate sections of the book to get your answers.

Twelve Common Myths and Misconceptions about Bilingual Children

MYTH OR MISCONCEPTION	WHAT WE ACTUALLY KNOW
Bilingual children start to speak later than monolinguals.	There is no scientific evidence supporting this. Bilinguals and monolinguals share the same wide window for normal development. (Chapter 7)
Bilinguals start out school behind monolinguals and they never catch up.	In fact, bilingual children tend to have faster growth curves than monolingual children. (Chapter 7)
Young children soak up language like sponges.	Children seem to have an easier time learning languages than adults, but we should not underestimate the effort it takes and should not expect them to learn perfectly from the beginning. (Chapter 3)
Bilinguals are just like two monolinguals in one person.	There are special capabilities that bilinguals have that monolinguals do not. Bilinguals very often have one (dominant) language that is comparable to that of a monolingual and another, weaker one, which they use less often. In any conversation, bilinguals choose whether to operate in a monolingual mode or a bilingual mode. (Chapter 3)
You have to be gifted in languages in order to learn two languages at once.	Early language learning is not like a talent and does not require a special gift; it's part of being human, like walking or seeing with two eyes. (Chapters 2 and 3)
If bilinguals score lower on standardized language tests, it shows they have lower aptitude than the average monolingual child.	Standardized tests examine just a part of a bilingual's language aptitude (i.e., just one language) and compare it to a monolingual's entire language aptitude. Average scores for bilinguals do not take into account different patterns of language dominance. There are, as of this writing, no standardized tests that are appropriate for use with bilingual children. (Chapter 7)

MYTH OR MISCONCEPTION	WHAT WE ACTUALLY KNOW
Latino immigrants in the U.S. resist learning English and want everyone to learn to speak Spanish.	Very few Latino immigrants do not speak English; there are not enough programs that teach English to accommodate the demand for them. Programs that use Spanish as well as English do so in part because it helps children learn English faster and better. (Chapter 7)
Some languages are more primitive than others and are therefore easier to learn. The reason so many people can speak English is that English has less grammar than other languages.	There is no such thing as a primitive language or a language without "grammar." All languages are infinitely complex and yet learnable. (Chapter 2)
Speaking a second language is its own reward.	This may be true, but we cannot expect children to see it that way. We must make it meaningful for them to know the language by providing contact with interesting people doing fascinating things in the second language. (Chapters 4 and 5)
Parents who do not speak a language perfectly will pass their errors and their accent on to their children.	This might be true only if the child never heard any other speakers, which is unlikely to happen with parents who are nonnative speakers of either a majority or a minority language. (Chapter 4)
If a bilingual child experiences any language problems in one or both languages, dropping one of the languages will fix the situation.	There is no evidence that this is so. Children who have problems with two languages generally also have them with one. (Chapter 6)
There's only one right way to raise a bilingual child.	Parents are the experts in this field. The only wrong way to raise a bilingual child is not to do it. If you haven't already, now is the time to start.

Resources

In this section, I list major sources of language exposure and information about language learning, as well as suggestions for tapping into them, organized loosely under

- language research and policy organizations,
- minority language schools,
- informal sources of personal interaction,
- media, and
- bilingual speech therapy.

The internet makes the relevant information easier to find than ever before, but also harder to capture in print, because it changes so often.

Language Research and Policy Organizations

Center for Applied Linguistics (CAL)
4646 40th Street NW
Washington, DC 20016
www.cal.org

The National Network for Early Language Learning (NNELL)
P.O. Box 7266, B201 Tribble Hall, Wake Forest University
Winston-Salem, NC 27109
http://nnell.org

Center for Advanced Research on Language Acquisition (CARLA)
University of Minnesota
Institute of International Studies and Programs
Minneapolis, MN 55455
www.carla.umn.edu

(CARLA provides links to listservs, organizations, and journals, as well as resources and advice for parents.)

Europa: Languages and Europe
http://europa.eu:80/languages

Minority Language Schools

Dual-Immersion Schools
Center for Applied Linguistics (CAL) Directory
www.cal.org/twi

(I received excellent cooperation from the parents at one school on their list in particular, the Amigos School in Cambridge, MA.)

Waldorf Schools
www.awsna.org

(Waldorf Schools teach two foreign languages in the elementary grades.)

The Association of American Schools in South America (AASSA)
www.aassa.com

Homeschooling in foreign languages
www.homeschoolingonashoestring.com/fornlang.html
www.homeschooldiner.com/subjects/foreign_language/main.html

(It's hard to find noncommercial sites, but they are there! Foreign language homeschooling has a huge web presence.)

For more information about bilingual education programs and schools, also try contacting language and education departments at local colleges and universities, as well as cultural attaches in embassies.

Informal Sources of Personal Interaction

To supplement your efforts, consider these sources of exposure to other languages outside the home. Embassies, cultural centers, and houses of worship can also put you in touch with others interested in the language and culture of other countries.

Camps
Concordia Language Villages
www.concordialanguagevillages.org

(These camps offer a variety of programs in a broad selection of languages at a wide range of prices, including full-family activities for those with children too young to go to camp on their own.)

KidsCamps.com
www.kidscamps.com/academics/language.html

(This database of camps across the United States and Canada allows the user to search by region for language camps, including a few immersion programs.)

Yugntruf Youth for Yiddish
www.yugntruf.org

(The organization offers a one-week program in Yiddish during the summer but has activities throughout the year.)

Danish Sisterhood of America
www.danishsisterhood.com/default.asp

(This specialized organization sponsors Danish language camps.)

Child-friendly study abroad
www.umflint.edu/departments/internatl/child.php

(A good source of information on international study programs for people with children.)

Newsletters and internet sites
Bilingual Family Newsletter
www.bilingualfamilynewsletter.com

(Since 1984, this newletter has been providing short articles for a worldwide community. Based in Britain, it now accepts PayPal, a real advance in ease of subscribing. The newsletter offers the comfort of something to hold in your hand but the ease of internet contact.)

The following internet sites provide constantly changing information, resources, and access to other parents.

www.multilingualchildren.org

(See especially their guide for starting a playgroup, "Peer pressure at its best.")

www.bilingualfamily.org

(Resources, support, information, and a marketplace. "Once a day" section encourages daily visits to the site. Also publishes an e-magazine, *Multilingual Living.*)

www.bilingualfamiliesconnect.com

www.bilingualbabies.org/modules/news

(*Bilingual Babies* is an international source based in Britain.)

www.nethelp.no/cindy/biling-fam.html

www.enfantsbilingues.com

www.mehrsprachige-familien.de

www.literacytrust.org.uk/talktoyourbaby/Bilingual.html

http://humanities.byu.edu/bilingua/index.html

(This website provides helpful information especially for nonnative parents.)

Household help
Au pair agencies

www.aupairusa.org

www.efaupair.com

www.euraupair.com

Advertising for household help through colleges or universities and houses of worship in neighborhoods with high concentrations of minority-language speakers will also give you contact with people who can become your network through which to find a household helper. Posting an advertisement in the language you want the person to speak may catch such a person's eye.

Media
There is an explosion of media available in different languages, as well as bilingually. (Note: I have no ties to any of these—except the Living Language section of the Random House website, *www.randomhouse.com/livinglanguage.*)

Books and other media for children
www.multilingualbooks.com/index.html

(More than just books can be found at this site.)

www.afk.com

(*Asia for Kids* provides access to Asian language-learning resources.)

www.csusm.edu/csb/english

(The *Barahona Center for the Study of Books in Spanish for Children and Adolescents* site features searchable databases of recommended books in Spanish and books about Latinos.)

www.lectorum.com

(*Lectorum* claims to be the oldest and largest Spanish-language book distributor in the United States.)

www.mantralingua.com

(This site offers bilingual books in English and any of twenty-two different languages.)

www.milet.com

(This site features lots of titles in lots of languages and accepts PayPal.)

www.alphadictionary.com/indow.ohtml

(Search online for dictionaries or for words directly from a selection of twenty-four languages.)

Songs
http://songsforteaching.com

(This site encourages using music to promote learning in all subjects, including languages.)

Toys
www.spanishtoys.com

(This site offers a good selection of toys, with lots of distribution points in the U.S.)

Books for parents
See the "For Further Reading" headings associated with each chapter in the References section.

Bilingual Speech Therapy

There are still relatively few speech and language therapists who have the background and training necessary to work with bilingual children. These sources should help you find someone in your area to consult, at least for a second opinion.

American Speech and Hearing Association (ASHA)
www.asha.org

Bilingual Therapies
www.bilingualtherapies.com/index.html

(This site belongs to a group of clinicians who have set up a practice. It features a clearinghouse of articles and links of interest.)

Glossary

accidental bilingual   Someone who becomes bilingual through circumstances that were not planned, such as a sudden move to a new country during childhood.

active bilingual   A bilingual who can speak and understand two languages (to some degree), as opposed to a *passive bilingual,* who understands and/or reads a second language but does not speak or write it.

additive bilingual   A person whose second language adds to his or her knowledge in the first; the growth of a second language does not undermine the growth of the first one.

ambilingual   A bilingual who is highly skilled in both languages.

aphasia   The loss of some or all functions of speech and language, usually resulting from brain damage.

associative learning   Associating a symbol with a concept through traditional learning (like memorization).

balanced bilingual   A bilingual whose knowledge of two languages is about equal, as opposed to having one dominant language that is much stronger and can be used in more domains than the other.

BFLA   Acronym for *Bilingual First Language Acquisition,* the process by which a baby or a young child learns two languages simultaneously, so neither can be called the "first" language or the "second" language.

BICS, Basic Interpersonal Communication Skills   Conversational fluency in a language that allows one to function adequately "on the playground," as opposed to more abstract language that is generally used for academic writing or schoolwork. (See *CALP.*)

bilingual mode	The manner of speaking in which two languages are used in alternation, often within the same sentence, as opposed to *monolingual mode,* the style of speaking that entails using only one language at a time.
CALP, Cognitive Academic Language Proficiency	A type of language behavior that includes the use of abstract concepts and tasks associated with school, as opposed to *BICS.*
code-switching	The language practice of changing from one "code," or language, to another within one sentence or conversation. Switches generally take place only at permissible places in the structure of the conversation or sentence.
communicative competence	The ability, beyond knowing the grammar and vocabulary of a language, to use language(s) in culturally appropriate ways.
community language	The language used by the majority of people outside the home, for public purposes, as opposed to the home language or *minority language.*
consonants	In contrast to vowels, the sounds of a language, like *p, f,* and *r,* that are made by shaping one's mouth, tongue, and lips to momentarily cut off or restrict the flow of air through the mouth and nose.
covert correction	A technique of responding to errors not by drawing attention to them but by modeling correct usage within the conversation.
critical period	An optimal period for learning during which stimulation produces a desired effect and after which stimulation no longer produces the same effect.
decontextualized language	More abstract language that does not rely on context in order to be understandable. It must be more explicit than talking about the here and now, which allows listeners to fill in gaps in their understanding by looking at the situation being discussed.
discourse	The level of language use that involves putting two or more sentences together in coherent ways, either

in conversation or in spoken or written texts (e.g., narratives, political speeches, etc.).

dominant language
The language of a bilingual that is stronger than the other, usually because it is or has been used more in the bilingual's environment.

dual-language programs
Educational programs that incorporate the use of two languages into the curriculum in structured ways. In the U.S., the more common term is "two-way immersion" program as opposed to "one-way" or "English-only" schooling.

dyslexia
A condition in which the ability to read develops poorly or is disrupted, which manifests in children of normal intelligence as difficulty with reading or the inability to read.

early bilingual
A bilingual who learns a second language before puberty, while the innate language-learning mechanisms are still available; an infant or childhood bilingual, as opposed to a *late bilingual*.

elective bilingual
An individual who chooses to learn a second language, usually a majority-language speaker who adopts the use of a minority language for personal reasons, as opposed to an *immigrant bilingual*, who is forced by circumstances to adopt a second language.

elite bilingual
An *elective bilingual* who, as is often the case from a socioeconomic point of view, comes from the wealthier, more educated, or "elite" segments of society. (See *elective bilingual*.)

expansion
A covert correction strategy that entails the expert speaker in a conversation responding to the other person's ungrammatical or improper language use by expanding on the content of that utterance in order to subtly correct the error or omission by modeling the proper structure.

expressive language (versus receptive language)
Speaking and writing, which require the individual to produce language. Using expressive language, or having "active" command of a language, is considered more challenging than using only

receptive skills, as in the "passive" tasks of reading and listening.

FLA (versus SLA) An acronym for *First Language Acquisition,* which uses innate mechanisms especially dedicated to language that allow knowledge of the first language to develop, as opposed to *SLA, Second Language Acquisition,* which also makes use of general learning mechanisms that are not specialized for language.

foreign language A nonnative language learned in a country where it is not the community language, as opposed to a *second language* that is the community language where the learner is living.

grammar The system of rules describing the structure of a language—its sound patterns, its words, how sentences are formed, and how they are used.

heritage language Usually a minority language, or the majority language of another country, associated with an individual's background. It does not express the popular culture of the community or country where the speaker or speakers are living, but often represents their family heritage.

immersion A living situation or curriculum in which only the target language (the language to be learned) is used.

immigrant bilingual See *elite bilingual.*

infant bilingual One who learns two languages from birth and has two first languages rather than a first language and a second language.

input Language that learners hear—as opposed to *output,* what the learners themselves say.

intentional communication (versus reflexive communication) Speakers' deliberate vocalizations and communication, as opposed to reflexive responses, e.g., an infant's crying.

L1; L2 An individual's first language; a second language or any subsequent languages that are not an individual's native language.

Language Acquisition Device, LAD	Within a theory that says language is hard-wired, or innate, the unseen mechanisms of the brain that allow children to acquire language by inferring the structure of a language solely from what they hear.
Language Acquisition Support System, LASS	As a complement to the innate *LAD*, the supportive social environment, like a family, that promotes language development.
language impairment	Any one of a number of processes that keep language from developing normally, whether they are specific to language (that is, only language is impaired) or more general, like deafness or very low IQ, which causes delays or deficiencies not only in language, but in many other areas as well.
language shift	The process within a community of shifting away from using one language and adopting another.
late bilingual	One who learns a second language after puberty, unlike an *early bilingual*, and therefore has a first language and a second language. Depending on one's living situation, the second language can become the person's primary language.
lexical	Having to do with the words of a language and the processes that build meaning.
lexicon	An individual's mental dictionary, the list of all the words a person knows and whatever information is associated with them.
literate language (versus oral language)	The characteristics of written language, which is more decontextualized and generally uses more complex structures than *oral language*.
majority language	The language that the majority of speakers in a community use, often with "official" language status if it is used for government, in education, and in other official or public domains.
mature (or canonical) babbling	The regular sequences of consonants and vowels produced by an infant, like "bababa," that contain the syllables that words can be made from, but which are not words because the child attaches no lexical meaning to them.

metalinguistic awareness	The conscious awareness of some basic properties and structures of language. For example, that the word "dog" has three sounds is a metalinguistic observation.
minority language	The language used by a subgroup of a population (or even just by one family), sometimes also called a *heritage language*.
Minority Language at Home, mL@H	One of the major strategies for organizing language use within one's household. With mL@H, the community or majority language is not used within the home.
Mixed Language Policy, MLP	One of the major strategies for organizing language practices within one's household. Multiple languages are used within the home, often in communicating with the same person.
monolingual mode	See *bilingual mode*.
morphosyntax	The level of grammar that includes forms indicating structural relationships between words. For example, some languages use a special suffix or form to show which word is the subject of a verb in a sentence and which is its object. English morphosyntax includes plural markers, verb endings, and the like.
native language proficiency (versus nonnative and near-native proficiency)	The ability to speak a language with the fluency and range typical of someone who has spoken it since birth, as opposed to *nonnative proficiency*, which implies less fluency and range, or *near-native proficiency*, language use with a high degree of fluency and range, but which contains subtle errors and is more susceptible to effects of fatigue and unfamiliarity.
non-converging dialogue	Conversation between two people in which each person uses a different language.
nonnative language	See *native language*.
One Parent–One Language, OPOL	One of the major strategies for organizing language use within one's household. Each parent (or person) uses a different language with the children for all of

their communication. Language choice is dictated by person, according to the language customarily used by the person being addressed.

oral language
Spoken language, as opposed to written language. See *literate language*.

output
The language an individual produces (as opposed to language that the individual hears). See *input*.

overextension
Common child error of using a term to include more meanings than its conventional definition allows—for example, calling all four-legged animals "dogs."

parentese
A manner of talking to infants, sometimes also called *motherese* or *caregiver speech*. Compared to *adult-directed speech*, its sentences are shorter, its pronunciation uses a wider pitch range, and it entails more repetition and longer pauses.

phonemic awareness
Awareness of the sound units of spoken words, a part of the reading process in which the sound units are matched up with individual letters of written words (in an alphabetic script).

phonology
The part of a grammar that describes the system of sounds and how they are used in a language.

recast
A covert correction strategy in which parents rephrase the child's utterance either to make it correct or to expand on it. See also *covert correction*.

receptive language (versus expressive language)
See *expressive language*.

reflexive communication (versus intentional communication)
See *intentional communication*.

scaffolding
The support provided to a novice speaker by an expert speaker to enable the novice to extend his or her turns in a story or conversation.

sequential bilingual (versus simultaneous bilingual)	One who learns one language first and then another, either a childhood bilingual or a late bilingual, as opposed to someone who learns two languages simultaneously from birth.
socioeconomic status, SES	The economic and educational level of individuals or families. It is usually calculated according to profession and years of education of the parents in a family.
simultaneous bilingual (versus sequential or successive bilingual)	See *sequential bilingual*.
SLA	See *FLA*.
Specific Language Impairment, SLI	Difficulty learning or using language despite otherwise well-developed cognitive skills. See *language impairment*.
speech sounds	Sounds used to pronounce the words of a language, as opposed to other noises that are not part of any language, like buzzes or pure tones.
standardized tests	Tests that are administered under consistent conditions and scored relative to either the performance of a representative sample group ("norm-referenced") or a predetermined set of standards ("criterion-referenced"). Scores on norm-referenced standardized tests are established by giving the test to a specially selected group and using the statistics of their performance on it as the baseline. On standardized IQ tests, for example, a score of 100 is average, the 50th percentile, with 15 points above or below defining the "average range" (statistically, one standard deviation in either direction from the mean).
syntax	The system of rules within a grammar that specify the structural relations of elements within a sentence and allow the speaker to produce and recognize how sequences of words and phrases are to be assigned meaning within the language.

target language	The language that a person is learning (as spoken by adults).
texts	Sequences of sentences organized coherently.
turnabout	A conversation strategy in which the expert speaker expands on the novice speaker's utterance and adds an open question to provide a possible direction for the novice's next turn.
Two-Way Immersion, TWI	See *dual-language programs*.
underextension	The common child error or learner error of using a term more restrictively than its conventional definition permits, such as using the word "shoes" for only one particular pair or type of shoes. (See *overextension*.)
zone of proximal development	The skills just beyond what a child can do independently, but which the child can do with help of an expert (a teacher or parent); the child will be able to acquire and exercise the next set of skills with help before using them independently.

References

Note: A full set of endnotes is available from the author.

Chapter 1
For Further Reading

Crystal, David. *The Language Revolution*. Cambridge, UK: Polity Press, 2004.

De Courtivron, Isabelle, ed. *Lives in Translation*. NY: Palgrave Macmillan, 2003.

Gordon, Raymond, Jr., ed. *Ethnologue: Languages of the World*, 15th edition. Dallas, TX: SIL International, 2005. http://www.ethnologue.com/.

Oller, D. Kimbrough, and Rebecca E. Eilers, eds. *Language and Literacy in Bilingual Children*. Clevedon, UK: Multilingual Matters, 2002.

Major Sources (in the order in which they occur)

Crawford, James. Census 2000: A Guide for the Perplexed. http://ourworld.compuserve.com/homepages/jWCRAWFORD/census02.htm.

Gupta, Anthea. "Bilingual and Multilingual Children: Another Perspective." *Ask-A-Linguist FAQ*. http://linguistlist.org/ask=ling/biling2.html.

Merrill, Jane. *Bringing Up Baby Bilingual*. NY: Facts on File, Inc., 1984.

Saunders, George. *Bilingual Children: From Birth to Teens*. Clevedon, UK: Multilingual Matters, 1988.

Wright, Lawrence. "The Agent." *New Yorker*, July 9, 2002.

Gathercole, Virginia C. M., ed. *Language Transmission in Bilingual Families in Wales*. Bangor,Wales: Report for Welsh Language Board, 2005.

Grosjean, Francois, P. Li, T. F. Münte, and A. Rodriguez-Fornells. "Imaging Bilinguals: When the Neurosciences Meet the Language Sciences." *Bilingualism: Language and Cognition* 6 (2003): 159–165.

McCardle, Peggy, and E. Hoff, eds. *Childhood Bilingualism: Research on Infancy through School Age.* Clevedon, UK: Multilingual Matters, 2006.

Bialystok, Ellen. *Bilingualism in Development: Language, Literacy, and Cognition.* Cambridge, UK: Cambridge University Press, 2001.

Lambert, Wallace E. "The Effects of Bilingualism on the Individual: Cognitive and Sociocultural Consequences." In *Bilingualism. Psychological, Social, and Educational Implications,* edited by P.Hornby, 15–28. NY: Academic Press, 1977.

Bialystok, Ellen, F.M. Craik, R. Klein, and M. Viswanathan. "Bilingualism, Aging, and Cognitive Control: Evidence from the Simon Task." *Psychology and Aging* 19 (2004): 290–303.

Bialystok, Ellen, F.M. Craik, and M. Freedman, "Bilingualism as a Protection Against the Onset of Symptoms of Dementia." *Neuropsychologia* 45 (2007): 459–464.

Boroditsky, Lera, W. Ham, and M. Ramscar. "What Is Universal about Event Perception? Comparing English and Indonesian Speakers." *Proceedings of the 24th Annual Meeting of the Cognitive Science Society,* Fairfax, VA, August 2002.

Gumperz, John J., and S. C. Levinson, eds. *Rethinking Linguistic Relativity.* Cambridge, UK: Cambridge University Press, 1996.

Lucy, John A. *Grammatical Categories and Cognition.* Cambridge, UK: Cambridge Univ. Press, 1992.

Wright, Steven C., and L. Tropp. "Investigating the Impact of Bilingual Instruction on Children's Intergroup Attitudes." *Group Processes and Intergroup Relations* 8 (2005): 309–328.

Fishman, Joshua, ed. *Can Threatened Languages Be Saved: Reversing Language Shift, Revisited.* Clevedon, UK: Multilingual Matters, 2001.

Welsh Language Board. http://www.bwrdd-yr-iaith.org.uk/.

Sommer, Doris, ed. *Bilingual Games: Some Literary Investigations.* NY: Palgrave Macmillan, 2003.

Wierzbicka, Anna. "Universal Human Concepts as a Tool for Exploring Bilingual Lives." *International Journal of Bilingualism* 9 (2005): 7–26.

Steiner, George. *Errata: An Examined Life.* New Haven, CT: Yale University Press, 1997.

Chapter 2

For Further Reading

The Human Language Series (film). Gene Searchinger (producer). Equinox Films, 1994.

Bruner, Jerome. *Child's Talk: Learning to Use Language.* NY: Norton, 1983.

Eliot, Lise. *What's Going On in There? How the Brain and Mind Develop in the First Five Years of Life.* NY: Bantam Books, 1999.

Gopnik, Alison, A. Meltzoff, and P. Kuhl. *The Scientist in the Crib.* NY: William Morrow, 1999.

Hart, Betty, and T. Risley. *Meaningful Differences in the Everyday Experiences of Young American Children.* Baltimore, MD: Paul Brookes, 1995.

Roeper, Tom. *The Prism of Grammar.* Cambridge, MA: MIT Press, 2007.

Major Sources

Chomsky, Noam. *Aspects of the Theory of Syntax.* Cambridge, MA: MIT Press, 1965.

Vihman, Marilyn M. *Phonological Development: The Origins of Language in the Child.* Oxford, UK: Blackwell, 1996.

Oller, D. Kimbrough. *The Emergence of the Speech Capacity.* Mahwah, NJ: Lawrence Erlbaum, 2000.

Saffran, Jenny R. "Statistical Language Learning: Mechanisms and Constraints." *Current Directions in Psychological Science* 12 (2003): 110–114.

Pinker, Steven. *The Language Instinct.* NY: William Morrow, 1994.

Werker, Janet, and R. C. Tees. "Cross-language Speech Perception: Evidence for Perceptual Reorganization during the First Year of Life." *Infant Behavior and Development* 7 (1984): 49–63.

Snow, Catherine, and C. Ferguson, eds. *Talking to Children: Language Input and Acquisition.* Cambridge, UK: Cambridge University Press, 1977.

Nelson, Katherine. *Making Sense: The Acquisition of Shared Meaning.* NY: Academic Press, 1985.

Gleitman, Lila, and H. Gleitman. "A Picture Is Worth a Thousand Words, but That's the Problem: The Role of Syntax in Vocabulary Acquisition." *Current Directions in Psychological Science* 1 (1992): 31–35.

Fisher, Cynthia. "Structural Limits on Verb Mapping: The Role of Abstract Structure in 2.5-Year-Olds' Interpretations of Novel Verbs." *Developmental Science* 5 (2002): 55–64.

Tomasello, Michael. "Can an Ape Understand a Sentence?" *Language and Communication* 14 (1994): 377–390.

Pepperberg, Irene. *The Alex Studies: Cognitive and Communicative Abilities of Grey Parrots.* Cambridge, MA: Harvard University Press, 2002.

Marcus, Gary, S. Vijayan, S. Bandi Rao, and P. M. Vishton. "Rule Learning by Seven-Month-Old Infants." *Science* 283 (1999): 77–80.

Hickmann, Maya. *Children's Discourse: Person, Space, and Time Across Languages.* Cambridge, UK: Cambridge University Press, 2003.

Hymes, Dell. "Models of the Interaction of Language and Social Life." In *Directions in Sociolinguistics: The Ethnography of Communication,* edited by J. Gumperz and D. Hymes, 35–71. NY: Holt, Rinehart, and Winston, 1972.

Fenson, Larry, et al. *MacArthur-Bates Communicative Development Inventory Technical Manual.* Baltimore, MD: Paul Brookes, 2003.

Cummins, Jim. "Cognitive/Academic Language Proficiency, Linguistic Interdependence, the Optimum Age Question and Some Other Matters." *Working Papers on Bilingualism,* 19 (1979): 121–129.

Sternberg, Robert J., and E. Grigorenko, eds. *Environmental Effects on Cognitive Abilities.* Mahwah, NJ: Erlbaum, 2001.

Vargha-Khadem, F., K. E. Watkins, C. J. Price, J. Ashburner, K. J. Alcock, A. Connelly, R. S. J. Frackowiak, K. J. Friston, M. E. Pembrey, M. Mishkin, D. G. Gadian, and R. E. Passingham. "Neural Basis of an Inherited Speech and Language Disorder." *Proceedings of the National Academy of Science* 95 (1998): 12695–12700.

Chomsky, Noam. "A Review of B.F. Skinner's 'Verbal Behavior.'" *Language* 35 (1959): 26–58.

Gathercole, Virginia C. M., and E. Hoff. "Input and the Acquisition of Language: Three Questions." In *The Handbook of Language Development,* edited by Erika Hoff and Marilyn Shatz, 107–127. Oxford, UK: Blackwell Publishers, 2007.

Burns-Hoffman, Rebecca. "A Discourse Analysis of Variation in Children's Language in Preschool, Small Group Settings." Ph.D. diss., University of Colorado at Boulder, 1992.

Anderson, Daniel R., and T. Pempek. "Television and Very Young Children." *American Behavioral Scientist* 48 (2005): 505–522.

Collins, Molly F., and J. Parish. "Electronic Books: Boon or Bust for Interactive Reading?" Poster presented at the Boston University Conference on Language Development, Boston, MA, November 2006.

Olson, David R. *The Social Foundations of Language and Thought*. NY: Norton, 1980.

Vygotsky, Lev. *Thought and Language*. Cambridge, MA: MIT Press, 1962.

Chapter 3
For Further Reading
Crystal, David, 2004. (See reference in chapter 1.)

Eliot, Lise. (See reference in chapter 2.)

Genesee, Fred, J. Paradis, and M. Crago. *Dual Language Development and Disorders*. Baltimore, MD: Paul Brookes, 2004.

Grosjean, Francois. *Life with Two Languages*. Cambridge, MA: Harvard University Press, 1982.

Kroll, J. F. and A. DeGroot. *Handbook of Bilingualism: Psycholinguistic Approaches*. NY: Oxford University Press, 2005.

Rymer, Russ. *Genie: An Abused Child's Flight from Silence*. NY: Harper Collins, 1993. Also, "Secret of the Wild Child," A NOVA Video Production by WGBH/Boston, 1994.

Tabors, Patton. *One Child, Two Languages: A Guide for Preschool Educators of Children Learning English as a Second Language*. Baltimore, MD: Paul Brookes, 1997. (2nd edition forthcoming.)

Major Sources
Wong-Fillmore, Lily. "Individual Differences in Second Language Acquisition." In *Individual Differences in Language Ability and Language Behavior*, edited by Charles Fillmore, D. Kempler, and W. S. Y. Wang, 203–227. San Diego, CA: Academic Press, 1979.

Hyltemstam, Kenneth, and N. Abrahamsson. "Who Can Become Native-like in a Second Language? All, Some, or None? On the Maturational Constraints Controversy in Second Language Acquisition" *Studia Linguistica* 54/2 (2000): 150–166.

Albert, Martin, and L. K. Obler. *The Bilingual Brain: Neuropsychological and Neurolinguistic Aspects of Bilingualism*. NY: Academic Press, 1978.

Karmiloff, Kyra, and A. Karmiloff-Smith. *Pathways to Language: From Fetus to Adolescent*. Cambridge, MA: Harvard University Press, 2001.

Wierzbicka, Anna, 2005. (See reference in chapter 1.)

Oller, D. Kimbrough, and R. Eilers, eds. (See reference in chapter 1.)

Leopold, Werner. *Speech Development of a Bilingual Child: A Linguist's Record* (4 volumes). Evanston, IL: Northwestern University Press, 1939–1949.

Volterra, Virginia, and T. Taeschner. "The Acquisition and Development of Language by Bilingual Children." *Journal of Child Language* 5, 311–326.

Grosjean, Francois. "Neurolinguists, Beware! The Bilingual Is Not Two Monolinguals in One Person." *Brain and Language* 36 (1989): 3–15.

Gupta, Anthea. (See reference in chapter 1.)

Clyne, Michael. *Dynamics of Language Contact*. NY: Cambridge University Press, 2003.

"American Tongues" video from the Center for New American Media. L. Alvarez and A. Kolker, Directors. NY: CNAM, 1987.

Gopnik, Alison, A. Meltzoff, and P. Kuhl. (See reference in chapter 2.)

Bornstein, Marc, and J. Bruner, eds. *Interaction in Human Development*. Hillsdale, NJ: Erlbaum, 1989.

Mayberry, Rachel I., E. Lock, and H. Kazmi. "Development: Linguistic Ability and Early Language Exposure." *Nature* 417 (2002): 38.

Kohnert, Kathryn J., E. Bates, and A. E. Hernandez. "Balancing Bilinguals: Lexical-Semantic Production and Cognitive Processing in Children Learning Spanish and English." *Journal of Speech, Language, and Hearing Research* 42 (1999): 1400–1413.

Kohnert, Kathryn J., and E. Bates. "Balancing Bilinguals II: Lexical Comprehension and Cognitive Processing in Children Learning Spanish and English." *Journal of Speech, Language, and Hearing Research* 45 (2002): 347–359.

Caplan, David. *Biological Studies of Mental Processes*. Cambridge, MA: MIT Press, 1980.

Hart, Betty, and T. Risley, 1999. (See reference in chapter 2.)

Gathercole, Virginia C. M. "Miami and North Wales, So Far and Yet So Near: A Constructivist Account of Morphosyntactic Development in Bilingual Children." *International Journal of Bilingual Education and Bilingualism* 10/3 (2007): 224–247.

Pearson, Barbara Z., S. C. Fernandez, V. Lewedag, and D. K. Oller. "Input Factors in Lexical Learning of Bilingual Infants (Ages 10 to 30 Months)." *Applied Psycholinguistics* 18 (1997): 41–58.

Werker, Janet, W. M. Weikum, and K. A. Yoshida. "Bilingual Speech Processing in Infants and Adults." In *Childhood Bilingualism: Research on Infancy through School Age*, edited by P. McCardle and E. Hoff, 1–18. (See reference in chapter 1.)

Chapter 4
Major Sources

De Houwer, Annick. "Environmental Factors in Early Bilingual Development: The Role of Parental Beliefs and Attitudes." In *Bilingualism and Migration*, edited by Gus Extra and Ludo Verhoeven, 75–95. Berlin: Mouton de Gruytere, 1999.

Leopold, Werner. (See reference in chapter 3.)

Vihman, Marilyn. "Language Differentiation by the Bilingual Infant." *Journal of Child Language* 12 (1985): 297–324.

Deuchar, Margaret, and S. Quay. *Bilingual Acquisition: Theoretical Implications of a Case Study*. Oxford, UK: Oxford University Press, 2000.

Barron-Hauwaert, Suzanne. *Language Strategies for Bilingual Families. The One Parent One Language Approach*. Clevedon, UK: Multilingual Matters, 2004.

De Houwer, Annick. "Parental Language Input Patterns and Children's Bilingual Use." *Applied Psycholinguistics* 28 (2007): 411–424.

De Houwer, Annick. "Home Languages Spoken in Officially Monolingual Flanders: A Survey." In *Methodology of Conflict Linguistics*, edited by K. Bochmann, P. Nelde, and W. Wolck, 71–87. St. Augustin: Asgard Verlag, 2003.

Pearson, Barbara Z., S. C. Fernandez., V. Lewedag, and D. K. Oller, 1997. (See reference in chapter 3.)

Hakuta, Kenji, and D. D'Andrea. "Some Properties of Bilingual Maintenance and Loss in Mexican Background High School Students." *Applied Linguistics* 13 (1992): 72–99.

Eilers, Rebecca, B. Z. Pearson, and A. Cobo-Lewis. "Social Factors in Bilingual Development." In P. McCardle and E. Hoff, eds., 2006. (See reference in chapter 1.)

Saunders, George, 1988. (See reference in chapter 1.)

Lambert, Wallace E., and D. M. Taylor. "Language in the Lives of Ethnic Minorities: Cuban-American Families in Miami." *Applied Linguistics* 17 (1996): 477–500.

Gathercole, Virginia C. M., 2005. (See reference in chapter 1.)

Pearson, Barbara Z. "Social Factors in Childhood Bilingualism in the United States." *Applied Psycholinguistics* 28/3 (2007): 399–410.

Crystal, David, 2004. (See reference in chapter 1.)

Gordon, Raymond, 2005. (See reference in chapter 1.)

Oller, D. Kimbrough, and R. Eilers, eds. (See reference in chapter 1.)

Grammont, Maurice. *Observations sur le Langage des Enfants (Observations on Children's Language)*. Paris: Melanges Meillet, 1902.

Sommer, Doris, ed., 2003. (See reference chapter 1.)

Muhammed, Jameelah. *The Global Child*. Washington, DC: BEE Books, 2003.

Lanza, Elizabeth. "Language Contact in Bilingual Two-Year-Olds and Code-Switching: Language Encounters of a Different Kind?" *International Journal of Bilingualism* 1 (1997): 135–162.

Pearson, Barbara Z., and A. McGee. "Language Choice in Hispanic-Background Junior High School Students in Miami: 1988 Update." In *Studies in Anthropological Linguistics*, edited by Ana Roca and John Lipski, 91–102. Berlin: Mouton de Gruytere, 1993.

Merrill, Jane, 1984. (See reference in chapter 1.)

Chapter 5
Major Sources

Saunders, George, 1988. (See reference in chapter 1.)

Talbot, Margaret. "The Baby Lab" (on Liz Spelke). *New Yorker*, September 4, 2006.

Tabors, Patton, 1997. (See reference in chapter 3.)

Merrill, Jane, Chapter 9, "Language Travel: Distant Shores." (See reference in chapter 1.)

Barron-Hauwaert, Suzanne, 2004. (See reference in chapter 4.)

Chapter 6
For Further Reading

Genesee, Fred, J. Paradis, and M. Crago, 2004. (See reference in chapter 3.)

Grosjean, Francois, 1982. (See reference in chapter 3.)

American Speech Language and Hearing Association. *http://www.asha. org/public/hearing/disorders/*.

Major Sources

Leonard, Laurence B. *Children with Specific Language Impairment.* Cambridge, MA: MIT Press, 1998.

Tomblin, Bruce, N. L. Records, P. R. Buckwalter, X. Zhang, E. Smith, and M. O'Brien. "Prevalence of Specific Language Impairment in Kindergarten Children." *Journal of Speech, Language, and Hearing Research* 40 (1997): 1245–1260.

Bruck, Margaret. "The Suitability of Early French Immersion Programs for the Language Disabled Child." *Canadian Journal of Education* 3 (1978): 51–72.

Paradis, Johanne, M. Crago, F. Genesee, and M. Rice, "French-English Bilingual Children with SLI: How Do They Compare with Their Monolingual Peers?" *Journal of Speech, Language, and Hearing Research* 36 (2003): 113–127.

Pearson, Barbara Z. "Assessing Lexical Development in Bilingual Babies and Toddlers." *International Journal of Bilingualism* 2 (1998): 347–372.

Peña, Elizabeth D., V. Gutierrez-Clellen, A. Iglesias, B. A. Goldstein, and L. M. Bedore. *Bilingual English Spanish Assessment (BESA).* In development.

Chapter 7
For Further Reading

American Speech Language and Hearing Association. *http://www.asha. org/public/speech/disorders/LBLD.htm*.

August, Diane, and K. Hakuta. *Improving Schooling for Language-Minority Students: A Research Agenda.* Washington, DC: National Academy Press, 1997.

Bruner, Jerome S. *Actual Minds, Possible Worlds*. Cambridge, MA: Harvard University Press, 1986.

First Words Project. Florida State University, Amy Wetherby, Ph.D. Director. http://firstwords.fsu.edu/.

Hakuta, Kenji. *The Mirror of Language*. NY: Basic Books, 1986.

Oller, D. Kimbrough, 2000. (See reference in chapter 2.)

Major Sources

Fenson, Larry, V. A. Marchman, D. J. Thal, P. S. Dale, J. S. Reznick, and E. Bates. *Users Guide and Technical Manual for MacArthur-Bates Communicative Development Inventories*, 2nd edition. Baltimore, MD: Paul Brookes, 2003. Information on international forms: *http://www.sci.sdsu. edu/cdi/adaptations.htm.*

Oller, D. Kimbrough, R. E. Eiler, A. B. Coco-Lewis, and R. Urbano. "Development of Precursors to Speech in Infants Exposed to Two Languages." *Journal of Child Language* 27 (1997): 407–25.

Pearson, Barbara Z., S. C. Fernandez, and D. K. Oller, "Lexical Development in Bilingual Infants and Toddlers: Comparison to Monolingual Norms." *Language Learning* 43 (1993): 93–120.

Doyle, Anna B., M. Champagne, and N. Segalowitz. "Some Issues in the Assessment of Linguistic Consequences of Early Bilingualism." *Working Papers on Bilingualism* 14 (1977): 21–30.

Petitto, Laura, M. Katerelos, B. G. Levy, K. Gauna, K. Tetréault, and V. Ferraro. "Bilingual Signed and Spoken Language Acquisition from Birth: Implications for the Mechanisms Underlying Early Bilingual Language Acquisition." *Journal of Child Language* 28 (2001): 453–496.

Genesee, Fred, J. Paradis, and M. Crago, 2004. (See reference in chapter 3.)

Meisel, Jürgen. *Bilingual First Language Acquisition: French and German Grammatical Development*. Amsterdam: John Benjamins, 1994.

Karmiloff, Kyra, and A. Karmiloff-Smith, 2001. (See reference in chapter 3.)

Werker, Janet F., W. M. Weikum, and K. A. Yoshida. (See reference in chapter 3.)

Werker, Janet F., and R. C. Tees. "The Organization and Reorganization of Human Speech Perception." *Annual Review of Neuroscience* 15 (1992): 377–402.

Sebastian-Galles, Nuria, and S. Soto-Faraco. "Online Processing of Native and Non-native Phonemic Contrasts in Early Bilinguals." *Cognition* 72 (1999): 111–123.

Werker, Janet F., C. T. Fennell, K. M. Corcoran, and C. L. Stager. "Infants' Ability to Learn Phonetically Similar Words: Effects of Age and Vocabulary Size." *Infancy* 3 (2002): 1–30.

Burns, Tracey C., J. F. Werker, and K. McVie. "Development of Phonetic Categories in Infants Raised in Bilingual and Monolingual Environments." In *Proceedings of the 27th Annual Boston University Conference on Language Development,* edited by B. Beachley et al., 173–184. Somerville, MA: Cascadilla Press, 2003.

Navarro, Ana, B. Z. Pearson, A. B. Cobo-Lewis, and D.K. Oller. "Assessment of Phonological Development in Bilingual Children at Age 36 Months: Comparison to Monolinguals in Each Language." Paper presented at the annual meeting of the American Speech Language and Hearing Association, Orlando, FL, December 1995.

Navarro, Ana. "Phonetic Effects of the Ambient Language in Early Speech: Comparisons of Monolingual- and Bilingual-Learning Children." Ph.D. diss., University of Miami, 1998.

Pearson, Barbara Z., and S. C. Fernandez. "Patterns of Interaction in the Lexical Development in Two Languages of Bilingual Infants." *Language Learning* 44 (1994): 617–653.

Boysson-Bardies, Benedicte, and M. M. Vihman. "Adaptation to Language: Evidence from Babbling and First Words in Four Languages." *Language* 67 (1991): 297–319.

Berman, Ruth, and D. Slobin. *Relating Events in Narrative.* Mahwah, NJ: Erlbaum, 1994.

Verhoeven, Ludo, and S. Stromqvist, eds. *Narrative Development in a Multilingual Context.* Amsterdam: John Benjamins, 2001.

Pearson, Barbara Z. "Narrative Competence in Bilingual School Children in Miami." In *Language and Literacy in Bilingual Children,* 135–174. (See reference in chapter 1.)

Pearson, Barbara Z., 2007. (See reference in chapter 4.)

Wong-Fillmore, Lily. "When Learning a Second Language Means Losing a First." *Early Childhood Research Quarterly* 6 (1991): 323–346.

Lambert, Wallace, 1977. (See reference in chapter 1.)

Hakuta, Kenji, and D. D'Andrea, 1992. (See reference in chapter 4.)

Nairn, Allan, and R. Nader. *The Reign of ETS: The Corporation that Makes Up Minds: the Ralph Nader Report on the Educational Testing Service.* Washington, DC: Center for the Study of Responsive Law, 1980.

Peal, Elizabeth, and W. Lambert. "The Relation of Bilingualism to Intelligence." *Psychological Monographs* 76 (1962).

Pearson, Barbara Z. "Predictive Validity of the SAT-Verbal Scores for High-Achieving Hispanic College Students." *Hispanic Journal of the Behavioral Sciences* 15 (1993): 342–56.

Pearson, Barbara Z., 1998. (See reference in chapter 6.)

Baker, Colin. "Normative Testing and Bilingual Populations." *Journal of Multilingual and Multicultural Development* 9 (1988): 399–409.

Umbel, Vivian, B. Z. Pearson, M. Fernandez, and D. K. Oller. "Measuring Bilingual Children's Receptive Vocabularies." *Child Development* 63 (1992): 1012–20.

Oller, D. Kimbrough, B. Z. Pearson, and A. B. Cobo-Lewis. "Profile Effects in Early Bilingual Language and Literacy." *Applied Psycholinguistics* 28/2 (2007): 191–230.

Gathercole, Virginia C. M. "Monolingual and Bilingual Acquisition: Learning Different Treatments of *That*-Trace Phenomena in English and Spanish." In *Language and Literacy in Bilingual Children*, 220–254. (See reference in chapter 1.)

Gathercole, Virginia C. M., and E. M. Thomas. "Input Factors Influencing the Acquisition of Welsh." In *Proceedings of the ISB4*, edited by J. Cohen et al., 852–874. Somerville, MA: Cascadilla Press, 2005.

MacArthur-Bates Inventarios del Desarrollo de Habilidades Comunicativas (Inventarios) Translated and adapted by Donna Jackson-Maldonado, Ph.D., Elizabeth Bates, Ph.D., & Donna J. Thal, Ph.D. Baltimore, Paul H. Brookes, 2003.

Chapter 8
For Further Reading
Steiner, George. *After Babel: Aspects of Language and Translation.* Oxford, UK: Oxford University Press, 1992.

Major Sources

Steiner, Rudolf. *The Genius of Language*. Herndon, VA: Anthroposophic Press, 1919–1920.

Pavlenko, Aneta. *Emotions and Multilingualism*. Cambridge, UK: Cambridge University Press, 2005.

Haugen, Einar. "The Stigmata of Bilingualism," In *The Ecology of Language, Essays by Einar Haugen*, edited by A. Dil, 308–324. Stanford, CA: Stanford University Press, 1972.

Steiner, George, 1997. (See reference in chapter 1.)

Ramírez-Esparza, Nairán, S. D. Gosling, V. Benet-Martínez, J. P. Potter, and J. W. Pennebaker. "Do Bilinguals Have Two Personalities? A Special Case of Cultural Frame Switching." *Journal of Research in Personality* 40 (2006): 99–120.

Sommer, Doris, ed., 2003. (See reference in chapter 1.)

Stavans, Ilan. "Love Affair with Spanglish," in De Courtivron, 129–146. (See reference in chapter 1.)

Dorfman, Ariel. "The Wandering Bigamists of Language," in De Courtivron, 29–38. (See reference in chapter 1.)

Hoffman, Eva. "P.S.," in De Courtivron, 49–54. (See reference in chapter 1.)

Tawada, Yoko. "Writing in the Web of Words," in De Courtivron, 147–156. (See reference in chapter 1.)

Wierzbicka, Anna, 2005. (See reference in chapter 1.)

Index

developmental errors. *See* errors
Dhomhniall, Nuala Ní, 11, 293
discourse
   definition of, 310
   development of, 59, 64, 261–262
divergent thinking
   bilinguals v. monolinguals, 23–24,
      276
diversity, linguistic. *See* linguistic
   diversity
dominant language
   compared with monolinguals' sole
      language, 260–261
   definition of, 311
   development of, 250
   false diagnosis of impairment and,
      227
   myths and misconceptions, 300
   skill levels in L1 and L2 by
      classification, 89–90
   table 6, 90
Dorfman, Ariel, 8, 293
Down syndrome
   bilingualism and, 130
   language impairment and, 222
Doyle, Champagne, and Segalowitz
   first words, monolingual v.
      bilingual, 247
dual-immersion programs
   bilingualism and, 266–268
   CS-6, 180–182
   CS-24, 204–205
   CS-25, 205–208
   CS-26, 208–209
   CS-27, 209–211
   definition of, 201–202, 311
   educational trends away from, 155
   evaluating strategies and, 211
   U.S. and EU, 118
dual-language programs. *See* dual-
   immersion programs
dyslexia
   CS-32, 231
   CS-33, 232–233
   definition of, 224, 311

earaches
   language impairment and, 225
earning potential of bilinguals v.
   monolinguals, 9
early bilingual
   definition of, 311
early language learning
   myths and misconceptions, 300
early SLA (Second Language
   Acquisition)
   stages of, 85–87
   v. BFLA, 84–84, 117, 264
elective bilingual
   CS-5, 178–180
   CS-6, 180–182
   CS-7, 182–184
   CS-8, 184–185
   definition of, 311
elite bilingual
   definition of, 311
   table 4, 88
   table 6, 90
emotional benefits of bilingual
   upbringing
   access to cultural heratige, 10–11
   benefits of an extended
      family, 10
   emotional motivations for bilingual
      upbringing, 9–13
   language of intimacy and affection,
      12–13
   parental role, 11–12
English achievement (bilinguals),
   264–266
English-only schooling. *See* one-way
   (English-only) schooling
errors
   developmental, 100–101
   FLA v. SLA, 100–101
   morphosyntax, 280–283
   overextension, 315
   transfer, 100–101
   underextension, 317
EU (European Union),
   multilingualism in, 4, 9

About the Author

Barbara Zurer Pearson, Ph.D., is a Research Associate in Linguistics and an Adjunct Professor in the Department of Communication Disorders at the University of Massachusetts–Amherst. Her Ph.D. in Applied Linguistics is from the University of Miami. She has over twenty years of research experience in the fields of language acquisition and bilingualism and did ground-breaking work on bilingual acquisition and assessment with her research group at the University of Miami. Those studies of bilingual infants and children have been published in the book *Language and Literacy in Bilingual Children*. Most recently, Barbara Zurer Pearson worked on the *Diagnostic Evaluation of Language Variation* (*DELV*), a project to develop an innovative language assessment for children funded by the National Institutes of Health.